Living Today with an
Eye for Eternity

~*LUMINAIRE STUDIES*~

Living Today with an Eye for Eternity

STUDIES IN 1 & 2 TIMOTHY and TITUS

Raymond O. Bystrom

WINNIPEG, MB CANADA   KINDRED PRODUCTIONS   HILLSBORO, KS USA

Kindred Productions is the publishing arm for the Mennonite Brethren Churches. Kindred publishes, promotes and markets print and mixed media resources that help shape our Christian faith and discipleship from the Mennonite Brethren perspective.

Scripture taken from the HOLY BIBLE: NEW INTERNATIONAL VERSION®. NIV®. Copyright © 1973, 1978, 1984 by International Bible Society. Used by permission of Zondervan.

Published simultaneously by Kindred Productions, Winnipeg MB R3M 3Z6 and Kindred Productions, Hillsboro KS 67063

Cover and book design by Fred Koop, Saskatoon, SK

Printed in Canada by The Christian Press

Library and Archives Canada Cataloguing in Publication

ISBN: 978-1-894791-12-0

Library and Archives Canada Cataloguing in Publication

Bystrom, Raymond O
    Living today with an eye for eternity : studies in the pastoral letters / Raymond O. Bystrom.

(Luminaire studies)
Includes bibliographical references.
ISBN 978-1-894791-12-0

    1. Bible. N.T. Pastoral Epistles--Commentaries. I. Title. II. Series.

BS2735.53.B97 2007   227'.83077   C2007-900215-3

TABLE OF CONTENTS

Introduction to the Pastoral Letters

The three letters to Timothy and Titus are unique within the body of New Testament writings commonly attributed to Paul. They are written to individuals, not communities like most of Paul's other letters, although the exhortations of these letters frequently concern the entire church, or groups within it. Also, they have a distinctive vocabulary and style that set them apart from the other Pauline letters. All three portray a deep concern for the pastoral oversight of the church, especially for specific leadership issues and functions within the faith community. For this reason, these three letters have, since the 18th century (Lock 1924: xiii), been called the "Pastoral" Letters or Epistles.

Who is the Author of These Letters?

Until the 19th century, the Pastoral Letters were commonly accepted as letters of Paul, written sometime toward the end of his life and ministry. Today, however, there are two approaches to the question of their authorship. First, most scholars view them as pseudonymous writings of the early second century due in large part to their unusual style and to the impression that they reflect a post-Pauline situation. Those who take this position today argue that the author calls the church back to its Pauline heritage, but he does so by presenting a theology that seems to go beyond the Paul of the undisputed Pauline writings. For example, in this view these letters seem to posit the creation of a fixed church structure with leadership by appointed officers replacing the more charismatic style of the earlier Pauline church. Also, they appear to encourage a way of life that conforms to the patterns of a second century secular society in order to prevent criticism and persecution, unlike Paul's earlier letters, which call for the church to be a contrast society (see Bassler 1996: 17-21).

A second view, that the Pastoral Letters are authentically Pauline, argues that they should be read in the context of Paul's ministry between 49–68 C.E. and interpreted in light of the other Pauline works, even though Paul may have used an amanuensis (secretary) to write them. Still other scholars within this camp nuance their position with the suggestion that a close associate may have used Pauline materials (oral or written) to continue Paul's influence with no intention of deceiving his readers (see Johnson 1996:26-33; Reicke 2001: 51-59, 68-75, 85-91).

In my view, this second approach to the question of the authorship of the Pastoral Letters is the better of the two sketched above. While it is not possible to prove Pauline authorship, and while I do not hold my position without reservation, I do believe it is possible to read these three letters within the context of Paul's own life and ministry; in particular, to read them as documents pertaining to the close of his life.

Are All Three Letters Alike?

It is important to note several ways in which these letters are alike, and equally important to observe the ways in which they are different. If we assume all three letters are alike, we may reduce our ability to hear each one's distinctive message.

Similarities. Here are some of the features common to all three letters. First, all three texts have a common literary form: they are all **letters.** This is important because, in the final analysis, form shapes function. We cannot demand of a letter what we have come to expect of a gospel. Also, ancient letters are typically comprised of various parts each with their own distinctive role to play within the whole. For example, the prayer or thanksgiving at the beginning often depicts themes and/or issues addressed later in the letter.

Second, all three texts are ***personal letters*** addressed to Paul's delegates, Timothy and Titus. Also, the personal attitudes and actions of these specific Pauline delegates constitute a major focus of all three letters. Paul is deeply concerned with what they are doing and teaching. To be sure, these letters are not simply, Paul's private correspondence to Timothy and Titus. The Apostle Paul writes these three letters to his co-workers with the task of proclaiming and living the gospel message. Paul's concern for them stems from their role within the Christian community as "men of God" (1 Timothy 6:11; 2 Timothy 3:17) or as "God's servants" (2 Timothy 2:24). Thus, while written to individuals, these letters are official in character.

Third, all three are **personal paraenetic letters**. The term *paraenesis* refers to moral exhortation. That is, Paul's primary concern is to exhort the community, various groups within it, and its leaders to embrace traditional teaching and certain modes of behavior. "Memory" and "reminding" are key elements of *paraenesis*, which stresses the imitation of models for cultivating virtues. An awareness of their literary form helps us to understand certain emphases in these three letters. For example, Paul urges Timothy to imitate him as a model (2 Timothy 1:13; 3:10) and to present himself in turn to his community as a model to be imitated (1 Timothy 4:12). Within this literary form, Paul's polemic against false teachers becomes a foil for emphasizing a faithful teacher's positive attributes. That is, his characterization of the opponents is the antithesis of the ideal Timothy and Titus should pursue.

Differences. Although these letters have common features, they also differ from one another in several respects. For example, it is often stated that the Pastoral Letters are all about **church order**. But 2 Timothy has nothing on the subject of church structure while the circumstances discussed in 1 Timothy and Titus are distinctive. First Timothy is written against the backdrop of a well-established Ephesian faith community needing some major adjustments in its local affairs. Titus focuses on a new and unpromising cluster of churches that need pretty basic instruction on the fundamentals of household life. The only item relating to church structure in Titus concerns the exhortation to appoint elders.

Likewise, it is often asserted that the Pastoral Letters are concerned with **tradition** as a deposit, but this concern is expressed in only two places (2 Timothy 1:12-14; 1 Timothy 6:20).

Further, the way Paul's **opponents** are treated differs in these letters. The opponents of 2 Timothy seem to be community members who teach that the resurrection has already happened (2:18) and whose false doctrines negatively impact various church members (3:2-8). In 1 Timothy, the opponents, also members of the community, pretend to have knowledge and learning of the law (1 Timothy 1:7; 6:20). In Titus, where the opponents are clearly from "the Jewish party" (Titus 1:10-11; 3:9), their relationship to the Cretan church is unclear (1:13-16). These differences are quickly lost if all three letter's opponents are lumped together into a generalized group.

Paul's **polemic** against the opponents differs in each letter. Often it is claimed that the "real" Paul responds to his opponents with theological arguments whereas the Pastoral Letters' Paul slanders them. But the Paul of the real letters is certainly capable of slander as well (see Galatians 6:12-13; Philippians 3:2, 18; 2 Corinthians 10:12; 11:13-15). The role of polemic in these letters must not be missed; it serves as an antithesis to the ideal behavior Paul covets for church leaders like Timothy and Titus.

Also, these letters differ in their use of *theology* to rebut the opponents. Paul clarifies proper teaching as a response to false teaching in 1 Timothy (see 1 Timothy 1:8-11; 4:3-5; 4:6-8; 6:5-10), a tactic lacking in 2 Timothy and only suggested in Titus 1:15.

Furthermore, Paul's *disposition* toward his opponents and his exhortations about them differ in each letter. In 2

Timothy, he encourages gentleness and patience, holding out the possibility of their conversion (2 Timothy 2:23-26). In 1 Timothy, he expresses no hope for his opponents and treats them in a rather dismissive manner (1 Timothy 1:20; 4:2; 6:3, 20). In Titus, the opponents are to be "silenced" (1:11). People within the faith community who listen to the opponents are to be "rebuked sharply" (1:13). Thus, Paul's attitude toward his opponents in each letter depends upon the community situation reflected therein.

Why Study the Pastoral Letters?

Pastors seldom preach from the Pastoral Letters. But there are good practical reasons for studying, teaching and preaching them in the church today. First, we study them because they challenge our presuppositions and preoccupations. We espouse egalitarianism, but these letters support hierarchy in the church; we believe women are equal to men and deserve an equal role in ministry, but these letters limit the role of women in the church; we advocate tolerance as a sign of maturity, but these letters exhibit a good deal of intolerance toward Paul's opponents; we are convinced that bad behavior stems from a troubled soul, but these letters suggest it is rooted in bad ideas; we think the state should care for the poor and needy, but these letters teach that individual communities and families should look after the needy within their ranks; we know from experience that spontaneity is liberating and tradition stifling, but these letters call us to embrace tradition. These letters challenge our conventional wisdom about life and the church and that is why they need to be preached today. We do not preach the Scriptures because they confirm our unassailable assumptions; we preach them because we believe God's Word is provocative. We preach the Pastoral Letters because they challenge our proclivities and platitudes.

Second, we study the Pastoral Letters because they

are part of the New Testament canon. Most modern scholars argue that the Pastoral Letters were not written by Paul but by later members of a Pauline school. As a result, many contemporary preachers shy away from these letters. They assume that, if Paul did not write them, they have no value for the church. But we read and preach the Pastoral Letters because they have value for us quite apart from our ability to verify their author. We read these letters for what they say to the 21st century church, not simply for what they can teach us about the first century church. We preach these letters because we believe in the biblical text's prophetic role. These texts interpret us, giving us reason to proclaim them in today's church.

Third, we study the Pastoral Letters because they force the contemporary preacher to struggle with its doubly mediated message. These letters were written to individuals, not communities. The usual equation between Paul and the preacher, as well as the automatic identification of Paul's audience with the preacher's congregation, is broken. The implied readers of these letters are Paul's delegates—Timothy and Titus. This forces the preacher to ask: is our situation analogous to the one implied by the text? Does what Paul says to his delegates apply to all of us, only to preachers, or to none of us? What enduring issues do these letters address, and what issues are truly only of historical interest? In short, the Pastoral Letters' literary character causes the preacher to struggle. However, out of struggle comes creative preaching.

What is the Focus of 1 Timothy?

The situation presupposed by 1 Timothy portrays Paul traveling on a mission. He has left the city of Ephesus in Asia Minor to go to Macedonia, leaving Timothy in Ephesus (1:3). He hopes to return to Ephesus shortly

(3:14; 4:13), although he might be delayed (3:15). That's it. These are all the details about Paul's circumstances and plans revealed in this first letter.

Ephesus is well known to Paul; it is a strategic city in his mission to reach the Gentiles for Christ (see Acts 18:18-21, 24-28; 19:8-20). Paul makes an important speech to the elders of the Ephesian church before departing for Jerusalem (Acts 20:17-38). In this speech he calls the elders "overseers" (Acts 20:28), revealing the same fluidity in terminology for church leaders we find in 1 Timothy and Titus.

Timothy, one of Paul's co-workers during his Ephesian ministry, serves as Paul's emissary (Acts 19:22; 20:4; 1 Corinthians 4:17; 16:10; 2 Corinthians 1:1, 19). Acts does tell us that Paul sends Timothy and Erastus to Macedonia in preparation for one of his own trips there (Acts 19:22), but it never mentions Paul leaving Timothy in charge of the Ephesian community while he himself is in Macedonia. Acts, of course, omits or generalizes other trips made by Paul (see 2 Corinthians 2:1; 13:1; Acts 18:23) and nothing in the text itself prevents us from placing 1 Timothy in the period of Paul's active Aegean ministry.

Timothy's role, during the time of Paul's absence from Ephesus, is clear: he is Paul's delegate to this local community (see also 1 Corinthians 4:17; Philippians 2:19-23). Specifically, Paul wants him to deal with problematic deviant teaching (1:3; 4:6) and community structure. He is not appointed by Paul as head of the local church but retains his role as delegate. He is to teach and command (4:11) in Paul's absence, seeing in particular to the "reading, preaching, and teaching" (4:13). If the text is read carefully, Timothy by no means establishes new structures and procedures. Instead, he responds to problems arising from structures already in place. Thus, this letter does not invent church order. Timothy is mandated by Paul to solve difficulties at a time when the Ephesian church is under stress from "certain persons" in the community who teach a different message from Paul's.

First Timothy's loose and inconsistent literary pattern matches the situation described in the letter. Its Greek style and vocabulary are distinctive and hence often deemed "un-Pauline" by scholars. It is best, in my opinion, to attribute much of the distinctive style to the special aim and subject matter of the letter.

Several of the elements common to personal *paraenetic* letters are found in 1 Timothy. For example, Paul presents himself as a model (1 Timothy 1:16) and Timothy is explicitly told to model speech and conduct for the church (4:12, 15). Also, the polemic against the opponents is presented in antithetical arrangement, in contrast to the behavior expected of Timothy (see 1:3-11, 18-20; 4:6-16; 6:3-16, 20-21). Timothy is to avoid and shun the opponents' practices (4:7; 6:11, 20). Furthermore, the opponents are slandered with more or less stereotypical charges.

Two things are especially noteworthy with respect to the opponents. First, the opponents are not only slandered, but rebutted. Paul repeatedly instructs Timothy in proper understanding of the issues the opponents opposed (see 1:8-11; 4:3-5, 8-10; 6:6-10). Thus, Paul is as concerned about the *content* of Timothy's teaching as he is about his *character* (see especially 1 Timothy 4:16). Second, Paul gives his delegate specific directives to resolve the community crisis. Timothy is to "command and teach certain things" (4:11). All of the commands are encapsulated in the verse which many scholars consider to be the theme of the whole letter: "how people ought to conduct themselves in the household of God" (3:15).

The letter's directives section tends to fall into separate thematic discussions: matters of worship (2:1-15), qualifications for local leadership (3:1-13), care of widows (5:3-16), payment and other problems of elders (5:17-22), slaves and masters (6:1-2), and the rich (6:17-19). These sections are disconnected from one another as they alternate with instructions relating to Timothy's personal duties and conflicts with the opposition (1:3-11, 18-20; 4:1-16; 5:21-25; 6:3-16; 6:20-21).

What is the Focus of 2 Timothy?

Even more than Philippians or Philemon, this is probably Paul's most personal letter. This is not the correspondence of a church planter with his congregation, but the personal communication of a spiritual father with one he calls "my dear son" (1:2). Second Timothy is laced with allusions to shared and/or common perceptions, values and even desires. Paul affectionately recalls Timothy as one who knows his family history (1:5; 3:15). They share knowledge (1:15, 18), past experiences (1:13; 2:2; 3:10) and present troubles (1:14-15). Thus, Timothy is likely able to "read between the lines" in Paul's letter to him.

Paul's own circumstances, according to 2 Timothy, are not very encouraging. He is in prison, likely in Rome (1:16-17). He has already made one defense from which he emerges as one "delivered from the lion's mouth" (4:17). In contrast to the other letters, Paul expresses no hope of being released (Philippians 1:12; 2:24; Philemon 22). He considers his life as drawing to a conclusion (4:6-7). He has little hope for human vindication, only divine (4:18). Furthermore, he experiences human abandonment and rejection. Everybody in Asia has abandoned him (1:15); nobody stands with him at his first defense (4:16). Some of his co-workers have left him for other mission fields, while others are in love with this world and have abandoned him entirely (4:10). Paul deeply appreciates the ministry of Onesiphorus who visits him in prison (1:16-17). He derives comfort from the hope of a visit from Timothy (4:9, 21), receiving the books and parch-

ments he forgot in Troas (4:13), and the prospect of bene-
fiting from the services of Mark, who will accompany
Timothy (4:11). Of course, Paul is not entirely alone. He
sends greetings to Timothy from some associates (4:21)
and Luke remains as his companion (4:11). Yet, what matters is that he feels alone and abandoned.

Paul's mission is also in jeopardy. The troubles of the
past (3:11) have come back to haunt him. Alexander, the
coppersmith who harmed Paul (4:14), continues to resist
Paul's rebuke; Timothy must be cautious of him (4:15).
The Pauline communities also experience the social dis-
ruption generated by troublemakers like Hymenaeus and
Philetus (2:17). Paul regards them contemptuously as
"charlatans" (3:13), like the magicians who opposed
Moses (3:8). Still, they have a negative impact, especially
among believers too weak to resist their influence such as
uneducated women easily seduced by flattering speech
(3:6-7). Paul fears that his opponents' distorted teaching
will prove more popular than the sound doctrine he and
his true followers proclaim (4:3-4). Thus, the opposition is
growing and progressing (2:16-17). After a lifetime of
laboring in God's vineyard (4:6), Paul faces personal
abandonment as well as his entire mission's possible failure.

To make matters worse, Paul's delegate, Timothy, is
not an especially strong co-worker, as earlier letters
already suggest (1 Corinthians 16:10-11). Indeed, we soon
learn that Timothy is discouraged in the face of the
Ephesian opposition, and may even be wavering in his
assignment (1:5; 1:7; 2:1; 3:12). Timothy appears to be
embroiled in his own fears, fragility and fatigue.
Nonetheless, Paul must somehow empower his belea-
guered colleague to stand fast and fight the good fight.

Given these circumstances, what kind of letter should
Paul write? Many scholars argue that 2 Timothy is a good
example of **testamentary** literature. It is a sort of farewell

discourse written in the style of Genesis 49:1-33: the dying hero shares wisdom with his successors. Testamentary literature often includes a prediction of the bad times just around the corner when opponents will emerge and flourish. Also, it includes instructions to stand fast in the traditions passed on by the elder and dying mentor. To be sure, some elements of 2 Timothy resemble this scenario quite well. But another literary category fits this letter much better.

Paul accesses to a conventional literary form which serves his purposes well. Handbooks on literary criticism call it a *"**paraenetic**"* letter. A good example is found in the Hellenistic moral writings called *To Demonicus*, where one who assumes the role of a father to a son reminds the younger man of traditional moral teaching so as to rekindle his commitment to it. Such *paraenesis* is personal; it is addressed to an individual, not a community. This literary form tends to have several common elements: memory, model and maxims. **Memory** is crucial for the living recollection of shared understanding. In particular, the proper moral attitudes and actions are recalled in a **model** from the past that embodies the higher standard in his own life. This *paraenesis* is developed by means of **maxims** or instructions found in an antithetical pattern: avoid these things but cultivate other things. Second Timothy has, in large measure, these classic elements of *paraenesis*. Thus, 2 Timothy, like 1 Timothy and Titus, is best termed a *personal paraenetic letter.*

What is the Focus of Titus?

While the letter to Titus reflects many of the features common to 1 & 2 Timothy, it does have its own distinctive setting, literary shape and importance. In comparison to Timothy, we know relatively little about Titus. He is a Greek upon whom Paul refuses to compel circumcision (Galatians 2:1-3). He may be the godfearing "Titus

Justus" of Corinth in whose house Paul stayed after being expelled from the synagogue, although this is simply speculation and depends on the variant reading of Acts 18:7. Titus seems to work quite extensively with Paul during his Aegean ministry, particularly as his delegate in raising funds for the Jerusalem collection (see 2 Corinthians 2:13; 7:6; 8:16, 23; 12:18). The text of 2 Timothy 4:10 suggests that Titus worked in Dalmatia, but in this letter he is stationed on the Island of Crete (Titus 1:5). The personal warmth Paul shows toward Timothy is lacking in the case of Titus. Titus is not called "beloved" (2 Timothy 1:2), yet he is presented as a true child in the faith (1:4). This letter's focus on the obligation to give money (Titus 3:14) reminds us of Titus's special role in the Pauline mission.

Nowhere else do we learn of Paul planting churches on the island of Crete except in this letter to Titus (1.5). According to Acts, Paul passes Crete as a prisoner on his way to Rome (27:7-12). Even if he does set foot on the island on this occasion, he certainly does not have the time to establish churches there. Still, it must be remembered that Acts is not an exhaustive report of all Paul's travels. For example, there is no mention in Acts of his founding churches in Galatia and Colossae, but few scholars doubt this fact. However, the statement of Titus 1:5 does not really require Paul's physical presence on the island of Crete. Rather than interpreting 1:5 to mean that Paul physically leaves Titus on the island, it could simply mean he leaves Titus in his current position on the island to straighten things out and appoint elders in every town.

At the time of its writing, Paul is actively involved in ministry. He is not imprisoned and he is planning to winter in Nicopolis, although we do not know to which of the many towns by that name he refers. In any case, while in Nicopolis, he anticipates a visit from Titus (3:12). By implication, Titus's assignment on the island of Crete is temporary. Titus himself is characterized as Paul's delegate who troubleshoots for the apostle. The letter suggests his gifts along these lines may be stretched by the Cretan situation: the church on the island is in its earliest days with elders still in the process of being appointed (1:5) and members who come from a less than reputable segment of the population. Furthermore, opposing teachers, possibly from Judaism (1:10), challenge these newly minted Gentile converts and are making progress among the faithful (1:11).

Titus resembles the literary structure of 1 Timothy. After an extensive greeting (1:1-4), Paul omits the typical expressions of thanksgiving and gets right down to business. *Paraenetic* features, while present, are minimized in Titus as compared to 2 Timothy. The theme of **memory** is found in 3:1 where Titus is encouraged to "remind" believers of their daily duties. Also, Titus, like Timothy (1 Timothy 4:12), is challenged to be a **model** to all the faithful (2:7), but Paul is not presented as an example. Polemic is heightened in Titus more than in the other two letters. Indeed, Titus is exhorted to take vigorous action against the opposing teachers (1:11; 3:10). The antithetical arrangement of the polemic is also minimized in contrast to 2 Timothy, although the opponents are contrasted to the overseer (1:7-10) and Titus (2:1; 3:9-11). Thus, the polemic in this letter highlights the basis for the instructions Titus must communicate to the faithful rather than supplying a contrast to the behavior and values of the ideal teacher.

Two lengthy theological warrants anchor the instructions Titus is to give to God's people on the island of Crete (2:11-14 and 3:3-7). Within this material, we encounter a high concentration of words and theological emphases that are distinctly Pauline, with a special focus on the educational power of God's grace. For those who read Titus to learn what it says to the contemporary church, this letter provides a coherent and challenging witness.

How is this Book to be Used?

This book has 13 chapters that explain the biblical text of 1 Timothy (chapters 1-6), 2 Timothy (chapters 7-10) and Titus (chapters 11-13). Small groups that meet either in the home during the week or adult education groups that meet on Sundays could elect to study the three Pastoral Letters over 13 weeks, assuming weekly meetings.

Each chapter is divided into five parts. First, **The Text** itself is reproduced, using the New International Version (1984). Of course, there is no substitute for the careful reading of the primary text. Hence, readers are encouraged to prepare for study by reading the text of 1 Timothy, 2 Timothy and Titus in advance of reading the commentary. Second, **The Flow and Form of the Text** seeks to identify the literary form and to map the biblical text's train of thought. Often the larger literary context is highlighted, especially literary connections to what precedes and follows the text under discussion. Third, **The Text Explained** treats specific units of thought within the chapter of a given letter without the overwhelming use of scholarly jargon, debate and footnotes. Any interaction with or reference to secondary sources is designed to provoke discussion and perhaps further research. Greek words are used sporadically to help the reader observe important nuances in the biblical text. Fourth, the section labeled **Application, Teaching/Preaching Points** attempts to bridge the first century setting of the Pastoral Letters with the 21st century. It is hoped, however, that the reader will not move too quickly to these points. The various chapters of these letters cannot be reduced to a central point or key idea. The way Paul writes to his delegates, Timothy and Titus, is inseparable from what he says to them. Thus, the reader is encouraged to hear the text anew and to resist reducing its meaning to points and propositions. Finally, the **Personal Reflection Questions** section provokes reflection upon the biblical text and dialogue about the text with other members of your faith community. In the final analysis, we study the Pastoral Letters not primarily to learn "the facts" about Paul and his delegates, but to learn what it means for us to be God's people today.

A **Select Bibliography** of further readings is supplied at the end of the book. Throughout the commentary, selected works are cited or referenced by placing the author's last name, date of publication and page reference within brackets in the following way: (Marshall 1999: 57-92).

CHAPTER ONE

Stop the False Teachers

The Text: 1 Timothy 1:1-20

Paul, an apostle of Christ Jesus by the command of God our Savior and of Christ Jesus our hope, [2] *To Timothy my true son in the faith: Grace, mercy and peace from God the Father and Christ Jesus our Lord.* [3] *As I urged you when I went into Macedonia, stay there in Ephesus so that you may command certain men not to teach false doctrines any longer* [4] *nor to devote themselves to myths and endless genealogies. These promote controversies rather than God's work—which is by faith.* [5] *The goal of this command is love, which comes from a pure heart and a good conscience and a sincere faith.* [6] *Some have wandered away from these and turned to meaningless talk.* [7] *They want to be teachers of the law, but they do not know what they are talking about or what they so confidently affirm.* [8] *We know that the law is good if one uses it properly.* [9] *We also know that law is made not for the righteous but for lawbreakers and rebels, the ungodly and sinful, the unholy and irreligious; for those who kill their fathers or mothers, for murderers,* [10] *for adulterers and perverts, for slave traders and liars and perjurers—and for whatever else is contrary to the sound doctrine* [11] *that conforms to the glorious gospel of the blessed God, which he entrusted to me.* [12] *I thank Christ Jesus our Lord, who has given me strength, that he considered me faithful, appointing me to his service.* [13] *Even though I was once a blasphemer and a persecutor and a violent man, I was shown mercy because I acted in ignorance and unbelief.* [14] *The grace of our Lord was poured out on me abundantly, along with the faith and love that are in Christ Jesus.* [15] *Here is a trustworthy saying that deserves full acceptance: Christ Jesus came into the world to save sinners—of whom I am the worst.* [16] *But for that very reason I was shown mercy so that in me, the worst of sinners, Christ Jesus might display his unlimited patience as an example for those who would believe on him and receive eternal life.*

¹⁷ *Now to the King eternal, immortal, invisible, the only God,*
be honor and glory for ever and ever. Amen. ¹⁸ *Timothy, my son,*
I give you this instruction in keeping with the prophecies once
made about you, so that by following them you may fight the
good fight, ¹⁹ *holding on to faith and a good conscience. Some*
have rejected these and so have shipwrecked their faith. ²⁰
Among them are Hymenaeus and Alexander, whom I have
handed over to Satan to be taught not to blaspheme.

The Flow and Form of the Text

After the traditional greeting of verses 1-2, the balance
of this passage (vv. 3-20) forms a chiastic (*abccba*) pattern
in which the false teachers (vv. 6-7) are contrasted with
faithful teachers (vv. 12-17) and the diseased teaching (vv.
8-10) is contrasted with healthy teaching (vv. 10-11). The
opening (vv. 3-5) and closing (vv. 18-20) charges to
Timothy bracket the two contrasts (see diagram below).

A "chiasm" describes the shaping of a passage in the
form of an "X" (the Greek letter "chi" is X-shaped, hence
"chiasm"). A chiastic structure places parallel words,
phrases or ideas at the top and bottom of the passage, sig-
naling beginnings and endings. Scholars mark the parallels by labeling them as A, B, C and C, B, A. In a chiastic
structure, attention is drawn to significant material by
means of repetitive parallels and by highlighting the center of the figure, the major thrust of the passage. The logic
of a chiastic structure helps an audience identify the key,
pivotal center and the major idea in the communication.
The central thrust of this passage is Paul's desire to root-
out the "diseased teaching," or whatever is contrary to
"healthy teaching," by stopping the false teachers (1:3).

> ### Chiastic Pattern of 1 Timothy 1: 3-20
>
> A. Charge to Timothy (vv. 3-5)
>   B. False Teachers (vv. 6-7)
>   C. Diseased Teaching (vv. 8-10)
>   C. Healthy Teaching (vv. 10-11)
>   B. Faithful Teachers (vv. 12-17)
> A. Charge to Timothy (vv. 18-20)

The Text Explained

Opening Greeting (1:1-2). Paul's greeting is typical of ancient letters and it follows a pattern familiar to us from his other letters. It identifies the sender, the recipient and concludes with a blessing. By means of these opening words, Paul establishes his authority, identifies himself closely with Timothy, and introduces his major theme of God's grace, mercy and peace.

At first glance it seems odd that Paul, the letter's sender, would tell Timothy he is an apostle. Surely Timothy knows about Paul's apostolic authority. Why not, "From Paul, your father in the faith?" It would fit nicely with the notion of Timothy as his son. Paul likely assumes Timothy will read this letter to all of God's people in Ephesus. Indeed, 6:21 suggests as much: "Grace be with you (plural)." Perhaps Paul wants the entire church to know that his delegate Timothy is functioning in Ephesus under apostolic authority. At the same time, given Timothy's mandate to root-out the false teachers in Ephesus (1:3), Paul is possibly concerned lest the church elders get a hold of his letter and suppress its message. After all, he is writing about the dangers of false teaching, a matter he had already warned the Ephesian elders about a few years earlier (see Acts 20:30). All of this may explain why the letter is not addressed to "the church at Ephesus" nor "to the overseers and deacons of the church of Ephesus" (cf. Philippians 1:1).

Paul underscores the basis of his apostolic authority
with the words "by the command of God" (cf. 2 Timothy
1:1—"by the will of God"). This a standard phrase used
of royal commands given to subordinates. No other apostle is mentioned in this letter and no one else is expected
to assume Paul's kind of authority. There is no concept
here of an office that is subsequently assumed by others.
While others may assume his role of teaching (cf. 2:7),
Paul is the singular apostolic link between God and this
church.

Only in the Pastoral Letters does Paul designate God as
"savior" (six times). In Philippians, Christ, not God, is designated "savior" (3:20; so also Ephesians 5:23; 2 Timothy
1:10; Titus 1:3-4; 2:13; 3:6). Why accent God's saving role or
function in this letter? While "savior" is a common word
among contemporary Christians, it is used only 24 times in
the whole of the New Testament. Its infrequent use in the
New Testament is possibly due to its common use among
pagan cults of the time, such as Roman emperor worship.
Hence, the early church uses the term sparingly. In the
Pastoral Letters, one greater than Caesar, the true King of
kings, commands Paul to be his apostle and special envoy.
It is also important to note that the designation of God as
savior is in harmony with the Old Testament portrait of
God: the savior who delivered Israel from Egyptian
bondage (Deuteronomy 32:15; Psalm 24:5). God our savior
stands behind the apostle's authority.

If God is presented as "savior," Christ is called "our
hope." When he thinks of Christ Jesus, Paul remembers
the great future salvage operation. One day Christ will
return to gather his people to himself and restore the
entire cosmos. Both expressions, God our savior and
Christ our hope, anticipate thematic emphases of this letter (see 2:3 and 4:10 as well as 4:10; 5:5; 6:15).

Timothy is called Paul's "true son in the faith." It is
difficult to determine whether this refers to spiritual

paternity, spiritual adoption or simply shared faith. A similar expression is used of Titus (cf. 1:4). Although it may refer to spiritual sonship, it is not clear from Acts that Timothy is Paul's convert. Also, Timothy is described in terms of his relationship to Paul, not in terms of his relationship to God. He is Paul's younger co-worker. The intimate language implies a bond of affection between them. Indeed, elsewhere Paul describes Timothy as one who serves with him in the work of the gospel "as a son with a father" (Philippians 2:22). Thus, Paul writes to Timothy with warmth and fatherly affection. He is a "true son," a description often used for a son born in lawful wedlock. Since Timothy's father is a Gentile and his mother a Jewess, his birth according to Jewish teaching is illegitimate, but his spiritual relationship to Paul is genuine. Paul may have led him to faith on his first visit to Lystra (see 2 Timothy 3:11; Acts 14:1-20; 16:1-3). What is important to note, given the difficult assignment facing Timothy, is that Paul's words are received as a vote of confidence. Paul's words serve as a stamp of approval upon Timothy.

Paul often concludes his letters' opening greetings with the words "grace and peace." Here he adds "mercy" to the mix (2 Timothy 1:2). If grace is God's supply of blessing to Timothy, mercy is God's undeserved forgiveness and constant loving care towards Jews and Gentiles alike. Mercy denotes God's special care of persons in need. Perhaps Paul adds it here because he is writing, indirectly, to a church troubled by doctrinal misunderstanding. "Peace" is the traditional Jewish blessing (*shalom*) that is not merely a quiet feeling, but the reality of right-relatedness to God, others and even God's creation.

The expression "from God the father and Christ Jesus our Lord" is common. But why is the personal plural pronoun ("our") absent in the case of the expression "God

the father"? It may indicate Paul's awareness of the difference between God's relationship to the world ("he
gives life to all things") and Christ's relationship to the
community of believers. In any case, the opening greeting makes two things clear: Paul is an apostle by God's
direct commission and Timothy is Paul's loyal delegate in
Ephesus.

First Charge to Timothy (1:3-5). Timothy's charge is
to command certain false teachers to stop teaching. Paul
clarifies the false teaching's nature (vv. 3-4), which
sharply contrasts with the stewardship of God's salvation
plan. Then he states the goal of his command to Timothy
(v. 5) and describes the false teachers' behavior (vv. 6-7).

Since his release from prison in Rome about A.D. 64,
Paul has been in Ephesus. But at some point he leaves
Ephesus and moves on to Macedonia (possibly Philippi),
leaving Timothy in charge of the work (cf. Philippians
2:24). Ephesus, a city located on Asia Minor's western
coast (modern Turkey), is famed for its cult and temple
dedicated to the worship of Artemis. There is also a large
Jewish colony in Ephesus, according to Acts 19.

Paul rushes right into the main reason for writing,
omitting his typical extended prayer and thanksgiving
for God's people (cf. Philippians 1:1-11). Verse 3 seems to
function as a key verse, explaining Paul's train of thought
and dealing with the crisis caused by the false teachers.
False teaching may be the central theme tying the whole
letter together. It is exciting when a young church plant is
growing rapidly. It is exhilarating as new Christians learn
the truths of God's love, mercy and grace, the meaning of
the cross, and the presence of Christ's Spirit. But young
believers may be inclined to accept new ideas uncritical-
ly. Perhaps something like this scenario was unfolding in
Ephesus.

Certain unspecified persons are teaching false doctrines. Their teaching is different from the message of the

Old Testament, of Christ (passed on to the Ephesians by Paul in oral form), and of the Apostle Paul. In the second letter to Timothy, we learn that the different teaching relates to the resurrection of believers (see 2 Timothy 2:18). Maybe there is confusion about the nature of our participation as believers in Christ's death and resurrection; some elders in Ephesus are teaching that the believers' resurrection has already happened. The contemporary health and wealth gospel, with its emphasis on the availability of salvation's benefits in the here and now, may be a dynamic equivalent to the Ephesian situation (see Fee 1985). The problem of false teaching appears to be the key that unlocks this letter's message. The apostle Paul withdraws the Ephesian elders' authority and appoints Timothy to sort out the mess.

Two things are important to keep in mind as we study this letter. First, Ephesus is Timothy's fourth solo assignment as Paul's delegate. His previous assignments included Thessalonica, Corinth and Philippi. Timothy's earlier experiences have equipped him for his assignment in Ephesus. Second, false teaching has cropped up elsewhere in the early church; it is not confined to the Ephesian church. For example, a different gospel was being preached in both Corinth (2 Corinthians 11:4) and Galatia (Galatians 1:6). John's letters to the seven churches of Asia Minor also remind us how widespread false teaching is in the early church (Revelation 2 & 3).

Paul does not spell out the exact content of the false teaching for he seems to assume his letter's recipient knows and understands the situation. Yet there are clues (v. 4), including: a) "godless myths" and "old wives tales" in 4:7); b) endless genealogies, presumably the habit of tracing one's ancestry back to Adam and Eve; c) speculation and controversies. Paul has good reasons for rejecting the false teaching—it does not serve God's saving mission in the world. It is not "the divine training that is known by faith," as the NIV translates the Greek text. God's redemption plan is known by faith, not by fanciful interpretations. In this way, Paul sets the false teachers' convictions outside the orbit of true faith in Jesus Christ and service to God. In a nutshell, the false teachers fail to manage God's household in a Christian manner.

Love that flows from a pure heart, clear conscience and sincere faith (v. 5) is Paul's primary objective. Paul wants to encourage wholeness in Christian thinking and living. Hence, he names three conditions for love to grow in the Christian community. A good conscience and a sincere faith are the polar opposites of a seared and corrupted conscience (cf. Titus 1:15). The standard of behavior set by the faith community is God's word properly interpreted.

False Teachers (1: 6-7). Paul portrays the false teachers as "wanderers" in three ways. a) They depart from Christian love characterized by a pure heart, a clear conscience and a sincere faith. b) They aspire to do great things; they strive to be "teachers of the law," a respectful title normally reserved for great teachers like Gamaliel who taught Paul the law (see Acts 5:34). But here it is a derisive name for the Ephesian elders who have no authority for what they are so confidently telling people. c) They do not understand what they are talking about.

False Teaching (1:8-10). Before Paul resumes the argument of verses 3-7, he makes two digressions (vv. 8-10 and vv. 11-17) that connect with his argument so far. The false teachers claim to be teachers of the law (Gk. *nomodidaskaloi*), but do not know what they are doing. Paul describes, in this first digression, the law's true purpose which, he argues, is for the ungodly. Paul is not arguing for a correct Christian use of the law here. Rather, he is pointing to the folly of the false teachers.

Paul begins his digression at a point of common knowledge by using a favorite Pauline phrase, "we know" (cf. Romans 2:2; 8:28). He says, in effect, "We all agree that the law is good." It is good because it truly does reflect God's will. Also, its goodness is related to its proper use; it must be used lawfully, that is, interpreted rightly. It must not be used as a source for legends and endless genealogies or ascetic practices. Instead, as Paul teaches elsewhere, it must be used to reveal sin (Romans 7:7-25) and restrain evil (Galatians 3:23-4:7). It is the law's restraining influence that is likely foremost in Paul's mind here.

By saying the Law was not intended for "the righteous," Paul reflects the point that is made in his letter to the Galatians: those who have the Spirit and bear its fruit have entered a sphere of existence in which the Law no longer performs its legal function (see Galatians 5:22-23). For example, as long as I obey the speed limit while driving my car, the speed limit law does not bother or summon me. Only when I violate the speed limit signs do I hear the siren and see the lights flashing behind me. In this way, the speed limit law corrects and curbs only drivers who violate it, no one else (Oden, 1983: 39). Similarly, the Law was not laid down for those who live according to its requirements, but as a restraint for the ungodly who violate its stipulations.

Virtue and vice lists are very common in the Pauline tradition and serve a basic parenthetical function; they offer examples of acceptable and unacceptable ethical behavior. The form itself is usually a listing of independent items, although considerable variation is possible. There are a few short vice lists in the Old Testament (e.g., Jeremiah 7:9) but such lists do not appear to be a well-developed literary form. Virtue lists are entirely absent in the Old Testament. Most scholars agree that the New Testament form, and often the very content, is borrowed from Hellenistic literature where it is very common. Apparently Paul feels free to borrow typical vices and virtues. He also freely shapes his list by both the particular situation and by the uniqueness of the Christian faith. Here in verses 9-10, Paul provides a vice list that is arranged roughly according to the two tablets of the Decalogue (Easton, 207), as illustrated below.

The Decalogue & the Vice List of 1 Timothy 1: 9-10	
I Timothy 1:9-10	**Exodus 20:3-17**
lawbreakers and rebels (v. 9)	You shall have no other gods before me (v. 3)
ungodly and sinful (v. 9)	You shall not misuse the name of the Lord your God (v. 7)
unholy and irreligious (v. 9)	Remember the Sabbath day by keeping it holy (v. 8)
those who kill their fathers and mothers (v. 9)	Honor your father and your mother (v. 12)
murderers (v. 9)	You shall not murder (v. 13)
adulterers and perverts (v. 10)	You shall not commit adultery (v. 14)
slave traders (v. 10)	You shall not steal (v. 15)
liars and perjurers (v. 10)	You shall not give false testimony (v. 16)

Of the sins or sinners listed, only immoral people and sexual perverts are found in earlier lists (see 1 Corinthians 6:9). The list seems to have two parts. First, there are three pairs by general classification. Thereafter, the list bears a remarkable similarity to the Ten Commandments. What is the reason for such a list here? It is certainly not a hidden reference to the sins of the false teachers who are guilty of their own kinds of sin, but not of these. Most likely the list is a conscious reflection on the Mosaic Law and expresses the kind of sins such a law was given to prohibit. It's as if Paul is saying, "Look, God did not give the Law for idle speculation and foolish discussion, but rather to reveal and restrain sin."

Healthy Teaching (10b-11). In his impatience to get on with his argument and his application to the present situation, Paul concludes with an equivalent to our "et cetera"—"and whatever else is contrary to the sound doctrine" (v. 10). As he moves on, he applies the list to the current Christian situation by his reference to sound teaching and to the gospel. A similar summary technique at the end of a vice list is used by Paul in Romans 13:9 and Galatians 5:21. Perhaps these Christians to whom Paul writes still consider themselves to be Jews and, for them, the Law has not passed away. Rather it provides the context within which the gospel is preached. Indeed, Paul even defends the Law by rejecting its improper interpretation.

"Sound doctrine" (v. 10) is an important phrase. Paul uses it eight times in the Pastoral Letters (6:3; 2 Timothy 1:13; 4:3; Titus 1:9, 13; 2:2, 8). The Greek word behind the English word "sound" is a medical term from which we get the word "hygiene." It is the opposite of sick and unhealthy and was used when lame people became perfectly whole (see John 5:15). Thus, we could say that Paul speaks of "healthy doctrine." If the Law is for the morally diseased, the gospel is health giving. By likening the false teachers' teaching to "an open sore that eats away the flesh" (cf. 2 Timothy 2:17), Paul may be imitating Greek philosophers who frequently referred to their opponents as people who were "sick in the mind." By extension, if the truth is being taught and learned and lived out in our churches, we should see healthy minds and wholesome lives. Error produces the opposite. Paul's metaphor focuses on behavior, not on the content of the doctrine. Healthy teaching leads to proper Christian conduct and behavior such as love and good works; diseased teaching leads to controversy, arrogance, abusiveness and strife (cf. 6:4).

God is called the source of all blessing (v. 11) and Paul is about to tell us how he has experienced this blessing for himself. He begins by reminding us that God entrusted the gospel to him.

Faithful Teachers (1:12-17). This paragraph takes the form of a personal testimony. Paul uses the personal pronoun "I" and "me" fourteen times. The entire unit is a digression, but it connects to the preceding unit and flows directly from the words "the gospel… which he entrusted to me" (v. 11). Paul reflects on his own calling out of sin into Christ's service. He presents himself as a model for Timothy, other church leaders, and all believers to follow. He also presents himself as the opposite of the false teachers, emphasizing his faithfulness. All church leaders should exemplify the qualities mentioned here by Paul. Since his testimony emphasizes God's lavish grace set forth in Jesus Christ, Paul breaks forth in a doxology or shout of praise to God, something that often happens in his writings (cf. Romans 11:33-36).

If we failed to identify with the warnings of this chapter's earlier portion, we readily identify with Paul's personal testimony in verses 12-17 where he speaks about his conversion experience. In contemporary parlance, he is telling his story. We are familiar with his conversion story from Luke's accounts in Acts 9, 22 and 26. Paul himself recounts his conversion story, with few details, in Galatians 1:11-17, Philippians 3:2-11 and 2 Corinthians 10-12. Here, however, his conversion story is front and center. Where the false teachers emphasize law, Paul emphasizes God's mercy and grace. At his conversion, he received mercy and grace from God, not law. He seems to be saying that the law has no power to save; only God's grace and mercy are adequate to rescue us.

Paul begins his testimony by underscoring two truths. First, the strength for Paul's ministry comes from Christ: "I thank Christ Jesus our Lord, who has given me strength" (v. 12). Paul knows from personal experience that Christ empowers us for ministry in his name (cf. Romans 15). Paul does not attribute his success in ministry to a seminary education, up-to-date methods or even personal charisma. Rather, he points to the empowering presence of Christ's Spirit working through him. Second, Christ authorizes Paul's ministry: "he (Christ) considered me faithful, appointing me to his service" (v. 12). Paul considers his appointment here to be his work as a servant or minister, not his role as an apostle. Paul does not claim God called him into ministry because he thought so highly of him. "Such an idea would contradict the whole passage," says Gordon Fee (1984, 16). Instead, Paul declares his amazement that God would even consider him for service in the first place. He says something like this: "I can't believe God would even deem me worthy of this assignment." But God did give him the privilege of serving, granted solely by Christ's virtue. So Paul's ministry is energized by and originated in Christ. In other words, Paul is completely dependent upon Christ Jesus as he ministers to the Gentiles.

In his continuing story, Paul notes his experience of God's grace and mercy. First, he describes himself in the past tense as a "blasphemer and a persecutor and a violent man" (v. 13). This refers to his persecution of the church when he not only denied Christ, but persecuted God's people and hence, Christ himself (see Acts 8:3; 9:1-12; 22:4-5; 26:9-11). He was an anti-Christian fanatic. He approved of Stephen's stoning, contributing to him becoming the first Christian martyr (Acts 7-8). Luke tells us he tried to destroy the church, going house to house and dragging away "Christian" men and women to put into prison (Acts 8:3; 9:1-2). Yet he experienced God's mercy.

Clearly, the wonder for him that magnifies God's grace is that Christ should even consider him for ministry at all. Second, Paul claims he was granted mercy because he acted in ignorance and unbelief. There is a kind of condition attached to God's mercy. Does his ignorance and unbelief let him off the hook? Does it make him less culpable? Paul does not reflect here on the distinction between "unwitting sins" and "purposeful sins" (cf. Numbers 15:22-31). Rather, he explains why he was the object of God's compassionate love. As Marshall says, "Here there is a clear recognition that non-Christians commit sins as a result of ignorance... of God's will" (1999: 393). This theological perspective is also reflected in our Lord's words from the cross: "Father, forgive them, for they do not know what they are doing" (Luke 23:34). Paul is a sharp contrast to the false teachers. Prior to his conversion, Paul acted in unbelief; he did not accept Jesus as Messiah. By contrast, the false teachers are leaders who once embraced Jesus, but now reject his message (see 1:19; 2 Timothy 2:18). Thus, their sin falls into a different category. Third, the experience of God's abundant grace results in a life of faith and love: "The grace of our Lord was poured out on me abundantly, along with faith and love that are in Christ Jesus" (v. 14). According to Paul, God initiates our salvation and our faith and love are simply a response to his grace and mercy. Also, faith and love are indications of God's grace in our lives. God bestows faith, which is a disposition of trust in him and belief in the gospel. Love also characterizes the believer in terms of loving and serving others in the style of Christ. Paul expresses that a genuine response to God's saving grace proclaimed in the gospel will result in a life of faith and love.

After Paul relates his own story about how God's grace was poured out on him as former persecutor, he is reminded of a well-known saying: "Christ Jesus came into the world to save sinners" (v. 15). It is introduced with the formula, "Here is a trustworthy saying that deserves full acceptance." This formula will be used four more times in the Pastoral Letters (3:1; 4:9-10; 2 Timothy 2:11-13; Titus 3:7-8). Here the formula (literally, "faithful is the saying") precedes the saying, although sometimes it follows the saying (see 3:1 and 4:9). Nothing quite like it is found elsewhere in the New Testament. Yet, the "faithful is God" formula is common in the Pauline writings (see 1 Corinthians 1:9). The emphasis is on the saying's reliability, as the NIV translation makes apparent: "a trustworthy saying that deserves full acceptance." The saying itself, a succinct summary of Christ's mission, makes two points about it. First, the historical ministry of Christ is the basis of salvation: "Christ Jesus came." Salvation is based solely on Christ and the message about him. In this way, Christ's incarnation is underscored. Second, the goal of Christ's incarnation is redemption: "… to save sinners." The word "sinners" is a universal term. All humanity shares this identity as Romans 3:19-20, 23 declare: "all have sinned and come short of the glory of God." But Christ came to save sinners. Indeed, God's salvation is the result of Christ's entrance into human history; this is the central point of the tradition or well-known saying.

Paul adds a personal remark: "I am the worst of them." Paul has an overwhelming sense of his own sinfulness and his utter helplessness before God. But he also has a deep appreciation of God's grace and mercy so lavishly given to him despite his sinfulness. Note also that Paul does not say, "I was," but "I am." As I. Howard Marshall says, "The converted sinner remains conscious that he is a sinner, saved by grace" (1999: 399-400). Thus, Paul recognizes that he is a sinner who has experienced God's redemption. But why does he say the "worst" (literally, "the first") of sinners? Paul is likely trying to establish the effectiveness of the gospel he has preached.

Indeed, the repeated references to himself as the worst of sinners is designed to emphasize the superabundance of the grace and mercy associated with the gospel message. It may also point to the fact that Paul was the "first" both in terms of the depth of his sin and his position in time at the beginning of salvation history.

With the addition of that last phrase, "of whom I am the worst," Paul gives us God's reason and purpose in saving him. In this way, he makes his final point about God's grace: "but for that very reason I was shown mercy so that in me, the worst of sinners, Christ Jesus might display his unlimited patience as an example for those who believe on him and receive eternal life" (v. 16). First, the reason Christ saves Paul is so he might be a primary exhibit for all other sinners who would later believe in Christ for salvation. Again, Paul says, "I was shown mercy" (1:13, 16). He underscores that if God could save him, given who he was and what he had done, there is hope for all of us! Second, by saving Paul, God displayed his patience in dealing with sinners. Patience as God's characteristic way of dealing with human rebellion (Numbers 14:18; Joel 2:13) is a thoroughly Pauline teaching (Romans 2:4; 3:25-26). "This forbearing patience is," according to Marshall, "also required as a quality in missionaries who must not despair of sinners but continue to seek to bring them to repentance and faith" (1999: 400). In a sense, Paul is God's pilot project for later believers. This converted persecutor is a pattern for future converts. His conversion demonstrates God's patience to all who come to faith in Christ. Third, salvation requires belief in Christ (v. 16). By "believe on him," Paul means personal faith in Jesus Christ, not simply adherence to dogma or creed. Finally, the goal of belief in Christ is eternal life (v. 16; cf. 4:8; 6:12). A believer's personal faith in Jesus Christ is the stepping-stone to the ultimate goal of eternal life.

Paul wraps up his personal testimony about God's

mercy with a doxology which is similar in content to the doxology of 6:15-16. He is moved to worship: "Now to the King eternal, immortal, invisible, the only God, be honor and glory forever and ever. Amen" (v. 17). Here Paul points to God's majesty and glory. His words emphasize God's otherness and eternity. It has a liturgical ring to it. It may reflect an actual doxology used in the Diaspora synagogue where Paul has his own roots and where he begins his missionary work. Eternal King (literally, "king of the ages") picks up the theme of eternal life in verse 16. God is eternal in that he is the ruler of the ages (both "this age" and "the age to come"). God is immortal or incorruptible. He is invisible, an Old Testament motif. He is the only God, again an Old Testament motif pointing to his oneness—God is one. Therefore, all honor and glory are due him forever and ever. The "amen" is pronounced in the synagogues as a way for the people to embrace or agree with the doxology. This practice passed into the early Christian church as evidenced by 1 Corinthians 14:16.

With the doxology of verse 17 Paul brings his digression to a conclusion. His two digressions (1:8-11 and 1:12-17) are a long way from his charge to Timothy to stop the false teachers. Yet every stitch of these two digressions relate directly to the false teachers and their diseased teachings (1:11) which emphasize Law and speculation rather than the gospel of God's mercy and grace that produces faith and love. Paul is concerned that God's salvation comes to us through the gospel of Jesus Christ. Paul is but an example of God's grace and mercy, not a hero figure whose behavior must be emulated. After all, Paul did not bring about his own conversion. He received mercy (passive voice). Truly, it is God who deserves the honor and the glory, even as our text claims.

Charge to Timothy (1:18-20). Paul now returns to the main purpose of writing his letter to Timothy. He repeats

the address, "Timothy, my son," and then reiterates his
standing orders concerning the false teachers. In effect he
says: "Now, my boy, this is what you have to do."

As he repeats the charge to Timothy, Paul does not
pull rank as an apostle or even as Timothy's spiritual
father, but simply reminds him that he has a reputation to
live up to. Prophecies have been made about Timothy.
Paul may be referring to the "prophetic" message given
to Timothy when the elders laid hands on him as reported in 1 Timothy 4:14. Or, he may have in mind that the
"brothers at Lystra spoke well of him," as Acts 16:2
reports. This might mean no more than that they gave
him a good reference, but it could mean that, at
Timothy's commissioning service, Christians from his
hometown of Lystra and from Iconium prophesied about
his future service and usefulness. As Towner says,
"Persons who accept positions of power and importance
in this world must also accept the obligations and responsibilities that go with them. The same (principle) is true in
the church" (1994:57). Timothy has an obligation to fulfill,
even if the circumstances are not ideal. Of course, in addition to a sense of obligation, Timothy can count on God's
support (see 1 Timothy 6:13-14). Paul reminds Timothy of
his earlier commitment and God's promise to support
him through "thick-and-thin."

Paul uses a military image to challenge Timothy calling him "to fight the good fight" (v. 18b). This image is
typical language for Paul, especially when he struggles
against opponents of the gospel. He portrays Timothy as
a soldier who must go to battle. Timothy's weapons,
however, are not clever arguments (see 2 Timothy 2:23-
25) nor the destruction of the enemy (cf. 2 Thessalonians
3:14-15), but "faith and a good conscience" (v. 19). By
good conscience, Paul undoubtedly invites Timothy to
show a godly concern for his opponents' spiritual well
being. His objective is to protect the faith of the people

being influenced by the false teachers and, if possible, to win back those who have strayed from the faith. As Paul has already illustrated, only the gospel is adequate for such work (1:11-16). Also, Paul is concerned that Timothy's faith remains intact as he takes on these opponents of the gospel.

The two people Paul hands over to Satan are likely former elders of the Ephesian church, the men Paul warned the church about on the Island of Miletus as reported in Acts 20:30. The name Hymenaeus appears again in 2 Timothy 2:17 where he is described as wandering away from the truth by claiming the resurrection had already taken place and by destroying the faith of some of God's people. He may have been claiming that Christians are already in heaven and will never die. Alexander could be the metalworker who did Paul a great deal of harm (see 2 Timothy 4:14-15) and who opposed his message. Or, he could be the Ephesian Jew of Acts 19:33. Might all three scriptures refer to the same Alexander? In any case, both false teachers have been "handed over to Satan." Likely, Paul has put them out of the church and they are now exposed, without the protection of God's promises to his people, to the dangers of sin. Metaphorically speaking, many people need to be thrown into the sea before they realize the advantages of being on the ship. This same phrase is used in 1 Corinthians 5:1-5 and 2 Thessalonians 3:14-15 where it seems to have the same purpose. All these cases express the same goal—the hope that these renegades will be changed, reformed and restored to fellowship in the church. There is no vindictiveness or punishment implied; only the hope of improvement. Thus, the discipline is temporary: until the sinner repents. Full recovery is the goal. Furthermore, the goal is also to preserve the entire faith community in Ephesus, the rest of the body of Christ.

Application, Teaching/Preaching Points

The opening chapter of Paul's letter to Timothy provides the contemporary church with a truckload of practical wisdom. Let me suggest several timely messages that derive from this first chapter.

Wanted: Relational Church Leadership. Is effectiveness in ministry diminished in any way by cultivating deep personal relationships with the persons one seeks to serve? Many people think so. It is often stated that a pastor's first priority is the person he or she seeks to serve, and the one serving should not expect their relationship with others in the congregation to be mutual or reciprocal in nature. However, the opening greeting of 1 Timothy underscores Paul's role as an apostle while simultaneously emphasizing his close and affectionate relationship with Timothy. He addresses Timothy as a friend, but in the same breath Paul views him as a person who serves under his apostolic authority. Office and person seem to be mixed in Paul's pastoral identity. As one commentator rightly notes: "The office of ministry does not imply interpersonal distance—quite the opposite. Pastoral authority at best elicits and celebrates personal closeness, the intimate ties that emerge in the relational life that is hid in Christ" (Oden, 1989: 18). If so, the renewal of the church today may depend upon leaders who teach the apostolic tradition with authority in the context of warm, caring relationships with the people they seek to serve and lead.

The Sacred-Secular Antithesis. The Ephesian church is not the first and only church to suffer from misleading fables (1 Timothy 1: 4). Today's church is not exempt from this disease; there are many misleading fables that plague contemporary Christians. For example, Dorothy Sayers identifies one of them when she says, "It is not right to accept that life is divided into time spent at work and time spent serving God." When we make false divisions "our inner lives tend to break up so that we live a divided instead of unified life.... This is the old sacred vs. secular antithesis. Many Christians are caught in its trap, " says A. W. Tozer. Such divisions violate our nature as whole people. Marriage, work, money, health—all suffer from this distortion. Spirituality is then seen as somewhere else; it becomes disconnected from everyday life and peculiar enough to be a specialty of the few whom we pay to do it for us commoners. In the early church of Paul's day, this heresy is called "godless myths" and "Gnosticism." It happens whenever people believe they have a special *gnosis*. Such knowledge experts must be challenged. The tendency in Paul's day and ours is for spirituality to be inward, exclusive and escapist. This well-intentioned but misguided spirituality actually denies God's good creation. To be true to our God-given spirituality is to practice dominion over and give thanks for all things (see 1 Timothy 4:4-5). We are also to train ourselves in true spirituality because godliness requires self-discipline and "has value for all things" (see 4:8). That's all things, not just a few isolated areas of our life or hours of the week. If you have abdicated certain things as untouchable or secularized some aspects of your life, reclaim them now for God.

Distinguishing False and True Teaching. According to our text, there are several differences between Christian teaching and false teaching. Christian teaching is "sound" teaching; it produces healthy people. Sound teaching is more than a ticket to heaven; it changes how we think about self, others and God. Sound teaching produces new people who are morally and mentally healthy, marked by love for self, others and God. Second, Christian teaching conforms to the gospel message; it squares with Christ's message and that of his apostles (see 1 Corinthians 15:1-13). Its center is the grace of God that propels us to love and serve others in the style of

Jesus Christ. Third, sound teaching carries apostolic authority, the gospel entrusted to Paul. False teaching lacks such a foundation. Thus, if any teaching conflicts with Paul's, its source is suspect and it is something other than the gospel God entrusted to Paul (see Galatians 1:6-9). Conformity to apostolic endorsement becomes the "canon" applied by the early church fathers to various writings to test their authority. This test remains appropriate today. We too can approach competing claims to authority by beginning with the Scriptures. Any teaching that does not conform to Scripture is clearly wrong. How one "feels" about the teaching is not the issue. A final conclusion about a particular teaching is a matter for the church. We have a measuring stick—the Scriptures. Therefore, teaching that is truly Christian (a) produces whole Christians, (b) flows out of the gospel of Jesus Christ, and (c) bears the apostle's stamp of approval. Still, we need to remember that there is no easy solution to some doctrinal disagreements. There are essentials that need to be addressed and non-essentials in which freedom to disagree must be granted. Above all, we should be committed to open dialogue, especially when Scripture is interpreted in more than one way.

Every Christian "Story" Speaks of God's Grace. Most of us would be somewhat reluctant to do what Paul does here in 1 Timothy 1:12-17. Certainly we are no match for the Apostle Paul. But if we set aside our humility for the moment, we must acknowledge that every Christian has a "story to tell" about God's grace and goodness. While we do not want to live in the past, it is appropriate at times to reflect on our own conversion story, allowing it to serve as a reminder of God's goodness. Paul's own experience of God's grace demonstrates God's goodness and the gospel's power. Paul knows in his heart and is fully convinced that the gospel message he preaches is true. It is important for every Christian to share a similar conviction, borne of personally experiencing God's grace. To be sure, this certitude about the gospel's truth cannot be based on mystical experiences with God; it must be supported by a changed life (see 1:14). Could the false teachers in Ephesus make the same claims about their gospel? Not likely! When the gospel of Jesus Christ is embraced by faith it produces a changed person, a new life.

Five "Trustworthy Sayings." Five times in the Pastoral Letters Paul uses the phrase, "Here is a trustworthy saying" (NIV translation). "Faithful is the saying" is a literal translation of the Greek phrase (*pistis ho logos*). There is evidence that the trustworthy saying of 2 Timothy 2:11 has a number of the key rhythmic elements of a hymn. If so, Paul may have been quoting well-known words from hymns, spiritual songs or church prayers. A sermon series on the five trustworthy sayings of the Pastoral Letters would communicate the heart of Christian preaching. Here they are in brief: 1) "Christ Jesus came into the world to save sinners" (1 Timothy 1:15); 2) "If anyone sets his heart on being an overseer, he desires a noble task" (1 Timothy 3:1); 3) "We have put our hope in the living God, who is the Savior of all, and especially of those who believe" (1 Timothy 4:9-10); 4) "If we died with him, we will also live with him; if we endure, we will also reign with him. If we disown him, he will also disown us; if we are faithless, he will remain faithful, for he cannot deny himself" (2 Timothy 2:11-13); 5) "When the kindness and love of God our Savior appeared, he saved us, not because of righteous things we have done, but because of his mercy. He saved us through the washing of rebirth and renewal by the Holy Spirit, whom he poured out on us generously through Jesus Christ our Savior, so that, having been justified by grace, we might become heirs having the hope of eternal life" (Titus 3:4-7).

Is Church Discipline Possible Today? The practice of discipline varies greatly in our churches today. In some fellowships, discipline is very strict and church members are given direction in very mundane matters. In other churches, discipline is a foreign concept and members politely ignore each other's failings—at least in public— and make a meal of gossip about them in private. But discipline is hardly a practice the church can afford to ignore today. Several New Testament passages spell out a very clear process. Matthew 18:15-17, 1 Corinthians 5:5, 2 Corinthians 2:5-11, and 2 Thessalonians 3:14-15 give clarity about how to proceed. Each step is designed to bring the erring believer to the point of admission and true change of mind and behavior.

Balancing "Inside" and "Outside" Ministries. We all know congregations that seem to be so preoccupied with internal affairs that they completely neglect evangelism and mission beyond the walls of the church. Some churches have even blamed Paul's emphasis here in the Pastoral Letters for this unfortunate situation. But it must be remembered that 1 Timothy, which is of necessity focused on false teaching and congregational order, does contain a very warm theology of salvation. Indeed, it stresses the mystery of the gospel and underscores the primacy of grace, as this first chapter reveals. Also, like the other Pastoral Letters, 1 Timothy encourages an attitude of Christian living that calls for obedience to a conscience operating in close connection with faith and sound teaching. This letter encourages a Christian lifestyle designed to win the respect of outsiders and commend the gospel. Indeed, Paul embraces a missionary theology wherein the apostle plants the church, but the church planter takes on the care of God's people and the preservation of the truth. I think we can safely assume that if the Ephesian church had been free of false teaching, the call to active evangelism would have been closer to the surface of Paul's concerns.

Personal Reflection Questions

- Paul tells his delegate Timothy (1:1) that he is an apostle! DISCUSS: Why do you think Paul didn't write, "From Paul, your father in the faith"? If Paul assumed his letter would be read to the congregation at Ephesus (see 6:21), why didn't Paul write directly to the church of Ephesus as he did in other letters (see Philippians 1:1 or 1 Corinthians 1:1)?

- False teaching is a major problem in the Ephesian church. DISCUSS: What have you learned about the false teaching to this point in the letter? What parallels do you see to our own day and time?

- The false teachers in Ephesus were introducing new ideas that conflicted with Paul's teaching. DISCUSS: How do we determine whether a new idea is true or false? How can local churches "stick to the knitting" and avoid endless dialogue about minor issues?

- Paul claims the law is good, if used properly. DISCUSS: How do we best use the law? That is, how do we work with the Scriptures so they pull us toward God and not away from our God-given vocation in the world?

- God's grace was poured out abundantly on Paul. DISCUSS: Is it possible that second and third generation Christians have grown too familiar with "being saved?" How do we keep alive our gratitude to God for his grace? What return can we make? What can we learn from Paul's testimony about drawing people's attention to God rather than ourselves?

- Two former elders of the Ephesian church wandered from the faith. DISCUSS: Do you know any Christians who have shipwrecked their faith? What is the root cause of wandering away from the faith?

CHAPTER TWO

Proper Conduct at Worship

The Text: 1 Timothy 2:1-15

I urge, then, first of all, that requests, prayers, intercession and thanksgiving be made for everyone—² for kings and all those in authority, that we may live peaceful and quiet lives in all godliness and holiness.³ This is good, and pleases God our Savior,⁴ who wants all men to be saved and to come to a knowledge of the truth.⁵ For there is one God and one mediator between God and men, the man Christ Jesus,⁶ who gave himself as a ransom for all men—the testimony given in its proper time.⁷ And for this purpose I was appointed a herald and an apostle—I am telling the truth, I am not lying—and a teacher of the true faith to the Gentiles.⁸ I want men everywhere to lift up holy hands in prayer, without anger or disputing.⁹ I also want women to dress modestly, with decency and propriety, not with braided hair or gold or pearls or expensive clothes,¹⁰ but with good deeds, appropriate for women who profess to worship God.¹¹ A woman should learn in quietness and full submission.¹² I do not permit a woman to teach or to have authority over a man; she must be silent.¹³ For Adam was formed first, then Eve.¹⁴ And Adam was not the one deceived; it was the woman who was deceived and became a sinner.¹⁵ But women will be saved through childbearing—if they continue in faith, love and holiness with propriety

The Flow and Form of the Text

The next major literary unit of this letter focuses on proper conduct in God's household, as 3:14-15 makes clear: "I am writing so that … you will know how people ought to conduct themselves in God's household…." The issues treated in chapters 2 and 3 are best understood as relating to the problems caused by the false teachers in the Ephesian church. First, Paul encourages the church to pray for all people as a way of participating in God's mission in the world (2:1-7). Second, he gives Timothy explicit instructions about the conduct of men and women at worship (2:8-15). Finally, he provides some guidelines for selecting church leaders, both elders and deacons (3:1-16).

In Paul's day, it was unthinkable for a household to be without authority, structure, rules of conduct and responsibilities. In this chapter, Paul draws on the household rules or codes of his time, applying them to the church conceived as "God's household." As Christians, we have a common Lord and relate to him as our Father. We are brothers and sisters in the faith. If human households require order to function appropriately, the household of God also requires proper behavior if it is to participate faithfully in God's mission to save the world. Unfortunately, today congregations often develop tunnel vision, becoming preoccupied with their own local agenda to the neglect of God's global plan. This is unfortunate because, as Towner aptly says, "the original plan, to reach all nations, calls for the parts to recognize the whole" (1994: 62).

Paul's application of the household code to the church undoubtedly has an apologetic function. He encourages behavior in the church that is deemed acceptable in Roman society to show that Christianity is not dangerous to the norms of the state. He encourages conduct in the church that promotes God's mission in the world in his day. For example, when he treats the matter of the church's prayers (2:1-7), he includes teaching about the church's need to show respect for the state. When he talks about the selection of church leaders, he emphasizes behavior that meets with the approval of outsiders. In this way, Paul reminds the church of God's global strategy.

The Text Explained
Pray for All People (2:1-2). Paul begins this first unit (2:1-7) by underscoring the importance of praying for all

people, including kings and persons in authority (2:1-2). Next, he gives the rationale for inclusive prayers by noting that the salvation of all people everywhere is God's will (2:3-4). Then he cites a creedal fragment of the early church that demonstrates the universal scope of God's desire to save all persons through Jesus Christ (2:5-6). Finally, he adds a personal reflection about his own call to be an apostle to the Gentiles as evidence of God's inclusive redemptive plan and the church's role in it (2:7).

The word "then" (2:1) indicates that what follows connects with the preceding paragraph. The false teachers in Ephesus may have been exclusive in their orientation. They called together a group of special people, creating an "in group" that excluded others who were not likeminded. But true Christianity is inclusive, embracing all people. Hence, Paul repeats the word "all" three times in seven verses: prayer should be made for all people (2:1); God wants all people to be saved (2:6); and Christ came to give his life as a ransom for all people (2:6). The inclusive emphasis in these verses is similar to Paul's words in Colossians 1:28 where he says, "We proclaim him, admonishing and teaching everyone with all wisdom, so that we may present everyone perfect in Christ." God treats all human beings with equal respect and love. Perhaps some of the Jewish Christians in the Ephesian church were having difficulty embracing their Gentile brothers and sisters. We too may think of ourselves as special people, a little better than those "pagan" outsiders. If so, we should note that Paul calls for prayer that is expansive in scope; he teaches Timothy and the church in Ephesus to pray for all people irrespective of their religion, race, social status or gender.

All kinds of prayers should be offered, including "requests, prayers, intercessions, and thanksgiving" (2:1). This is not a four-step program of prayer. Rather, Paul simply speaks about prayer in a comprehensive way—all kinds of prayers should be made for all kinds of people. In other words, our prayers should be large in scope, attending to all the details of people's lives, interceding for all people, giving thanks for all people, making requests on behalf of all people, and praying for all people irrespective of their social category.

Indeed, inclusive and comprehensive prayer by God's people is a ministry of first importance: "first of all" (2:1). By implication, we need to give careful attention to the place we give to this task when we gather together as God's people. We need to keep in mind the context here—God's mission in the world is at stake and an important aspect of our calling is to pray for all people.

What is especially clear is that our prayers should include persons in government; they should include prayers for the state, a feature that makes 21st century Christians a bit uncomfortable. However, the Jews of the dispersion set an example for us since they prayed for a pagan government even when it was oppressive (cf. Jeremiah 29:7). We should follow their example. The New Testament does encourage us to respect our rulers, as evidenced by Romans 13:1 and 1 Peter 2:13. Indeed, a submissive posture by the church toward government often lends credibility to the church in the eyes of the world (1 Peter 2:15). We are called to pay our taxes (Romans 13:7), honor the ruling authorities (Romans 13:7), and now in the Pastoral Letters, pray for kings and all those in authority (1 Timothy 2:2). The fact that Paul attaches such importance to the church's prayers for all people should prompt contemporary Christians to re-assess how we conduct ourselves in God's house.

The rationale for this manner of prayer is: "so that we may live peaceful and quiet lives in all godliness and holiness" (2:2). The goal of such inclusive praying is to create the best possible context for God's mission in the world through the church. If rulers have no reason to suspect Christians of disloyalty, they will be able to practice their faith without interference. The Roman government's enforced peace over a huge area enabled Christians like Paul to take the gospel across frontiers with a great deal of freedom. What's interesting here is that Paul does not ask the church to pray that God would liberate the land from Rome. Rather, he calls the church to pray for the Romans to responsibly administer the land.

Paul's description in verse 2 of the nature of Christian living ("in all godliness and holiness") points to the church's witness in the world. Godliness is one of Paul's favorite terms for authentic Christian living. It appears eight times in the Pastoral Letters. It refers to both right teaching and right living; that is, it calls us to be Christian where we work, live and play. Holiness, or seriousness, suggests a lifestyle that wins the respect of outsiders (cf. 1 Timothy 3:7; 6:1; Titus 2). Paul assumes that our manner of life as Christians will be evaluated by the watching world. If we embody the gospel's truth in our individual and corporate lives, we have a better chance of commending our faith and Christ's gospel to those who are outside the orbit of the Christian faith.

God's Inclusive Mission (2:3-5). The church's prayers for all people are grounded in God's own concern for all people: "This is good, and pleases God our Savior who wants all men to be saved and to come to knowledge of the truth" (vv. 3-4). A peaceful and quiet life in the land is not the only Christian motivation for our inclusive prayers. The practice of praying for all people is also rooted in the very character of God who wants all people to be saved. He wants all people to experience *Shalom*, a right relatedness to self, others and himself.

Since "savior" was the common title given to the rulers of empires from the time of Ptolemy I of Egypt, Paul might be indicating that earthly rulers actually do

God's will by protecting the people. Or, perhaps Paul is contrasting the earthly rulers for whom we pray with the Savior to whom we pray. Whatever the case, it is God's desire that all men "come to knowledge of the truth" (2:4). This is a technical expression that describes conversion as a rational decision about the gospel message. God wants the gospel preached to all nations so that all men might turn and embrace salvation through faith in Christ Jesus. In this context, to be saved means to experience freedom from sin, death and judgment.

The church's inclusive prayers are not an optional activity. Prayers for all people are intrinsic to the church's participation in God's world mission. The church exists for God's cosmic mission, which includes the goal of saving all people. One way we participate in God's mission in the world is through the ministry of prayer, especially prayer that includes all people. Such prayer seeks the gospel's penetration into every sphere of society in every region around the globe.

Christ's Inclusive Sacrifice (2:5-6). With verse 5, Paul introduces a well-known formula that may be part of an early Christian hymn or creed. His initial readers may recognize it as such. Verses 5-6 sound like an extract from a creed since they represent four compact, balanced, rhythmical phrases.

---

1 Timothy 2:5-6: An Early Creedal Fragment
For ...
there is one God;
there is also one mediator between God and man,
the man Christ Jesus,
who gave himself a ransom for all.

Verse 5 makes two major points. First, the universal scope of God's saving mission in the world is a logical corollary of his character: "For there is one God and one

mediator between God and men, the man Christ Jesus."
The Jews of pre-Christian times used the expression,
"there is one God" as a reflection on Deuteronomy 6:4
which they repeated daily. It was designed to counteract
the polytheistic claims of the many pagan gods surrounding them. There are not three gods, but one God,
and therefore one gospel (cf. Romans 3:29-30). This is
important for us when talking with Jews and Muslims
today, for some of them accuse us of believing in three
gods. If there were many gods, there would be many
gospels. Religious pluralism offers us a supermarket of
religions that are all deemed relatively true. But this is
nonsense according to Paul. There is only one God and
only one gospel. Of course, Paul draws on the "oneness
of God" theme to underscore the truth that there is one
God for Jews and Gentiles alike (cf. Romans 3:29-30;
Ephesians 4:4-6).

Second, the reference to "one mediator" indicates that
God's universal salvation is available only through
Christ Jesus. Jesus is the middleman or go-between; he is
the bridge person. Jesus stepped in between God and
man to make possible a new relationship between the
two parties. What he "mediated" was the new covenant
as spelled-out in Jeremiah 31:31-34. The false teachers, by
contrast, are inclined to invent extra mediators: Moses,
angels, supernatural powers, saints, etc. But if anything
or anyone comes between God and people except Jesus
Christ, our one mediator, something has gone wrong: we
should suspect error.

While God's salvation is inclusive of all people, there
is an exclusive dimension implied by Paul's logic.
Salvation is linked solely to the one mediator, Christ
Jesus. Indeed, the final phrase, "the man Christ Jesus,"
locates his mediating activity in his earthly career, life
and ministry in Palestine around A.D. 30-33.

The final line of verse 6 ("who gave himself as a ran-

som for all men") includes a thought that echoes Jesus'
own words about himself (see Mark 10:45). The media-
tion ministry of Christ was accomplished through his
death on the cross. There are at least six important theological emphases in this short verse. First, the change
from "many" in Mark 10 to "all" in 1 Timothy 2:6 underscores Christ's inclusive sacrifice. The earliest Christian
teaching available to us states that Christ's death was
intended to reach "all" people (cf. 2 Corinthians 5:14-15).
Second, Christ's death was voluntary; "he gave himself."
His death was not unexpected, nor a senseless accident.
He was in full control of his earthly career, including his
death (cf. John 10:18; Acts 2:23; 2 Corinthians 5:19). His
death was an integral dimension of God's redemptive
plan. Third, Christ's sacrifice was a payment to obtain the
release of slaves: it was a ransom. A ransom means an
exchange price paid to set a slave free. Since his life was
worth more than all creatures put together, Christ's death
provides a sufficient ransom to set us all free, not just a
few specially chosen elite people. Fourth, Jesus died as a
representative. The fact that the man, Christ Jesus, stood
between God and sinful people as our mediator indicates
the intimate nature of his representation. The significance
of Christ's mediating work is spelled out by the preposition "for." He died for the benefit of humankind. Fifth,
this verse may also indicate the substitutionary nature of
his sacrificial death. The Greek word *anti* is added to the
word *lytron* (translated "ransom" by the NIV in Mark
10:45 but without the preposition *anti*), which implies
that Christ died in place of humanity. Thus, Jesus gave
himself in our place. Sixth, the final phrase is difficult to
interpret: "the testimony given in its proper time" (2:6).
"Proper time" is a term repeated elsewhere in the
Pastoral Letters (1 Timothy 6:15; Titus 1:3). Here the
phrase may mean "the time that God knows to be the
right one," the decisive moment in history. If so, God

actively implemented his will for all to see, and the life and ministry of Christ was God's testimony given in its proper time. In other words, God initiated the proclamation of the Good News through the words and works of Jesus Christ.

Paul's Inclusive Ministry (2:7). Paul's call to be an apostle to the Gentiles is based on the character of God: "For this purpose I was appointed a herald and an apostle..." (2:7). He seems to reason like this: If this is what God is like, and what Jesus is like, then no wonder he has appointed me, Paul, as a missionary to the Gentiles. The same logic ought to motivate us today. A "herald" authoritatively declares royal news that people have not heard before. "Herald" has the same basic meaning as "evangelist." The work of proclamation that God initiated through the life and death of Jesus was passed onto the Apostle Paul, whose ministry as a "sent one" (Gk. *apostolos*) focused on the Gentiles indicating, once again, the universal scope of God's saving mission.

Paul underscores his message's reliability by saying, "I am telling the truth, I am not lying" (2:7). The false teachers in Ephesus may have been trying to limit the gospel message to Jews alone. If so, Paul responds to Jewish doubts about his effort to win Gentiles and baptize them without circumcising them first. Paul is a teacher of "the nations" (2:7), an expression that corresponds to "all people." As some observe, these three terms together (herald, apostle and teacher) describe the spiritual gifts needed for the three successive stages of missionary work: evangelistic preaching, apostolic church planting and the teaching of disciples.

Men and Women at Worship (2:8-10). Although the NIV translation omits it, verse 8 begins with a "therefore" in the Greek text. Paul now develops his remarks about praying for all people by giving guidance on how men and women ought to pray in the context of corporate

Christian worship. "Everywhere" does not mean "in every house church of Ephesus," but rather "among the nations" as Malachi 1:1 prophecies (cf. 1 Corinthians 1:2; 2 Corinthians 2:14; 1 Thessalonians 1:8). Indeed, when Gentiles pray to the Lord the prophecy of Malachi is fulfilled.

Paul gives men a singular guiding principle: "lift up holy hands in prayer" (2:8). It is customary in Jewish prayer for men to lift up their hands (1 Kings 8:54; Psalm 63:4). The only other New Testament reference to this custom describes Jesus lifting up his hands to bless his disciples at his ascension (Luke 24:50). But the physical act of raising hands is not the important feature of this Pauline injunction. Paul's emphasis is upon "holy" hands (cf. Psalm 24:3-4; Isaiah 1:15). As Isaiah points out, God will not listen to our prayers if our "hands are full of blood." If we are full of bitterness and unresolved anger, the physical lifting up of hands will not suffice. Positively, when we pray, we are to be in a right relationship with other people; we are urged to pray "without anger or disputing" (2:8; cf. Matthew 5:23; 6:12, 14-15; James 4:3; 1 Peter 3:7). A divisive spirit has invaded the corporate worship services of God's people in Ephesus. Paul likely has the false teachers in mind; they are causing dissension with their disputes and arguments (1 Timothy 1:4; 3:3; 6:4). Hence, Paul calls for a return to healthy interpersonal relationships that are so crucial for the prayer life of God's people.

Women are also commanded to pray in the worship service. However, the command to women is obscured by the NIV translation that omits the term "likewise" (2:9). In effect, Paul says, "Just as I want the men to pray in an appropriate way, I want the women to pray in an appropriate way." As 1 Corinthians 11:5 makes clear, Paul does not exclude women from praying in the worship setting. The Bible in general values the prayers of women

(1 Samuel 2:1-10; Luke 1:46-55; Acts 1:14; 16:13). The issue here is not whether women should pray, but how they dress when they do.

Paul uses three similar words to prescribe the manner of dress appropriate for women in worship: "modestly, with decency, and propriety" (2:9). Paul may be concerned about women who dress in a sexually explicit way, distracting the men during the worship service. But this may be too narrow a meaning. Paul's focus here may also be for the feelings of poor people who are upset by wealthy women flaunting their social status by means of dress. Indeed, Paul gets quite specific, discouraging "braided hair or gold or pearls or expensive clothes" (2:9), fineries that characterize the wealthy women of Paul's day. Thus, even as men who are argumentative disrupt the worship service, so also women who overdress can negatively influence corporate Christian worship.

What is important is that women at prayer should clothe themselves "with good deeds, appropriate for women who profess to worship God" (2:10). Biblical parallels to this Pauline emphasis are abundant. For example, the New Testament reminds us that Dorcas "was always doing good and helping the poor" (Acts 9:36). The Old Testament recalls Abigail's kindness (1 Samuel 25). It is not extravagant dress but good deeds that make a woman's piety visible to the watching world. Good deeds speak of genuine Christianity.

No Women Teachers (2:11-12). Together with 2:13-15, these verses are at the center of the current debate on the place of women in the church, if not also their role in the home and society. More has been written on 1 Timothy 2:11-15 than any other passage in the Pastoral Letters (see Mounce 2000: 94-102). Here, the "text explained" section of the commentary will focus on the meaning of this passage in the first century. For a consideration of this passage's meaning for the 21st century, please see the

"Application, Teaching/Preaching Points" section of the commentary.

In verses 11-12 Paul gives a positive command for a woman to learn in quietness, followed by a prohibition against women teaching men. The tone of command dominates as Paul shifts from persuasion ("I urge" in 2:1 and "I want" in 2:8) to authoritative command ("I do not permit" in 2:12). These two verses form a chiastic pattern (ABCBA), drawing attention to the central portion (C) of the passage as Paul's pivotal concern (see Bailey and Vander Broek 1992: 178-183). The repeated commands to quietness or silence (Gk. *hesychia*) frame the entire unit and recall the earlier appeal for prayers that foster the quiet life (2:1-2). But the emphasis here is on verbal silence and subordination. The positive command to subordination in verse 11 ("in full submission") is repeated in negative form in verse 12 ("or not to have authority over a man"). The restrictions on female speech and the exercise of authority reinforce and surround the central prohibition of verse 12: "I do not permit a woman to teach." The chiastic structure of these verses, as illustrated below, helps the audience identify the key, pivotal center and major idea of the communication.

Chiastic Pattern of 1 Timothy 2:11-12

A. A woman should learn in quietness
    B. and full submission
        C. I do not permit a woman to teach
    B. or to have authority over a man
A. she must be silent.

Paul does not explicitly identify the social context for the quiet and submissive behavior prescribed for women. But the "everywhere" of 2:8, plus the reference to "God's household" in 3:15, suggests that the prohibition applies primarily to the gathered Christian community in any place, or to the public worship service. The command derives its content from the household codes and cultural context of Paul's time. Hellenistic moralists spelled out with clarity the proper conduct of the various members of a household. Paul has simply adapted these regulations, applying them with some modification to the church, which he regards as "the household of God" (3:4, 3:15, 2 Timothy 2:20-21; Ephesians 2;19). In the ancient world of Paul's day, wives are expected to behave in a manner that reflects their subordinate status to their husbands; they are encouraged to be silent and submissive to their husbands (Ephesians 5:22-33; Colossians 3:18-19; 1 Peter 3:1-7; Titus 2:5). Paul slightly modifies the Greco-Roman household codes as he applies them to the church. His requirement is not that wives should be silent and submissive to their husbands during the worship service, but that all women are expected to be quiet (or silent) and submissive to all other men in the setting of the worship service, thereby reflecting their subordinate status. To put it bluntly, in the Ephesian church of the first century no woman is to exercise authority over a man in the setting of the church gathered. Thus no woman should participate in the teaching ministry of the church during public worship.

There are several things to note about verse 11: "A woman should learn in quietness and full submission." First, the generic singular, "a woman" (Gk. *gune*), refers to women in general even though the married state is regarded as normative (2:15). Paul's term is not limited to wives but refers to women in general. Second, the term "learn" (Gk. *manthano*) refers to instruction in the Christian way of life by a teacher in the setting of the gathered community. Indeed, all who participate in Christian corporate worship services can be characterized as "learners" (see I Corinthians 12:7-11, 28-30; 14:1-33) except, of

course, the teachers. Thus, it is normative for women to
learn along with the men; there is nothing alarming or
uncomfortable about Paul's remarks so far. Third, the
expression "in quietness" (*en esuchia*) is more ambiguous.
It could mean absolute silence, or silence in the sense of
not teaching, or simply learning in quietness as the NIV
translates—accurately, I think. Normally, "in quietness"
simply means enjoying tranquility (1 Timothy 2:2;
2 Thessalonians 3:12) or showing deference to teachers by
remaining silent when they are teaching (Acts 23:3).
However, "to learn in quietness" does not exclude a
healthy and respectful exchange between learner and
teacher (1 Corinthians 14:35). What Paul dislikes is rude,
disruptive remarks that interfere with the legitimate
teaching of God's people during corporate worship.
Thus, Paul enjoins women to learn quietly by showing
deference to their male teachers. Fourth, the phrase "in
full submission" (Gk. *en pase hypotage*) reinforces Paul's
call for women to show deference to their teachers in the
worship setting. It is not a call for a wife to submit to her
husband unless, of course, the teacher happens to be her
husband. Submission here is consonant with our common calling as God's people to submit to the gospel's
teaching (2 Corinthians 9:13). Paul commands women to
accept their male teachers' authority, an attitude deemed
appropriate for learning in the context of Christian worship. By implication, men who are not teachers are also
expected to learn in quietness and full submission to the
congregational leader (1 Corinthians 16:16; Galatians 6:6).

If verse 11 is problematic for 21st century readers,
verse 12 creates even more discomfort: "I do not permit a
woman to teach or to have authority over a man; she
must be silent." Paul shifts from talking positively about
a woman's appropriate role in worship (2:11) to a prohibition against certain activities by women in worship
(2:12). Several things should be noted about this notori-

ous verse. First, the verbal idea "I do not permit" is in the present tense (first person singular), meaning, "I am not permitting." The tense itself certainly does not support the notion that this command is applicable in all Christian settings for all time. Paul's injunction here is fresh and unencumbered with the weight of church tradition (see Marshall 1999: 455).

Second, the verb "to teach" (Gk. *didaskein*) begs the question: forbidden to teach whom (someone) and what (something)? What are women prohibited from teaching? Repeatedly in the Pastoral Letters, this verb refers to the authoritative task of teaching the gospel message in the setting of the gathered community (1 Timothy 4:11; 6:2; 2 Timothy 2:2), even as the noun form "teaching" (Gk. *didaskalia*) habitually refers to the gospel message (1 Timothy 1:10; 4:6, 13, 16; 5:17; 6:1, 3; 2 Timothy 3:10, 16; 4:3; Titus 1:9; 2:1, 7, 10). In dealing with the problem of false teaching in these letters (1:3-7), Paul wants to stop the false teaching from spreading, a situation some women may have been exacerbating. Thus, Paul does not want women teaching the gospel message in the church setting. However, this is not a blanket prohibition against women teaching anyone anywhere (see Titus 2:3-4; 2 Timothy 1:5; 3:15; Acts 18:26; Colossians 3:16). Rather, it is a command for women to refrain from teaching the Christian tradition and Scriptures in public worship in the Ephesian church of Paul's day.

Next, whom are the women forbidden to teach? Both the context and the grammar of verse 12 make "man" the object of the two verbs "to teach" and "to have authority over" (see Mounce 2000: 123). However, since women are allowed to teach in some circumstances, Paul likely means in this context that they are not to teach the gospel message in the setting of the gathered community; that is the responsibility of the overseers (see 1 Timothy 3:2; 2 Timothy 2:2, Mounce 2000: 124).

The next phrase, "to have authority over a man," is notoriously difficult. Behind this English phrase is the much disputed Greek term *authentein*, a verb that occurs nowhere else in the New Testament and only four times prior to the Christian era. Three interpretations of this verb's meaning in its present setting have been proposed: first, the neutral sense, "to exercise authority over a man" (Kostenberger 1995: 65-80); second, the erotic or seductive sense, "to proclaim herself the author of man" (Kroeger and Kroeger 1992: 87-104, 185-88); third, the negative sense of exercising autocratic or domineering power, "to exercise overbearing authority over a man" (Marshall 1999: 456-460). The second meaning is conjecture based on reconstructing the Ephesian background (the influence of the Artemis cult). It is difficult to see how the verb could mean, "to proclaim oneself the author of man" (see Marshall 1999: 457-459). The third meaning raises serious contextual problems for it is doubtful Paul would prohibit only women (and not men also) from teaching in a domineering or overbearing manner. Thus, the NIV translation, "to have authority over," without any strong negative or erotic connotations, is probably the best of the three options for this setting. If it means, "to have or exercise authority over," it provides an adequate parallel to the idea of "in full submission," its counterpart in the five-line chiasm of verses 11-12. Thus, Paul prohibits women from teaching the gospel message in the public setting of the worship service. Instead, they are to be learners who submit to the overseer's authoritative teaching.

Salvation through Childbirth (2:13-15). Paul supplies two biblical warrants for his prohibition, both from Genesis. The first is based on the order of creation (2:13) and the second is based on the woman's susceptibility to deception (2:14). Paul's instruction ends in verse 15 with an exceptive clause that defines a woman's role domestically.

The first warrant ("for Adam was formed first, then Eve") refers to the sequence of creation as described in Genesis 2:18-24. It rests on the assumption that the "first formed" has superior status and rightful authority over siblings born subsequently (see Genesis 27:29; Deuteronomy 21:15-17; Hebrews 1:6; Genesis 25:23; 37:9-11; 1 Samuel 16:6-13). By implication, women who teach and thereby exercise authority over men, are violating the social order established by God at creation. In 1 Corinthians 11:8, Paul relies on the same Creation account to support his argument that women should stay veiled when prophesying or praying in public worship: "man is not from woman but woman from man." However, he immediately qualifies his remarks with the recognition that "in the Lord" men and women are interdependent and men also derive from women (1 Corinthians 11:11-12). But in 1 Timothy 2, there is no such qualification of the creation order by the order of life "in the Lord." Unfortunately, Paul's argument works against him because, as Johnson writes, "the creatures of God created first were always inferior to those created later. The logic would imply that women, created later, are actually superior" (1996: 141).

The second warrant ("And Adam was not the one deceived; it was the woman who was deceived and became a sinner") is more developed and refers to the account of the temptation and transgression of God's command in Genesis 3. The key for Paul is the matter of Eve's deception (Genesis 3:17) rather than Adam's. It links Eve with the women who are being deceived (2 Timothy 3:5-7) as well as with Paul's opponents who are deceivers (1 Timothy 4:1; 2 Timothy 3:13; Titus 1:10). Presumably this means that women have a peculiar weakness and are less capable than men of discerning the truth and rejecting falsehood. If this is true, it's no wonder Paul's opponents have so much success with women!

Also, if this is true, it's no wonder Paul does not want women to exercise the critical role of teaching the gospel message in the public worship setting. After all, unlike men, women are vulnerable to deception and hence might unknowingly spread false teaching in the church (cf. 5:13). Again, Paul's argument is flawed. According to the story of Genesis 3, the woman was deceived by the serpent that is described as "more crafty than any of the wild animals the Lord God had made" (3:1). Whereas Adam, who was not influenced by the serpent, ate the forbidden fruit as soon as it was offered to him by the woman (3:6). Moreover, the Lord blamed the man for eating the fruit (3:17), not the woman. Paul's soft science exegesis of the creation account suggests he is simply "supporting his own culturally conservative position on the basis of texts that seem to him to support the greater dignity and intelligence of the male and, therefore, the need for women to be subordinate to men at public functions" (Johnson 1996: 141).

The exceptive clause of 2:15 ("But women will be saved through childbearing—if they continue in faith, love and holiness with propriety") defines a woman's way to salvation through childbirth and a virtuous life (see also 5:14; Titus 2:4). In effect, Paul's statement transforms the punishment of Genesis 3:16 into a means of salvation. Paul is quite likely trying to counter the ascetic tendencies of his opponents who forbid people to marry (see 4:3). In the proviso ("if they continue in faith, love and holiness with propriety"), Paul shifts from the singular verb ("she") to a plural ("they"). As the larger context indicates, his concern is with the behavior of women (cf. 2:9), not with the behavior of the woman's children as some commentators suggest. This qualifier functions as a warning. It also brings this remarkable statement into line with the letter's basic theological posture (see 1:14).

Application, Teaching/Preaching Points

Although this chapter is the source of much debate within the church, it is rich in its relevance for today's faith communities. Here are several issues for God's people to consider.

Does God Always Get What He Wants? Our text claims that God wants all people to be saved. So what is the relationship here between God's will and human disobedience? Some passages of Scripture seem to suggest that God does indeed always get what he wants. For example, Job concludes, "You can do all things; no plan of yours can be thwarted" (42:2). In some religions like Islam, the "inthwartability" of God is a fundamental principle: he determines the whole of history as well as our individual lives. But the God of the Bible is different. Even in Job, God himself underscores Job's free response to his suffering—Job can curse God and die (2:9), or he can maintain his spiritual integrity. Scripture shows that God longs for his people to repent (cf. Isaiah 65:2). Yet it seems that God has chosen to limit himself, refusing to overrule us even when we reject him. At the same time, surely the omnipotent God could arrange things so we have free will and he gets his own way too. Like the little girl who asked, "If God can do anything, can he make a stone so heavy that he cannot lift it?" Our understanding runs dry at this point. Unless our choice has some significance, we have no power of choice at all; just the pretense of choice. The New Testament apostles treat people as though they have the choice to respond, accept or refuse the gospel message. Thus, God gives us the freedom to repent and believe or to remain hostile to him and his Son. He has made us "in his image" and he respects us, not as his equals, but as responsible persons.

A Christian Attitude Toward Government. In the Pastoral Letters, the church is portrayed as settling in for the long haul with little, if any, emphasis on the expectation of Christ's imminent return. There is concern that believers present the Christian community to their society in a favorable light. These letters maintain an ethic of subordination, not only in domestic relationships, but also in the relationship between church and state. For example, in 1 Timothy 2:1-2, Paul encourages the practice of prayer for everyone. But those who are particularly singled out for prayer are "kings and all those in authority" (2:1). This refers to civil authorities, including the emperor. This sharply contrasts with Paul's other letters, which make no appeal for public prayer on behalf of officials or the emperor (although the prayer appeal here seems consistent with the spirit of the letter to the Romans). The practice of prayer on behalf of the emperor and empire is a regular feature of Jewish religious life in New Testament times. Indeed, prayers are offered daily in the Temple for the welfare of the empire until the fall of Jerusalem and the Temple in 70 C.E. Also, Jewish communities in the *diaspora* (outside of Palestine) make strong affirmations of loyalty to the empire. Thus, the call for Christians to pray for those in authority is not without precedent.

As in Judaism, the appropriateness of such prayer becomes problematic only when the state becomes hostile to the faith community. Then the question arises: should the persecuted church continue to pray for those in authority? The New Testament gives different answers to this question. In 1 Timothy 2:2, Paul explains that Christians should pray for those who hold political office because it will lead to quiet and peaceable lives. This concern for peaceful life reflects the hope that Christians be seen as model citizens instead of troublemakers. It also links to the author's concern for evangelism: by their exemplary conduct as loyal and praying citizens, Christians will promote the cause of the gospel. Nowhere do we get the feeling in the Pastoral Letters that there might be any inherent conflict between the Christian community and the state. Thus, prayer for those in authority seems the right thing to do.

Should Women's Roles Be Restricted Today? Debate about the place and role of women in ministry continues in many Christian denominations today. There are good people and excellent arguments on both sides of the question. Some argue for an "egalitarian" approach that releases women for all forms of Christian ministry inside and outside the church. Others adopt a "complimentarian" approach that subordinates women to men in selected roles within the church. I believe we need to acknowledge that both the "complimentarian" and "egalitarian" positions exist side by side in the Bible. In my judgment, equality is the biblical ideal (Galatians 3:28) reflecting how God acts, as depicted throughout the Bible. However, patriarchy is often allowed and regulated by God who has larger kingdom purposes in mind; 1 Timothy 2:11-12 is a case in point. In this letter to Timothy, Paul expresses deep concern for the success of God's mission in Ephesus. He restricts the role of women in ministry so that the behavior of God's people in that setting does not interfere with God's desire to save all people (1 Timothy 2:4). As Stackhouse states: "When society was patriarchal, as it was in the New Testament context and as it has been everywhere in the world except in modern society in our day, the church avoided scandal by going along with it—fundamentally evil as patriarchy was and is" (2005: 56). However, in North America today, an egalitarian approach to ministry would not hinder God's missionary cause in this setting. Indeed, the opposite is the case. North American churches entrenched in patriarchy reduce the gospel's attractiveness to outsiders. Stackhouse aptly states, "Now… that modern society is at least officially egalitarian, the scandal is that the church is not going along with society, not rejoicing in the unprecedented freedom to let women and men serve

according to gift and call without an arbitrary gender
line. The scandal impedes both the evangelism of others
and the edification... of those already converted" (2005:
56). Thus, in the final analysis, Paul's restriction of
women in public worship was necessary in the first century when society was generally patriarchal and
women's roles were limited in public affairs. If women
were to teach in public worship in Ephesus in the first
century, it would have been regarded as an unacceptable
breach of behavior patterns among Jews and also among
some Gentiles. Accordingly, the restriction can be interpreted as a culturally shaped prohibition that is no longer
binding in a different cultural context.

What about Paul's Appeal to Scripture? What com-
plicates Paul's commands in 1 Timothy 2:11-12 is the religious warrant attached to them. In 1 Timothy 2:13-15, he
appeals to Genesis to justify his restriction of women in
ministry using the Bible to back up his prohibition!
Verses 13-15 seem to have a twofold argument that Adam
was created prior to Eve (hence, men are superior!) and
that it was Eve who was deceived by the serpent (hence,
women are more easily deceived than men!). All of this
seems to be theological, not cultural. However, other factors need to be considered before embracing the validity
of Paul's argument. First, if it were not for this passage in
1 Timothy (and 1 Corinthians 14:33-36), very few faith
communities would be restricting women from teaching
in the church today. Second, in Paul's day, illiteracy (only
3% of the general population was literate!) and a lack of
education was the norm; women especially suffered from
these disadvantages. Third, there is considerable evidence in 1 Timothy 5:13 and 2 Timothy 3:6-7 that suggests
women were especially vulnerable to false teaching in
these Ephesian congregations. Fourth, the notion that
women are for all time more easily deceived than men
because Eve was deceived is baseless. If the serpent had

spoken to Adam rather than Eve, he would likely have fallen just as quickly as Eve. Fifth, the notion that priority in creation places men in a position of superiority over women (and husband over wife) so that women should not teach is groundless. Sixth, if Eunice and Lois are commended for teaching the Christian faith to the young Timothy, it means that teaching *per se* is not the problem. Seventh, the very unusual verb "to have authority over" (Gk. *authentein*) may express an unacceptable form of women dominating men in the Ephesian context. Eighth, some women in the Ephesian setting may be arguing that to be saved they need to teach in the public gathering, whereas Paul claims that childbearing is a legitimate fulfillment of their Christian calling.

In the final analysis, while we do not have certainty about the interpretation of this difficult text (2:11-15), there is sufficient doubt about the validity of the patriarchal interpretation as a prohibition for our day to make it an unwise imposition on the church. A helpful comment by F. F. Bruce is worth quoting here: "In general where there are divided opinions about the interpretation of a Pauline passage, that interpretation which runs along the line of liberty is much more likely to be true to Paul's intention than one which smacks of bondage or legalism." (see Griffith 1996:59).

Personal Reflection Questions

- Prayer is given a place of first importance by Paul. DISCUSS: Do we need to rethink the role that prayer plays in our corporate gatherings? Is our corporate prayer sufficiently expansive or is it somewhat limited in focus? How can we broaden our concerns so we do not simply pray for a chosen few?

- Paul mandates the church to pray for persons in authority. DISCUSS: Does your local church actively pray for persons in government at the local, provincial/state and national level? How could it improve its prayer ministry in light of 2:2-3? To what degree are Christians called to obey government? What happens when Christians are forbidden to meet together, teach or practice their faith?

• The text gives proper conduct in corporate worship top billing. DISCUSS: How can you improve your approach to corporate Christian worship in terms of your attitude, preparation and attire? What can we apply from this passage about prayer in the early church?

• The question of the role of women in church ministry is a problem for some today. DISCUSS: Compare the role of women in the church with that of women in politics, business and public life? If so, why? For example, how acceptable is it for a woman to serve as the president/prime minister of a nation but unacceptable for a woman to serve as the senior pastor of the church? Has historic Christianity contributed to the emancipation of women? Compare a culture that has been influenced by the Christian tradition with one that has not.

CHAPTER THREE

Qualifications of Church Leaders

The Text: 1 Timothy 3:1-16

Here is a trustworthy saying: If anyone sets his heart on being an overseer, he desires a noble task. [2] *Now the overseer must be above reproach, the husband of but one wife, temperate, self-controlled, respectable, hospitable, able to teach,* [3] *not given to drunkenness, not violent but gentle, not quarrelsome, not a lover of money.* [4] *He must manage his own family well and see that his children obey him with proper respect.* [5] *(If anyone does not know how to manage his own family, how can he take care of God's church?)* [6] *He must not be a recent convert, or he may become conceited and fall under the same judgment as the devil.* [7] *He must also have a good reputation with outsiders, so that he will not fall into disgrace and into the devil's trap.* [8] *Deacons, likewise, are to be men worthy of respect, sincere, not indulging in much wine, and not pursuing dishonest gain.* [9] *They must keep hold of the deep truths of the faith with a clear conscience.* [10] *They must first be tested; and then if there is nothing against them, let them serve as deacons.* [11] *In the same way, their wives are to be women worthy of respect, not malicious talkers but temperate and trustworthy in everything.* [12] *A deacon must be the husband of but one wife and must manage his children and his household well.* [13] *Those who have served well gain an excellent standing and great assurance in their faith in Christ Jesus.* [14] *Although I hope to come to you soon, I am writing you these instructions so that,* [15] *if I am delayed, you will know how people ought to conduct themselves in God's household, which is the church of the living God, the pillar and foundation of the truth.* [16] *Beyond all question, the mystery of godliness is great: He appeared in a body, was vindicated by the Spirit, was seen by angels, was preached among the nations, was believed on in the world, was taken up in glory.*

The Flow and Form of the Text

The metaphor of the church as God's household continues as the governing motif of 3:1-16: "I am writing these instructions so that ... you will know how people ought to conduct themselves in God's household" (3:15). Paul has already urged God's people to make their prayers expansive, including all people within their scope (2:1-7). And he has mandated the manner in which men and women ought to pray in public worship, adding that women are prohibited from teaching in the worship service (2:8-15). Now Paul turns his attention to the character qualifications of church leaders, specifically overseers and deacons (3:1-13), and concludes with a comment on the letter's purpose (3:14-16). Thus, Paul continues to focus on proper conduct in public worship. Since he has just prohibited women from leadership roles in public worship, Paul quite naturally describes the kind of persons who are to be approved for congregational leadership.

Lists of virtues and vices are very common in the Pauline writings (see Romans 1:29-31; Colossians 3:12; Galatians 5:19-23) and 1 Timothy 3 is a case in point. Paul's lists offer examples of acceptable and unacceptable ethical behavior, usually in the form consisting of a list of independent items. Vice and virtue lists do not appear to be a well-developed literary form in the Old Testament; there they are quite infrequent. Most scholars agree that the New Testament form, if not also the content, is borrowed from Hellenistic literature and rhetoric. Hellenistic Jews adopt this literary form to condemn Gentile sinfulness, especially idolatry and immorality (see Wisdom of Solomon 14:2-31; cf. Romans 1:29-31). A graphic example of the nature of a virtue list is given by Burton Easton, quoting a first century Greco-Roman writer named Onosander who lists the qualifications of a military leader:

I say that the general should be chosen as sober
minded, self-controlled, temperate, frugal, hardy,
intelligent, no lover of money, not too young or
old, if he be the father of children, able to speak
well, of good repute (Easton 1982: 10-11 as quoted by Bailey and Vander Broek 1992: 66).

A quick comparison with 1 Timothy 3:2-7 suggests
that a general and an overseer require similar qualifications. Paul and Onosander have a common view of the
virtues required of individuals in leadership. Paul has
likely borrowed a typical virtue list and then shaped it
according to the unique needs of the Ephesian church
and the Christian faith (see Bailey and Vander Broek
1992: 67).

In chapter three, Paul begins by commending the pur-
suit of church leadership, calling it a noble task and listing the qualities of an overseer (3:1-7). Second, he lists the
qualities of male and female deacons, underscoring their
character as persons (3:8-13). Third, he reminds Timothy
of his motivation for writing, quoting a fragment of an
early Christian hymn that summarizes the church's message of salvation (3:14-16).

The Text Explained

Qualifications of Overseers (3:1-7). Paul first lists the
qualities of a person the Greek text describes as an *episkopos*, which the NIV translates literally as "overseer"
(NRSV "bishop," NEB "leader," NJB "president"). It is a
term widely used in the Greco-Roman world to refer to
persons who provide the general oversight of a civil or
religious organization. Hence, it is an appropriate term
for persons who exercise leadership in the emerging
churches of the first century. Paul maintains that the role
of overseer is a noble task or, literally, a beautiful work, a
worthwhile job. It is not acceptable to set one's heart on

money (6:10), but it is just fine for a person to aspire to
church leadership, especially if the church thinks they are
fit for the task.

The church of Ephesus has had overseers for several
years, according to Acts 20:28. But some leaders have
proved unfit for the task and have been put out of the
church (cf. 1:20). Perhaps the role of overseer has come
under suspicion and disrespect because of the leadership
problems in the Ephesian church. If so, Paul seems to be
restoring nobility to the task of church leadership. He
aims to contrast the qualities of those who lead appropriately with those who do not. Also, he is especially concerned that overseers are qualified to deal with the dangers of false teaching. Hence, he anchors the teaching
responsibility of the church with leaders appropriately
selected and set apart for authoritative teaching in the
gathered community.

The word "overseer" (Gk. *episkopos*) occurs in four
other places in the New Testament (Acts 20:28;
Philippians 1:1; Titus 1:7; and in I Peter 2:25 of Jesus). If
Acts 20:28 is compared with Titus 1:5 and 7, one must
conclude that in both passages "overseer" and "elder"
are different titles for the same person. All overseers are
likely elders, but not all elders are necessarily overseers,
with the term "elder" emphasizing "maturity" while the
term "overseer" stresses "role" or "function."

In all cases in the church of Paul's day, leadership is
plural (cf. Acts 14:23; 20:17; Titus 1:5). Although
1 Timothy 3:1 uses the singular form, it has a plural
meaning, just as our expression "committee member"
implies one who belongs to a wider group. The New
Testament uses the word for one among many leaders
within the local church. Although the issue of an overseer's duties is not Paul's primary concern here, two
things are evident from the New Testament picture of
church leadership. First, elders, called overseers, are

responsible for teaching (1 Timothy 3:3; 5:17; Titus 1:9). Second, elders must "manage" or "care for" the household of God, which includes feeding, tending or shepherding the Lord's church (see Acts 20:28). Indeed, the Pastoral Letters teach that an overseer is to encourage the faithful by teaching sound doctrine and refuting the opponents of the gospel (see Titus 1:9).

What follows in 3:2-7 is not a "job description" but a character profile of the kind of person who is fit to lead in God's household. It is a discussion of what church leaders ought to be, not what they ought to do. In essence, Paul gives God's people a do-it-yourself guide for selecting leaders. The flow of thought in the list moves from personal to church life, from domestic to official functions. Also, the qualities are listed antithetically—a "this, not this" pattern is evident in 3:2-3. That there is nothing comparable to this list in the Pauline letters outside the Pastoral Letters may be due to the problems surrounding the false teachers in the Ephesian church. However, a remarkable parallel to Paul's arrangement here is found in Polycarp's *Letter to the Philippians* (see 4.2-6.1).

The first quality on the list, "above reproach" (Gk. *anapilempton*), summarizes all the qualities that follow; it functions as an "umbrella" quality for the remaining items on the list. The specific virtues that follow also clarify what the general principle, "above reproach," means in this first century context. The last mentioned quality of church leaders on Paul's list forms an *inclusio* with this first quality, bringing the list full circle: "he must have a good reputation with outsiders…" (3:7). In other words, the first and last qualities mentioned frame the entire list, while all the other items in between amplify the meaning of the umbrella quality "above reproach" or "of good reputation."

The NIV translation, "husband of but one wife," is a literal rendering of the Greek *mias gunaikos andra*. This phrase has been used to exclude persons married after divorce and after the death of a spouse, as well as persons involved in polygamy or promiscuity. Since this is the first concrete item on the list, it may have special significance for the Ephesian situation. If so, it may underscore the expectation that a church leader will be married, in contrast to the prohibition against marriage by the false teachers (see 4:3). Since Paul seems to allow, if not encourage, the remarriage of a surviving partner (1 Corinthians 7:39-40), it is not likely that he excludes persons who remarry after the death of their spouse. It may exclude persons who have remarried after divorce. If so, it must be remembered that there may be exceptions in the case of adultery (see Matthew 5:32; 19:9) or in the case of desertion by the unbelieving partner (1 Corinthians 7:15). Perhaps it is best to see this qualification as a reference to fidelity in the marriage relationship. As Towner says, "most of us would probably admit that one's marriage sheds a good deal of light on one's character.... What one does or is in one's private life has consequences for the church" (1994, 84).

The next three virtues (temperate, self-controlled, respectable) are characteristic of the ideal of moderation promoted broadly in Greco-Roman moral teaching and throughout these letters (see 2:9; 3:11; Titus 2:2-5). Also, one of Paul's primary concerns is for good order and peace within the context of public worship, "for God is not a God of disorder but of peace" (1 Corinthians 14:33).

Hospitality is also widely promoted in Greco-Roman culture. Given the spread of the gospel by itinerant preachers (see 5:10; Romans 12:13; Hebrews 13:2; Philemon 22; 1 Peter 4:9; 3 John 5-8), hospitality receives special emphasis within the Christian community. It's presence here on the list of qualities for an overseer points to the leader's responsibility to extend hospitality to others as a representative of the church, not simply as the head of a household.

The final positive quality on this antithetical list, "able to teach," receives special significance by virtue of the Ephesian situation. Paul critiques the false teachers (1:6-7; 4:1), prohibits teaching by women (2:12), and encourages Timothy to teach in an appropriate manner (4:11-16). Further, Paul posits a double honor for elders who are responsible for preaching and teaching (5:17). Also, in Titus the overseer's role as a teacher is specifically linked to refuting opponents (1:9; see also 2 Timothy 2:24-26). Clearly, an overseer's teaching/preaching task is of paramount importance for Paul, especially in the Ephesian context where false teachers are distorting the essence of the gospel message.

Four vices are to be avoided by an overseer. He is not to be "given to drunkenness, not violent but gentle, not quarrelsome, not a lover of money" (3:3). These vices are repeated in Titus 1:7-9 and 2 Timothy 2:24-25 and are typical items on Greco-Roman virtue and vice lists. Here they are designed to encourage the peaceable life admired by Paul (2:2; cf. 1 Corinthians 14:33) and to discourage the qualities so characteristic of the false teachers (see 2 Timothy 2:23; Titus 3:9). Absence of greed is an especially prominent concern in 1 Timothy (see 3:8; 6:9-10, 17-19) where it addresses Paul's charge that the false teachers are motivated by avarice (6:5).

The last three items on the list—managing one's household well, spiritual maturity, and a good reputation with outsiders—are emphasized by adding comments to them that clarify their relevance for an overseer. The expectation that an overseer must manage his own household well is a common requirement of men in the Greco-Roman world. Paul adopts it here and applies it to the care and management of the church, God's household (3:15).

The next requirement, that an overseer's children must be submissive and subordinate (see also Titus 1:6), also echoes Greco-Roman expectations. In this setting, the requirement complements the subordination of women to men required in 2:11-12 (see also Titus 2:5, 9; 3:11). Even more, an inability to deal with rebellious children in the context of one's home may foreshadow an overseer's inability to deal with rebellious false teachers in the church (see 1:3-4; Titus 1:10).

The stated motivation for excluding a new convert (Gk. *neophytos*, which means literally "newly planted") is the concern that such a person will "become conceited" (Gk. *typhotheis*). The Greek word translated "conceited" can also have the meaning, "deluded or blinded" (see 6:4; 2 Timothy 3:4, 13-15). This implies that an overseer who is a new convert could easily become blinded by false teaching and then, in his capacity as a teacher, lead the church astray. The Greek word translated "devil" (*diabolos*) means literally "slanderer" and refers either to a human agent or to Satan. Paul has God's archenemy in mind here (see 2 Timothy 2:26), although he does use the word in the more mundane sense a few verses later (see 3:11; 2 Timothy 3:3; Titus 2:3). The NIV translation, "fall under the same judgment as the devil," is an interpretation; the literal translation of the Greek is "fall under the condemnation of the devil." It could mean either the condemnation reserved for the devil or the condemnation the devil inflicts. However, it is probably not a reference to the condemnation that Satan inflicts because Christ alone is the ultimate judge (2 Timothy 4:1). This phrase refers instead, as the NIV translation posits, to the same condemnation Satan faces (see Revelation 20:1-3) or as in 1 Timothy 1:20, to the condemnation of being handed over to Satan. In both cases, it is an ominous threat.

Paul concludes his treatment of an overseer's qualifications with a comment on the leader's relationship with outsiders: "he must also have a good reputation with outsiders" (3:7). The New Testament frequently registers concern for the reactions of outsiders (1 Corinthians 14:16; 1 Thessalonians 4:12; 1 Peter 2:11-12; 3:1-2). This concern is especially strong in the Pastoral Letters (1 Timothy 5:14; 6:1; Titus 2:5-10) where there is a corresponding call for Christians to embody the best virtues of Greco-Roman society. Of course, here the focus is on the overseer or church leader who represents the church as its most prominent member. As in the previous verse, Satan has something to do with the importance of this requirement. The "devil's trap" snares the unwary and unrighteous (see 2 Timothy 2:26; cf. Job 2:1-5). If a church leader is disgraced in the eyes of outsiders, his disgrace as an individual brings a corresponding disgrace upon the Christian community, and that is the devil's trap! When the community's representative is disgraced, the whole Christian community suffers disgrace. This final qualification also summarizes the content of the entire list. In short, it requires a church leader's behavior to be "above reproach" (3:2) in the eyes of God and society.

Qualifications of Deacons (3:8-13). Paul treats the deacons "likewise," indicating a parallel class of church leaders. "Deacon" (Gk. *diakonos*) is very much a Pauline term, signifying one who performs acts of service for and on behalf of another. Throughout his letters, Paul describes a whole host of people as deacons, including Timothy (1 Thessalonians 3:2), Phoebe (Romans 16:1), Apollos (1 Corinthians 3:5), himself (2 Corinthians 6:4), and even Christ (Romans 15:8). In this way, he seems to define leadership roles within the Christian community in terms of service. Paul does use the word deacon in the Pastoral Letters to describe a position within the community for which one is tested (3:10) and by which one gains certain benefits (3:13). He does not specify the deacons' responsibilities, indicate the manner by which they are to be tested or list the precise nature of the position's benefits. In Philippians 1:1 overseers and deacons are linked,

although the differences between them are not spelled
out. In the Pastoral Letters, this chapter comes the closest
to providing us with a specific "church order" or community structure. Still, as in the case of the overseer, Paul
focuses exclusively on personal qualifications for the
position.

Paul's list of deacon qualifications follows a similar
but shorter pattern to that of the list for overseers. In general, the list tends to reinforce the cultural and ecclesial
ideal of moderation (3:8-10, 12-13). "Men worthy of
respect" is an interpretation of the Greek word "*semnos*"
which means "inspiring respect, high-principled, honorable" (see Zerwick 1979: 630). The implication is that
male deacons inspire respect in the following ways: first,
by being "sincere" (Gk. *me dilogos*). That is, they do not
say one thing to please one person and the opposite to
please another. Second, they gain respect by "not
indulging in much wine." That is, by not being addicted
to wine. Third, they gain honor in the community by "not
pursuing dishonest gain." This last item conveys the idea
of "doing something for profit" and "having no shame."

Unique to this list is the peculiar Christian requirement that deacons "keep hold of the deep truths of the
faith with a clear conscience" (3:9). The Greek expression
"*musterion tes pisteos*" that lies behind this NIV translation is likely formulaic, referring to the content of the
Christian faith which will be summarized shortly (see
3:16). Thus, deacons are to keep hold of the content of the
faith, an obvious contrast to the false teachers whose consciences are seared and whose faith has suffered ship-
wreck (1:19, 4-6; 4:2).

The word "test" (Gk. *dokimazo*) indicates a screening
process to determine the candidate's public conduct,
character and general fitness for the deacon's role in the
church. Had the Ephesian congregation been more careful in appointing leaders in the first place, they might not

have the current leadership crisis. Also, the NIV translation ("if there is nothing against them") obscures the meaning of the Greek term *anengkletos* ("blameless, irreproachable, without accusation") which is virtually identical with the umbrella term ("above reproach") applied to overseers in 3:2. The quality of being "irreproachable" is understandable when the behavior of some community leaders endangers the church's stability and reputation. The warning to test prospective deacons for "blamelessness" is especially intelligible if some leaders in the Ephesian church are being charged with indiscretions (see 5:13, 19-20).

Paul's instructions now shift to speaking about the wives of the deacons (from the NIV translation, "their wives") or women deacons. The Greek term, *gunaikas*, can be translated either "women" or "wives." The location of this verse in the midst of a discussion of the qualifications for men who are prospective deacons supports their identification as the wives of male deacons. Still, for several reasons, it is best to regard these women as "women deacons." First, there are women deacons in the Pauline churches (see Romans 16:1). Second, the qualities desired in the *gunaikas* tend to match those of the male deacons: "worthy of respect" in 3:11 matches "worthy of respect" in 3:8, and "trustworthy in every way" (3:11) matches "nothing against them" in 3:10. Third, the repetition of "likewise" (Gk. *hosautos*) suggests a distinct yet parallel group of persons is being addressed. The text gives no indication of the responsibilities of women deacons, although the prohibition of 2:12 precludes the possibility of them teaching in public.

Paul quickly returns to the topic of male deacons and continues their list of qualifications. These final items ("A deacon must be the husband of but one wife and must manage his children and his household well") echo the overseer's domestic requirements (see 3:2, 4) and assume that a deacon, like an overseer, will be married. The final clause is strange. Paul seems to provide practical motivation for seeking the position of deacon, even as 3:1 supplies motivation for becoming an overseer (it is a "noble task"). Perhaps the false teachers' behavior in Ephesus has generated a low opinion of deacons. If so, Paul seeks to restore confidence in the role. Thus, deacons (male or female) who serve well will receive a twofold reward: first, they will gain an excellent reputation within the community and before God; and second, they will grow closer to Christ in both faith and personal assurance.

There are several things about Paul's list of qualifications for overseers and deacons that are quite surprising. No theological basis is given for these positions or roles in the church, no specific list of responsibilities named and, apart from 3:9, no spiritual requirements mentioned: "They must keep hold of the deep truths of the faith with a clear conscience." Instead, the two lists for overseers and deacons promote the highest moral virtues of the Greco-Roman world. Paul's objective is likely apologetic (Balch 1981: 63-116). Church leaders represent the church and the Christian faith to an unbelieving society. If their lives are exemplary, they can reduce, if not negate, the hostility new religious movements often encounter (Bailey & Vander Broek, 1992: 69). If church leaders maintain stable household units and a community behavioral code (church) compatible with Roman society, it provides evidence of their leadership skills and silences any suspicion among outsiders that this new religious movement undermines the family structure and thereby threatens the empire's foundations.

Very significantly, Paul seems to assume that the truth of the church's teaching and preaching is either confirmed or denied by the conduct of its members (1:9-11). He stresses the church's witness in the world. The exemplary behavior expected of church leaders undoubtedly has tremendous importance for a new religious movement by encouraging a way of life the rest of society does not consider dangerous and may even admire. If so, Paul's aim and God's passion—that everyone "come to knowledge of the truth" (2:4)—is not hindered, but promoted by the behavior of church leaders.

Finally, the expectation that church leaders manage their household well essentially excludes slaves from leadership, for they are not masters of their own households. For a similar reason, women are excluded, except for the special role of deacon (3:11), since they are considered subordinate members and owe their obedience to the head of the household. This represents a departure from Paul's other churches, where women play various leadership roles (see Romans 16:1-2; Galatians 3:28) and where "slave" is an honorable epithet for Christ (Philippians 2:7) and for church leaders (Romans 1:1; Galatians 1:10; Philippians 1:1).

In short, church leaders who are overseers and deacons must not do anything to jeopardize God's mission in the world through the church. Rather, they should be the kind of people who instill confidence in fellow Christians and garner respect from outsiders to the faith. Paul does not mean church leaders are without defects. Rather, the list of qualifications for overseers and deacons suggests maturity in Christ. Paul wants people in leadership to give evidence of the Spirit's presence in their lives; he wants men (and women deacons) in leadership positions to keep in step with the Spirit in the sense that their behavior demonstrates obedience to God's Spirit.

Paul's Reason for Writing (3:14-16). Paul makes two comments that underscore the importance of his instructions: the first is on the nature of the church (3:15). The second is on "the mystery of godliness" which he summarizes by quoting a fragment of an early Christian hymn (3:16). In this way, Paul reiterates the important

connection between belief and behavior (see 1:8-11). In
these three verses, we encounter one of the most important passages of this letter, one that reminds us of Paul's
purpose, defines the nature of the church and summarizes the Christian faith.

Apparently, Paul expects to return to Ephesus: "I
hope to come to you soon" (3:14; cf. Romans 1:13;
Philippians 2: 24; 1 Thessalonians 2:18). However, he is
concerned about the consequences of a delay: "if I am
delayed" (3:15). Hence, he writes this letter to his delegate Timothy so that he "will know how people ought to
conduct themselves in God's household" (3:15). This
verse provides a second explanation of the letter's purpose, one that complements the aim stated in 1:18. In 1:18
Paul speaks about equipping Timothy for his task of
"fighting the good fight." Paul anticipates Timothy's
struggle with the false teachers whom he is mandated to
silence (1:3-4). Here Paul speaks about behavior "in the
household of God" (3:15). He leaves no doubt about its
referent, "the church of the living God" (3:15). This is a
phrase repeatedly used by Christians and Jews to contrast their God with the pagan world's lifeless idols
(Jeremiah 10:9-10; Daniel 6:20, 26; 2 Corinthians 6:16;
1 Thessalonians 1:9).

Paul does not use the metaphor of "the household of
God" elsewhere in his writings. Instead he prefers the
image of the "body of Christ" (I Corinthians 12:12-31;
Romans 12:4-8), or "the temple of God" (1 Corinthians
3:16-17; 2 Corinthians 6:16). Yet, he does describe the
church as "the family of the faith" (Galatians 6:10; cf.
Ephesians 2:19; 1 Peter 4:17). While the Greek phrase can
mean "house of God" or "household of God," the NIV
translation rightly opts for the latter. The first translation
option implies a sacred space, whereas the second implies
a social entity belonging to God. It is this latter sense that
dominates the Pastoral Letters (see 2:8-15; 5:1-2; 6:2;

Titus 2:1-10; 3:1-7; 2 Timothy 2:20-21) and which, in turn, reveals Paul's pervasive concern for proper behavior and appropriate relationships among all of God's people for the sake of the gospel's success in the world.

When Paul speaks of the church as "God's house-hold" (Gk. *oikos theou*), he introduces a metaphor of singular importance to the Pastoral Letters (Bailey & Vander Broek 1992: 71). He employs a form familiar to Greco-Roman society where the family is viewed as a microcosm of the empire. Greek and Roman philosophers frequently spoke about the household, claiming that a strong family leads to a strong society (see Balch 1981: 21-62). However, the household of these philosophers was the patriarchal household so normative in Greco-Roman culture where wives, children and slaves are considered subordinate members and owe their obedience to the household head. Paul employs this typical literary form, embellishing it by adding Christian rationales for some requirements (see 3: 5, 7, 9, 13). Thus, the overseer is expected to manage the household of God in the same way that a husband/father rules the traditional household (see 3:4-5, 12; Titus 1:6-7). Other members of God's household are assigned their proper place within a hierarchy that embraces both natural and ecclesial "households." Women, slaves and children are subordinate and hence expected to be submissive (2:11; 3:4, 12; 6:1; Titus 2:5, 9). Also, younger members are expected to respect the older (5:1-2, 4) while older women are to behave appropriately (Titus 2:3), with all members subject to and respectful of the Roman authorities (2:1-2; Titus 3:1).

As 21st century North American Christians, what do we do with Paul's remarks, given this explanation of its background? Two comments are appropriate here. First, in interpreting these Scriptures, we must evaluate the hierarchical assumptions of these household codes in light of the unity and equality enunciated by Paul in

Galatians 3:28 and by Jesus in the Gospels. Even as we do not call for the reinstitution of slavery just because the New Testament household code assumes the master/slave relationship, so we must critically assess the code's interpretation of the husband/wife relationship, as well as that of the parent/child. And frankly, at times it may be necessary to disagree with some parts of Scripture, based on our understanding of the whole (see Bailey &Vander Broek 1992: 71).

The final phrase describes the church as the "pillar and foundation of the truth" (3:15). Today, the land of Asia Minor is littered with ancient pillars, the remains of the Greco-Roman era. The pillars of the great temple of Diana in Ephesus, three times as large as the Parthenon in Athens, likely inspired Paul's metaphor for the church. The temple lies in ruin today, but its pillars may still be seen in St. Sophia in modern Istanbul: the Emperor Justinian had them carried by barge from Ephesus to be used for the construction of his great basilica. As for Paul's words, both architectural metaphors ("pillar and foundation") contribute to the image of the church as a stable structure firmly supporting truth in the face of opposition (see Jeremiah 1:18). Throughout the Pastoral Letters the opponents are associated with falsehood and deceit (4:1-2; 6:5; 2 Timothy 2:18; 3:8) whereas the church exists to protect and promote the truth. Here Paul undoubtedly thinks of the church as the gospel's guardian and communicator. Since the church plays such a key role in protecting and communicating the gospel, believers must conduct themselves appropriately so that the gospel message is not discredited. Thus, the success of God's mission in the world rests not only upon the preservation of the gospel message, but also upon the behavior of God's people who embrace the gospel. The church is called to embody the truth of the gospel message it embraces and proclaims.

"Beyond all question, the mystery of godliness is great," writes Paul (3:16). The expression "the mystery of godliness" requires some study. A "mystery" (Gk. *muste-rion*) is a previously unknown truth now made known. Specifically, in this context, it denotes the historical appearance of Christ who revealed God's plan of salvation through his life, death and resurrection. The term "godliness" (Gk. *eusebeias*) in the context of the Pastoral Letters is a reference to living Christianly. Thus, Paul's expression links the appearance of Christ with Christian living; it indicates that God's people cannot disconnect belief and behavior, as the false teachers were doing with damaging results.

By means of a six line hymnic fragment, Paul summarizes the "mystery's" content. The six lines likely form three couplets as follows:

---

1 Timothy 3:16: A Fragment of an Early Christian Hymn

Line 1	appeared in a body
Line 2	was vindicated by the Spirit
Line 3	was seen by angels
Line 4	was preached among the nations
Line 5	was believed on in the world
Line 6	was taken up in glory.

Line 1. "(He) appeared in a body" (or, "he was manifested in flesh") refers to the incarnation of Christ. God revealed himself to the world through the flesh of Jesus Christ, that is, the human form of Jesus Christ (cf. John 1:14).

Line 2. "Was vindicated by the Spirit." Here Christ's vindication through his resurrection is in view. In the first couplet (lines 1 and 2) the "body-Spirit" or "flesh-Spirit" antithesis in the New Testament suggests that "Spirit" references the supernatural realm that Christ entered by virtue of his resurrection from the dead. Indeed, in many New Testament passages, it is the resurrection event that demonstrates his vindication before hostile powers (see Acts 2:22-36; 3:11-15; Romans 1:4; 1 Corinthians 2:1-9; Ephesians 1:20-21). Thus, the first couplet, lines 1 and 2, encompasses both the human form and the supernatural realm.

Line 3. "Was seen by angels." This phrase likely refers to a revelation of Christ to angelic beings, not the passive observation of angels. At some point Christ appeared victorious before the angels. The time frame does not seem to be important for the hymn (cf. John 20:12).

Line 4. "Was preached among the nations." Christ's victory is proclaimed in the world. This line also indicates the church's role in preaching the gospel message in the world. The second couplet (lines 3 and 4) underscores the communication of Christ's victory in both heaven and earth. Paul may have quoted this fragment of a hymn to counter the tendencies of the Ephesian false teachers who limited the scope of God's salvation.

Line 5. "Was believed on in the world." This line reports the result of the gospel's proclamation mentioned in Line 4. Jesus is proclaimed and believed on, not only in Jerusalem, but to the ends of the earth.

Line 6. "Was taken up in glory." This line clearly refers to the ascension. It is especially obvious since the verb used here (*analambano*) is the same one used to describe the ascension in Acts 1:2, 11, 22 and Mark 16:19. If the previous couplet (lines 3 & 4) moved from angels in heaven to nations on earth, the third and final couplet (lines 5 and 6) moves from believers in the world to glory in heaven.

Application, Teaching/Preaching Points

What on earth are preachers supposed to do with Paul's long list of qualifications for leadership? What could be less interesting to the person in the pew than a homily on the qualities of church leadership? Well, maybe that's part of its value for today. Here are some important points about this passage for today's church.

Dynamic Equivalent Qualifications for Church Leaders. It has been suggested that our list of qualifications for 21st century North Americans leaders would be different from Paul's (see Kraft, 1978: 259). It is assumed, rightly I think, that Paul's list is culturally appropriate for a first century Ephesian setting, but it needs to be interpreted for our own time and context. Kraft writes: "We suggest that this passage designates (and illustrates for that culture) at least irreproachability, self-control and good will to others as requirements. In a dynamic-equivalence church the leaders are therefore to manifest such characteristics as will communicate these meanings to the people of their culture" (1978: 261). So what would a dynamic-equivalent list of qualifications for church leaders look like? It would likely include items like serious, self-controlled, courteous, a good teacher or preacher, not a drunkard, not quarrelsome, upright and doctrinally sound. But being hospitable, dignified and no lover of money may or may not be included on a list for North American church leaders. Why not? We would not necessarily insist that leaders demonstrate an ability to manage a home or family well. These qualities may be deemed important for older church leaders, but we tend to choose younger leaders than the church of Paul's day. Nor would North Americans say, as is necessary in Paul's Greco-Roman context, that "above reproach" demands that a person never have more than one marriage. We tend to allow, and even encourage, a person to remarry after the death of a spouse. But many North American churches (not all) disqualify a person who has remarried after a divorce. A North American list would include most of the items on Paul's list in 1 Timothy 3:2-7 but we would likely add a few qualities such as administrative ability and perhaps even youthfulness. Thus, the lists would be fairly similar owing, in part, to the many similarities between North American culture and the culture of the Greco-Roman world.

Church Leaders with Rebellious Teenagers. Are church leaders with rebellious teenagers disqualified from serving? Paul seems to expect church leaders to manage their families well. Ironically, it seems that children raised more strictly then their friends often react more violently against parental control, especially in their teen years. Many loving and godly parents feel guilty if their teenagers become spiritually disobedient, feeling it reflects badly on them, their church and the Lord. Some parents therefore feel they should not accept appointments or even resign from leadership positions when their children rebel or fail to come to faith in Christ. It seems to me that while a person's household management may be a helpful rule of thumb when first appointing leaders, we should not regard subsequent rebellion of grown children a basis for disqualification.

The Importance of Simple Structures. At times, the purpose of the Christian church has been distorted by an over-emphasis on structure, frequently appearing like little more than a factory for salvation. At other times, it has been seduced by charismatic figures who completely ignore the inherent value of suitable structures. This third chapter of 1 Timothy is so simple and straightforward that it sits in judgment on faith communities whose fervor is drowning in procedures, meetings and paperwork or whose structures are ignored by her charismatic leaders. Sound structure is not incompatible with spiritual fervor, and an interest in suitable structures does not signal the church's imminent demise. The contemporary experience of sectarian movements of all kinds demonstrates that structure and *charism* can and do coexist in mutually reinforcing ways. Also, the virtues of sobriety and marital fidelity may seem trivial to those who embrace a romantic outlook on life. But the majority of people for whom escape into alcohol or drugs is more than a little attractive, or for whom a sexual adventure with someone other than their spouse is very desirable, find that these virtues represent a quiet heroism of daily life. When embodied by people who must be visible to the world and to the faith community on a daily basis, such virtues are even more remarkable. Finally, these fundamental organizational needs should not be neglected when faith communities are in the process of making decisions about their leaders. Often when a community has suffered from a lack of effective preaching and teaching, it covets an overseer or pastor with charismatic gifts. Or, it seeks both charisma and effectiveness. These gifts do not normally come in the same person. A little reflection on Paul's list in 1 Timothy chapter three provides a helpful starting point for the debate and discussion required by the local church to make a sound decision about its future leadership.

Church Structures: Ancient and Modern. As we have noted, 1 Timothy develops the notion of the church as the household of God. Elsewhere, Paul uses the metaphor of the body (see Romans 12 and 1 Corinthians 12) which says very little about leadership and structure. Indeed, if anything, the image of the church as a "body" underscores its charismatic or organic nature. By contrast, the metaphor of the church as a "household" emphasizes the importance of direction in the church. The structure proposed by our text resembles the society's pattern at the time of its composition, but the letter does not teach that this form or structure is appropriate for all places at all times. It seems to me that today's congregations need to consider and apply both the metaphors of the church: as a body and as the household. It is important to recognize today that neither metaphor is necessarily superior to the other, nor should one metaphor be followed to the exclusion of the other. We need to hold both in fruitful and creative tension.

Personal Reflection Questions

- Qualifications for church leaders is the focus of this chapter. DISCUSS: Make your own list of qualities you expect of church leaders today. Compare it with those given in 1 Timothy 3:2-7. Give good reasons for any differences. Compare the list in 1 Timothy 3 with Titus 1:5-9. In what ways are the purposes of the two lists the same or different?

- Church leadership is a noble task according to Paul. DISCUSS: If you aspire to the "noble task" of church leadership, to what extent do you feel that you meet Paul's umbrella requirement of being "above reproach" and having "a good reputation with outsiders?" What changes would you need to make in your life to qualify? How has your church reacted to a church leader who has been publicly exposed for scandalous behavior? How should we respond, as individuals and as churches? Recall your service in the church. How has your ministry/service strengthened your own faith?

- Women in ancient Ephesus played a limited role in corporate worship. DISCUSS: To what extend does your church give women an opportunity to serve and lead? Why should your church have more or fewer women serving and leading? What could be done, practically speaking, to improve the situation regarding women in ministry?

- The church is the pillar and foundation of the truth. DISCUSS: Can you think of a recent experience in your church that illustrates this Pauline declaration? Consider the ancient hymn that Paul quotes. Re-write it in your own words, and then, if possible, use it in your public worship service.

Training in Godliness

The Text: Timothy 4:1-16

*The Spirit clearly says that in later times some will aban-
don the faith and follow deceiving spirits and things taught by
demons. [2] Such teachings come through hypocritical liars,
whose consciences have been seared as with a hot iron. [3] They
forbid people to marry and order them to abstain from certain
foods, which God created to be received with thanksgiving by
those who believe and who know the truth. [4] For everything God
created is good, and nothing is to be rejected if it is received
with thanksgiving, [5] because it is consecrated by the word of
God and prayer. [6] If you point these things out to the brothers,
you will be a good minister of Christ Jesus, brought up in the
truths of the faith and of the good teaching that you have followed. [7] Have nothing to do with godless myths and old wives'
tales; rather, train yourself to be godly. [8] For physical training
is of some value, but godliness has value for all things, holding
promise for both the present life and the life to come. [9] This is a
trustworthy saying that deserves full acceptance [10] (and for this
we labor and strive) that we have put our hope in the living
God, who is the Savior of all men, and especially of those who
believe. [11] Command and teach these things. [12] Don't let anyone
look down on you because you are young, but set an example
for the believers in speech, in life, in love, in faith and in purity. [13] Until I come, devote yourself to the public reading of
Scripture, to preaching and to teaching. [14] Do not neglect your
gift, which was given you through a prophetic message when
the body of elders laid their hands on you. [15] Be diligent in these
matters; give yourself wholly to them, so that everyone may see
your progress. [16] Watch your life and doctrine closely. Persevere
in them, because if you do, you will save both yourself and your
hearers.*

The Flow and Form of the Text

The assertion that "everything God created is good" (4:4) builds on the previous affirmation of the earthly realm in the hymn fragment, especially line 1: "he appeared in a body" (3:16). The first part of this chapter is also the most detailed treatment of the teaching of Paul's opponents who appear to be very antagonistic toward the world of the flesh. Paul begins by refuting the false teaching that Timothy has been commanded to stop (4:1-5) and then he identifies the marks of a good servant of Christ Jesus, emphasizing the importance of training in godliness (4:6-10) and Timothy's gifts and responsibilities (4:11-16). He wants Timothy to understand the nature of the false teaching in Ephesus and to combat it by means of sound teaching and an exemplary personal life.

The Text Explained

Prediction of False Teaching (4:1-5). Paul begins by reminding Timothy that false teaching in the church should not catch him by surprise. God's Spirit has given ample advance warning: "The Spirit clearly says that in later times some will abandon the faith…" (4:1a). Indeed, Paul forewarns the Ephesian elders about people who "will arise and distort the truth in order to draw away disciples after them" (see Acts 20:28-31). Of course, he echoes Jesus' teaching concerning false prophets who appear as ferocious wolves in sheep's clothing (Matthew 7:15; Mark 13:22-23; 2 Thessalonians 2:3; cf. Revelation 13). The presence of false teaching seems to go with the turf of living between the times, or the "later times," a reference to the entire period between Christ's first and second comings (called the "last days" in 2 Timothy 3:1). Opposition to the truth revealed in Jesus Christ, and defection from it, are "signs of the times." New Testament cities are not as isolated from one another as we are inclined to think. False prophets travel as fast as true apostles. In conjunction with this observation, it is interesting to note that the false teaching in several different New Testament urban churches has a number of common features (see the table below). Thus, the situation in Ephesus should not come as a surprise. Neither does it mean that God's mission in the city has failed (see 2 Timothy 2:19-21).

Summary of False Teaching in Key New Testament Cities				
False Teaching	Ephesus	Corinth	Colossae	Asia Minor
Legalism	1 Tim. 1:7-9		Col. 2:16,17	
Ascetism	1 Tim. 4:3		Col. 2:16-23	
Speculations	1 Tim. 1:4			
Resurrection	2 Tim. 2:18	1 Cor. 15:12		
"Knowledge"	1 Tim. 6:20	1 Cor . 8:1-2	Col. 2:3-8	
Exclusivism	1 Tim. 2:4-6	1 Cor. 1:12	Col. 1:28	
Satanism	1 Tim. 5:15	1 Cor. 10:20		Rev. 2:9, 13, 24
Sexual Sin	2 Tim. 3:6	1 Cor. 6:9		Rev. 2:14, 20

The association of these heresies with demons and deceitful spirits is standard, illustrating the cosmic horizon of this situation: "… and follow deceiving spirits and things taught by demons" (4:1). Satan, who has been known to disguise himself as an angel of light (see 2 Corinthians 2:11; 11:14), empowers the false teachers. Demonic attack is a common experience in Asia Minor, at least according to the letters to the churches at Smyrna, Pergamum, Thyatira and Philadelphia (see Revelation 2:9, 13, 24; 3:9). History reveals that a person may sincerely believe he is being faithful to the truth, while being deceived by the devil (see 1 Kings 22:19-23). Paul knows from personal experience that false teachers are really "Satan's servants" (2 Corinthians 11:15).

The human agents of this false teaching are described as "hypocritical liars whose consciences have been seared ith a hot iron" (4:2). For centuries Christians have used the term "conscience" to refer to the part of the person that guides moral choice. So the reference to the searing of the conscience likely suggests that these persons lack proper moral guidance. These false teachers pretend to be super-spiritual but their consciences are seared. Hippocrates, a Greek authority on medicine, used these words to refer to a cauterizing instrument. The image suggests that the false teachers were numb to the truth (cf. Ephesians 4:19) and marked by the Devil's own branding iron. Satan has his agents who are committed to his service and who have his mark of ownership, like slaves in the ancient world who were branded with a hot iron. These servants of Satan are enslaved to sin and their ability to discern rightly has been damaged. It is important to understand that Paul connects a good conscience with the Christian faith (see 1:15), implying that rejecting the faith may lead to a seared conscience.

Even as the good conscience is linked with good conduct, the seared conscience is connected with perverted conduct. The ability to make good decisions has something to do with the conscience, in Paul's mind. The conscience enables the believer to translate his or her faith into behaviors and convictions into conduct. Godly living flows from a good conscience whereas ungodly living stems from a seared conscience. Although the acid test of orthodoxy is not necessarily orthopraxis, ungodly living should certainly raise questions about the claims of any movement calling itself "Christian."

Paul gives two examples of the false teaching in order to demonstrate how distorted these teachers are: "they forbid people to marry and order them to abstain from certain foods" (4:3). Forbidding marriage is a widespread tendency in the first century among false teachers, as the New Testament indicates (1 Corinthians 7:1; Hebrews 13:4). Since Paul encourages young widows to remarry

(1 Timothy 5:14), it must be a problem in Ephesus too. Perhaps the Ephesian false teachers are influenced by the Greek notion that matter is evil. Hence, our bodies are unclean and sex is unclean, making it better to be a virgin and never marry. Such teaching fails to grasp the truth that God made us male and female; he created our sexuality. It is good and the source of much joy when expressed within the marriage relationship (Proverbs 5:15-19).

The false teachers also command abstinence from certain foods. This error is also widespread (see 1 Corinthians 10:23-33; Romans 14:1-23; Colossians 2: 16, 21). As Christians, we are liberated from the bondage of rules and regulations. God wants us to receive his gifts with grateful hearts and not reject them on the basis of legalism or superstition. These errors are to be countered by positive teaching: "for everything God created is good, and nothing is to be rejected if it is received with thanksgiving ..." (4:4). In the Greek text, the word "everything" is emphasized. "Good" means beautiful to look at. Paul's words remind us of God's words in the creation narrative of Genesis. Seven times the text says, "God saw that it was good." Because the earth is the Lord's creation, it is good. Nothing is to be rejected or treated as taboo. The believers in Ephesus probably know that Jesus declared all foods clean (Mark 7:19) and had taught Peter the same truth in a special vision (see Acts 10:15).

There is a single stipulation given to believers: all of God's gifts are to be received with thanksgiving. No wonder giving thanks before meals is a Christian custom (Romans 14:6; 1 Corinthians 10:30). "Saying grace" is more than a traditional formality; it is the heart's way of responding to God's goodness.

Paul gives a final rationale for using all foods: "because it is consecrated by the word of God and prayer" (4:5). His words imply that all we have to do to sanctify any food is to make a prayer of thanksgiving, thereby recognizing the giver. The expression "the word of God" likely refers to the use of Scripture in the prayer of thanksgiving, a common Jewish practice.

Training in Godliness (4:6-10). All the imperatives of this chapter are addressed specifically to Timothy. In fact, these imperatives are the first of this letter to be directed to him. Although they focus on Timothy's strategy for tackling his opponents, Paul has a larger aim in mind. In Greco-Roman ethical writings it is common to define desired behavior by contrasting personal examples. Paul uses this device here (see also 1 Timothy 1:18-20; 6:3-16; Titus 1:5-16). His exhortations to Timothy depict the ideal church leader whose doctrine and life pose a sharp contrast to the teachers Paul has just pilloried (4:1-5). Thus, after the opening sentence that portrays Timothy as a strong contrast to the false teachers (4:6), Paul gives two instructions—one negative and the other positive—that sharpen the contrast (4:7). The balance of the passage provides support for the second of these two instructions (4:8-16).

Summary references like "these things" (Gk. *tauta*) are frequent in 1 Timothy (1:18; 3:14; 4:6, 11; 6:2), serving a transitional function. It's referent here, however, is ambiguous. It likely refers to the theological message of verses 4-5 with its call to oppose the asceticism of the false teachers. But it may also include the instructions of the entire letter. Paul is not questioning Timothy's compliance when he says, "if you point these things out to the brothers" (4:6). Rather, he simply contrasts a "good servant" with a "hypocritical liar" (4:2). The NIV translates the Greek word *diakonos* as "minister," not "deacon," implying ministerial service in general (cf. 1 Corinthians 3:5; 2 Corinthians 6:4). Paul links a "good" (Gk. *kalos*) minister with adherence to "good" (Gk. *kale*) teaching.

Elsewhere in the Pastoral Letters we learn that Timothy was trained in the faith by Paul (2 Timothy 1:13; 3:10) and nourished in the faith by his mother and grandmother (2 Timothy 1:5). However, a "good minister" must not only be trained and nourished in the faith; he must also continually follow it closely. The Greek verb "to follow" (*parakoloutheo*) includes the idea of a kind of understanding that comes only through obedience.

The threat posed by the false teachers undoubtedly motivates Paul's two instructions to Timothy. First, Timothy must avoid their teaching: "Have nothing to do with godless myths and old wives' tales" (4:7a). Paul already dismissed these teachings as myths (see 1:4) and now he discredits them by calling them "old wives' tales," or unreliable gossip that is a sharp contrast to "the truths of the faith" and "the good teaching" Timothy follows.

Second, Paul instructs Timothy to train himself in godliness: "train yourself to be godly" (4:7b). Greek writers frequently use the image of physical or athletic training (Gk. *gymnasia*) to depict the effort required to achieve moral or spiritual maturity (see Hebrews 5:14). Paul uses it here, applying it to spiritual fitness for service in Christ's name. Like an athlete, Timothy should keep in rigorous spiritual shape. Gymnasts train hard for hours each day, practicing over and over until they are perfect. Likewise, servants of Christ should work diligently to know and live the faith. When Paul acknowledges the relative value of physical fitness ("physical training is of some value"), he turns the metaphor against his opponents. In this context, it is a disparaging remark about the ascetic demands of his opponents. By contrast, training in godliness "has value for all things" (4:8). Genuine godliness is essentially a lifestyle lived in obedience to God's word. It has unlimited value, holding promise for both the present and the future life (see Luke 18:30).

The letter's third "trustworthy saying" (see 1 Timothy 1:15; 3:1) appears next (4:9-10). The formula may refer to the preceding comment in 4:8, confirming the superior value of godliness over profane myths and false asceticism. However, it is best to view it as a reference to verse 10: "... we have put our hope in the living God, who is the Savior of all men, and especially of those who believe." The "we" refers to Paul and Timothy in their struggle against the false teachers on behalf of the gospel, not the common struggle of all believers to achieve salvation. Only a "living God" can offer the real promise of life in the present and the future (4:8). The next clause, "the Savior of all men," returns to this letter's strong emphasis on the inclusive nature of God's salvation (see 2:4, 6; 3:16; 6:13) and contrasts sharply with Paul's opponents who restrict salvation to an ascetic elite. The final clause, "especially those who believe," is somewhat difficult. The word "especially" seems to imply salvation of some kind for all, even those who do not believe. But this does not fit with Paul's perspective of salvation, inclusive though it is (see 1:20; Titus 1:16; 3:10-11). Some theologians argue that the clause teaches that God is potentially the Savior of all, but in reality is the Savior of only believers. Others claim that the term "especially" (Gk. *malista*) means something like "that is to say" (the living God is the Savior of those who believe), thereby correcting the theologically magnanimous scope of the preceding clause.

Timothy's Gifts and Responsibilities (4:11-16). This next unit contains a list of duties Paul invokes on Timothy (4:11-16), all couched in the second person singular imperative. While some of these imperatives call Timothy to function as an ethical role model for the faith community (4:12, 16), most address his responsibility as the church's worship leader with his teaching role receiving prominent attention (4:11, 13, 16). There is also ample motivation given for obedience (see 4:15b, 16b) and a powerful reminder of the moment the church called Timothy to serve and lead (4:14), an event that functions as the theological anchor of Paul's instructions here.

The opening mandate, "Command and teach these things," concludes 4:6-10 and introduces 4:11-16. The expression, "these things," (Gk. *tauta*) echoes 3:14 and 4:6. While the specific referent is ambiguous, the refrain pulls together all of Paul's exhortations, making them one of the thematic centers of the letter. Indeed, a comparable statement to 4:11 is found in 6:2b ("These are the things you are to teach and urge on them"). These two sentences together function as "bookends" for the entire section 4:11 to 6:2.

The reference to Timothy's youth is somewhat surprising since the letter has presented him thus far as a mature, responsible church leader. Elsewhere, Timothy is portrayed as Paul's younger colleague (Philippians 2:22) who was to be accepted as one who serves the Lord (1 Corinthians 16:10-11). But here Timothy's age seems to be a problem, for some are "looking down" (Gk. *kataphroneo*) on him because he is young. Perhaps this remark reflects the situation of the early church where overseers and deacons do not have explicit age requirements (see 3:1-13). If so, the normative subordination of youth to age (see 5:1-2) may be reversed on occasion by the appointment of a young church member to a position of leadership. Early in the second century, Ignatius of Antioch admonished the church of Asia Minor "not to presume on the youth of the bishop, but to render him all respect" (*Ignatius Magnesia* 3.1). All of this indicates that Timothy's age may be a problem for some of the Ephesian church elders.

Paul's concern for the emotional impact such a problem may have on Timothy prompts him to give some advice on how to garner respect. He uses the common ethical motif of "example" (Gk. *typos*; see also Philippians 3:17; 2 Thessalonians 3:9; 1 Peter 5:3). First, speech and conduct form a pair. Next, a triad of virtues are named— love, faith and purity. The triad recalls the triad of 1 Corinthians 13:3—faith, hope and love, with purity replacing hope as the third member. Purity (Gk. *hagneia*) probably refers broadly to morally blameless conduct, not simply sexual chastity.

The three leadership responsibilities enjoined in verse 13 ("devote yourself to the public reading of Scripture, to preaching, and to teaching") embrace a major portion of a typical public worship service that may also include hymns, prayers and the Lord's Supper (see 1 Corinthians 11:17-31; 14:26). Teaching ends this short list and, together with preaching, reappears in the description of the elder's work (5:17) and in the instructions to Timothy in 6:2b. The importance of these three leadership roles undoubtedly reflects the false teachers' abuse of them.

Paul mentions these three key leadership responsibilities to set the stage for his reference to the gift (Gk. *charisma*) Timothy has received. This context also helps to define the gift's purpose: namely, ministry. The next clause ("which was given you through a prophetic message") can be interpreted as a proclamation by Christian prophets identifying Timothy as God's person for church leadership and ministry, or as their exhortation to him (see 1:18). The ritual of laying hands on a person has its roots in the ancient conviction that the human hand could transmit God's blessings (Genesis 48:14). Rabbinic Judaism developed a rite by which a teacher would pass on his authority to his students at the conclusion of their course of studies by laying his hands on their heads. The Christian antecedent of the rite described here is likely the baptismal laying on of hands after the candidate has been immersed (see Acts 8:14-17; 19:1-6), symbolizing the transmission of the Holy Spirit or his gifts (see 2 Timothy 1:6-7).

Our text names "the body of elders" as the ones who placed their hands on Timothy and thereby transmitted to him the gifts necessary for ministry. By means of a similar ritual, the elders themselves are set apart for ministry within the church (see 5:22; Acts 6:6; 13:3). In 2 Timothy, Paul alone is named as the one who laid his hands on Timothy (2 Timothy 1:6), a remark that likely reflects Paul's close personal relationship with Timothy. Here in 1 Timothy 4:14, the focus seems to be on the role played by "the body of elders" during the rite rather than on the Spirit or even God. By contrast, a similar ritual mentioned in Acts focuses on the role of prayer with no mention of the impartation of gifts (see Acts 6:6; 13:1-3; 14:23). The Pastoral Letters mention no spiritual gifts apart from persons who have participated in this rite of the laying on of hands by the elders. In fact, the rite appears to guarantee the continuity of the church's leadership (Titus 1:5), and hence the authenticity of the church's teaching (6:20). In a church troubled by false teachers and false teaching, these are important matters.

The manner in which spiritual gifts (Gk. *charisma*) are depicted in the Pastoral Letters differs from Paul's other letters. Here there is only the one gift, not many diverse gifts, for ministry. Also, the gift is inextricably linked with the rite involving the body of elders that appoints one for ministry, implying that the gift is imparted through the laying on of hands. Furthermore, these letters tend to view the gift as something that is "in you" (4:14) or "within you" (2 Timothy 1:6), even a latent power within you that can be rekindled (2 Timothy 1:6) or neglected (4:14). Thus, it appears to be a gift that is always present but not always operational. While the rite is crucial for imparting the gift, it does not guarantee responsible use of it. Indeed, it is in responsibly exercising the gift that a person is effectively transformed into an agent of God's salvation (4:16).

The final two verses simply reinforce Paul's previous exhortations: "Be diligent in these matters; give yourself wholly to them, so that everyone may see your progress" (4:15). The notion of progress (Gk. *prokope*) fits Paul's repeated emphasis on the importance of diligent effort (see 4:7; 2 Timothy 2:3-6, 22). His opponents also progress but, like gangrene, they progress from bad to worse (see 2 Timothy 2:17; 3: 13). By contrast, Timothy is to move toward more fully exercising his gifts for ministry among God's people, something that will be salvific for him as well as the church members. That is, God needs faithful leaders who are nourished by the truth and who in turn nourish others. In doing this, they will save themselves and their hearers.

On the surface, Paul's instructions in 4:6-16 appear to be for Timothy alone. But his message is likely aimed at a wider audience. His instructions to Timothy (4:6-16) are a vehicle for denouncing his opponents (4:1-5). Paul assumes God's people will be encouraged by the portrait of Timothy created by the instructions addressed to him, instructions designed to promote godliness, exemplary conduct and speech as well as faithful teaching. These are all central features of the Pastoral Letters. Two complimentary theological claims anchor the instructions: the first points to God's saving nature (4:10). The second describes the human agents of God's salvation: namely, servants who are loyal to their roots (4:14) and focused on their task of faithful teaching (4:6, 16).

Application, Teaching/Preaching Points

Paul's treatment of the false teaching in Ephesus and his call for Timothy to combat it by means of sound teaching and an exemplary personal life offer the contemporary church many practical lessons.

Does Prayer Make God's Creation Good? Paul's response to the false teachers (1 Timothy 4:3-4) echoes the strong position he adopts in 1 Corinthians (chapters 8-10) where he asserts that no part of the world is in itself evil or contaminating. Therefore, the use of our bodies in sex and in matters of diet must be regulated by "conscience." That is, we are called to balance freedom with responsibility to God, others and self. Here, however, Paul makes an even more universal and positive statement than in 1 Corinthians: "everything God created is good and nothing is to be rejected if it is received with thanksgiving" (4:4). What was stated in Genesis 1:31 still holds true: "God saw everything that he had made, and behold, it was very good." In 1 Timothy 4:3-4, Paul seems to qualify this conviction by twice affirming, "if it is received with thanksgiving" (4:3, 4). Does a simple thanksgiving prayer change God's physical creation so that something previously unacceptable becomes acceptable? If we think so, then we have misunderstood what Paul means by "thanksgiving" (Gk. *eucharistia*). Like his fellow Jews, Paul sees the prayer of thanksgiving as an *anamnesis*, a way of recalling the presence and claims of God upon us. Thanksgiving is more than a formal recitation of words, it blesses and glorifies God by acknowledging that all things come from God and return to him: "there is one God, the Father, from whom are all things and for whom we exist" (1 Corinthians 8:6). This sort of thankful recognition does not change God's creation physically. Rather, it gives expression to our conviction that we, and all things, come from God. And with such recognition, we help to establish the truth that this world is indeed God's good creation. Of course, the world is still God's and it is quite independent of our recognition of it. But Scripture teaches that when we forget that this is God's good world, things become grotesque and distorted: "although they knew God they did not honor him as God or give thanks to him, but they became futile in their thinking and their senseless minds were darkened" (Romans 1:21).

However, when we celebrate food and sexual love by
gratefully receiving them as God's good gifts, Paul claims
they are "consecrated" in a twofold fashion: by the word
of God which created it, and by the power of thanksgiving which celebrates it as God's good work (4:5).

What is Christian Spirituality? Paul wants Timothy
to "train (himself) to be godly" (4:7). But Paul has no
patience with those who promote physical asceticism
(4:8), a style of forbidding things that he castigates elsewhere: "Such regulations indeed have the appearance of
wisdom, with their self-imposed worship, their false
humility, and their harsh treatment of the body, but they
lack any value in restraining sensual indulgence"
(Colossians 2:23). The term "body" or "flesh" has nothing
to do with physical excess but much to do with spiritual
arrogance. These false teachers in Colossae tended to
judge, condemn and disqualify people who did not meet
their standards of maturity (Colossians 2:16, 18). They
revealed that they were hostile and unloving (see
1 Corinthians 3:3; Galatians 5:19-21). So Paul makes an
important distinction between two kinds of spirituality in
1 Timothy 4:7-8. One kind identifies "the spirit" with the
human psyche and seeks to realize its full potential by
controlling the body and employing mental gymnastics.
Paul believes this form of spirituality narcissism can
become self-centered, closed to both God and others.
Paul says it has little value because it functions mainly as
a way of perfecting ourselves so that we can measure our
accomplishments against others. By contrast, Paul
appeals to Timothy to pursue "training in godliness."
This form of spirituality views the struggle and labor of
human existence as a continuing openness to God's call
and to the needs of the neighbor. A spirituality focused
on physical asceticism is useful only for this life, but spirituality focused on God's own life holds promise and
unlimited value for both the present and the future life.

Christian Worship in the Early Church. Our text describes public worship as involving three practices: public reading of Scripture, preaching and teaching (1 Timothy 4:13). It is the custom in the synagogue of Paul's day to follow the public reading of the Law and the Prophets by an exposition or explanation of them. In Pisidian Antioch, the elders ask Paul and Barnabas for a "word of encouragement" (Acts 13:5), translated here in verse 13 as "preaching" (NIV translation). Hence, "preaching" here is the same spiritual gift translated as "encouragement" in Romans 12:8. It does not mean cheering people up so much as exhorting them from Scripture to be Christian where they live, work and play. It is what Jesus did in the Nazareth synagogue (Luke 4:17-22). If this "exposition" focused on the Scriptures just read, then the third component, the teaching, would seem to mean instruction from the whole wealth of the Christian canon. This is the model followed by the early church. Reading and expounding Scripture take central place. In one sense, God's words to us should come before our songs to God. Today we may be more centered on the people who lead our corporate worship than on God whom we gather to worship.

When Are Spiritual Gifts Given? Timothy seems to have the gift of teaching and its reception is linked to Paul laying hands on him. Is this how gifts are always given? Scripture suggests several different ways in which we receive gifts. First, we receive gifts by divine providence at birth. God knew Jeremiah and formed him in his mother's womb (1:5). Paul says God "set me apart from birth" (Galatians 1:15). His natural gifts of leadership and initiative are evident before his conversion. God our Creator is the same as God our Redeemer. He is not taken by surprise at our conversion! The Holy Spirit sanctifies our natural gifts of being a competent organizer or a clear speaker as the spiritual gifts of administration and teaching. Natural gifts are not the same as spiritual gifts, but neither are they totally unrelated to them because God is the giver of both. Second, we receive gifts by divine sovereignty at conversion. Paul's own conversion experience gives us a model here (Acts 9:15, 20; 22:15; 26:16; 1 Timothy 2:7). God appoints him at that time to be a herald, apostle and teacher. The Bible teaches us that all Christians are members of the body of Christ with God-given and God-determined functions to perform (1 Corinthians 12:6, 7, 11, 18). It starts with conversion. Third, we receive gifts by divine provision in the church. Some of us dislike the notion that God might use a rite like laying-on of hands, as though performing this ceremony automatically bestows spiritual gifts. However, 1 Timothy 4:14 and 2 Timothy 1:6 say that God does use this way. Moses laid hands on Joshua (Numbers 27:18-23; Deuteronomy 34:9). The early church laid hands on the Seven, and also in appointing Barnabas and Saul as missionary apostles (Acts 6:6; 13:3). It seems proper that the Sovereign Giver should use the church as a means of transmitting his grace to that church. All of this raises the question of whether it is proper for individuals to "seek gifts" for themselves (1 Corinthians 12:31—"Eagerly desire the greatest gifts"). If Paul teaches that each of us should accept our role as hands, feet, ears or mouths, it contradicts the metaphor of the church as the body if we all want to be hands or mouths! What we are to seek is the more excellent way of love—appreciating the differing gifts given to each one by the Lord. Furthermore, in 1 Corinthians 12, Paul encourages the congregation to seek the greatest gifts for they enable the local church to participate faithfully in God's world mission.

Personal Reflection Questions
• Everything God created is good. DISCUSS: How can we encourage one another to enjoy God's creation?

Create a list of activities that foster the enjoyment of God's good creation.

• God's good gifts should be received with gratitude. DISCUSS: How do these verses underscore the importance of "giving thanks" at mealtime? What should we do about "giving thanks" in public places like restaurants?

• Train yourself to be godly, Paul tells Timothy. DISCUSS: Is godliness more important than physical fitness? Does physical fitness play too great or too small a role today? How can you achieve balance between a fit mind and a fit body?

• Young Timothy is exhorted to exercise his gift. DISCUSS: How can we encourage and release the ministry gifts of young adults in our churches? How is your church doing on this score?

• Paul's delegate is to devote himself to the public reading of Scripture, preaching and teaching. DISCUSS: Does 1 Timothy 4:13 conflict with 1 Corinthians 14:26-33? If so, how would you reconcile them?

CHAPTER FIVE

Caring for All People

The Text: 1 Timothy 5:1-6:2

Do not rebuke an older man harshly, but exhort him as if he were your father. Treat younger men as brothers, [2] *older women as mothers, and younger women as sisters, with absolute purity.* [3] *Give proper recognition to those widows who are really in need.* [4] *But if a widow has children or grandchildren, these should learn first of all to put their religion into practice by caring for their own family and so repaying their parents and grandparents, for this is pleasing to God.* [5] *The widow who is really in need and left all alone puts her hope in God and continues night and day to pray and to ask God for help.* [6] *But the widow who lives for pleasure is dead even while she lives.* [7] *Give the people these instructions, too, so that no one may be open to blame.* [8] *If anyone does not provide for his relatives, and especially for his immediate family, he has denied the faith and is worse than an unbeliever.* [9] *No widow may be put on the list of widows unless she is over sixty, has been faithful to her husband,* [10] *and is well known for her good deeds, such as bringing up children, showing hospitality, washing the feet of the saints, helping those in trouble and devoting herself to all kinds of good deeds.* [11] *As for younger widows, do not put them on such a list. For when their sensual desires overcome their dedication to Christ, they want to marry.* [12] *Thus they bring judgment on themselves, because they have broken their first pledge.* [13] *Besides, they get into the habit of being idle and going about from house to house. And not only do they become idlers, but also gossips and busybodies, saying things they ought not to.* [14] *So I counsel younger widows to marry, to have children, to manage their homes and to give the enemy no opportunity for slander.* [15] *Some have in fact already turned away to follow Satan.* [16] *If any woman who is a believer has widows in her family, she should help them and not let the church be burdened with them, so that the church can help those widows who are really in need.* [17] *The elders who direct the affairs of the church well are worthy of double honor, especially those whose work is preaching and teaching.* [18] *For the Scripture says, "Do not muzzle the ox while it is treading out the grain," and "The worker deserves his wages."* [19] *Do not entertain an accusation against an elder unless it is brought by two or three witnesses.* [20] *Those who sin are to be rebuked publicly, so that the others may take warning.* [21] *I charge you, in the sight of God and Christ Jesus and the elect angels, to keep these instructions without partiality, and to do nothing out of favoritism.* [22] *Do not be hasty in the laying on of hands, and do not share in the sins of others. Keep yourself pure.* [23] *Stop drinking only water, and use a little wine because of your stomach and your frequent illnesses.* [24] *The sins of some men are obvious, reaching the place of judgment ahead of them; the sins of others trail behind them.* [25] *In the same way, good deeds are obvious, and even those that are not cannot be hidden.*

6:1 All who are under the yoke of slavery should consider their masters worthy of full respect, so that God's name and our teaching may not be slandered. [2] *Those who have believing masters are not to show less respect for them because they are brothers. Instead, they are to serve them even better, because those who benefit from their service are believers, and dear to them. These are the things you are to teach and urge on them.*

The Flow and Flow of the Text

Instructions pertaining to three groups of people within the church—widows, elders and slaves—are given in 5:3-6:2a. The introduction (5:1-2) to this extensive passage is grammatically part of Paul's personal mandate to Timothy from the previous chapter (4:6-16), is theologically rooted in the metaphor of the church as God's household (3:15), but its content anticipates 5:3-6:2.

Paul's rationale for treating elders together with widows and slaves is not immediately clear. The other two leadership positions—overseer and deacons—are treated together in chapter three, but now elders are considered in conjunction with widows and slaves. Widows do not appear elsewhere in the Pastoral Letters and the discussion of slaves seems to be isolated from its usual context of the household management tradition (see Titus 2:1-10; Ephesians 5:22-6:9). To be sure, the discussion of these three groups is superficially linked by the motif of "recognition" or "respect." Thus, as the NIV translates, "proper recognition" (Gk. *timao*) is to be given to widows (5:3), double "honor" (Gk. *time*) is to be given to elders who direct the affairs of the church, and slaves are to consider their masters worthy of full "respect" (Gk. *time*). But deeper issues have likely prompted Paul to consider these three groups of people together.

Numerous comments by Paul about the widows and elders imply that specific problems have emerged in the church in conjunction with these two groups. Although the instructions for slaves are brief (6:1-2a), there are indications that problems have arisen among them as well. Thus, Paul admonishes problematic groups within the church that have in some way been linked with the false teachers. Since widows receive the most extensive treatment (14 verses), elders next (4 verses), and slaves the least (2 verses), the sequence in which they are treated may indicate the relative gravity of the problems associated with each group. Also, if Paul is concerned about church order, he is clearly more concerned with the moral fiber of the people comprising these groups than with how the church is actually structured. Paul seems to subscribe to the dictum that faith must show itself in everyday life. No wonder the next chapter castigates the false teachers for their lack of moral character and warns of their eventual demise (see 6: 3-10).

Paul employs a wide range of literary forms in chapter five, including exhortation (5:1-2, 21-23), especially to Timothy and by implication to the church, vice and virtue lists (5:9-10, 13-14), quotations from Scripture (5:18), and a short saying or aphorism typical of Wisdom literature (5:24-25).

The Text Explained

Respect Age and Beauty (5:1-2). Paul's initial directive is conventional ancient advice: "Do not rebuke an older man harshly, but exhort him as if he were your father. Treat younger men as brothers, older women as mothers and young women as sisters with absolute purity" (5:1-2). Similar statements can be found in Plato (*Republic* 463c) and in the Old Testament Wisdom literature (Proverbs 15:28; 30:11-12). The content of this advice could have been spoken by anyone in antiquity. Paul simply repeats a common and widely embraced value. What is peculiar about his remarks is their application to relationships within the church conceived as God's household. Timothy, and by extension every other person in authority—if not every member of the congregation—is expected to relate to fellow church members as he would the members of his own family. The directive is hortatory, a form common to these letters. The content of these directives assumes Timothy's relative youthfulness and provides a concrete example of how the younger Timothy is to model love and purity in all of his relationships in the church (4:12; 5:22).

The Greek word (*presbuteros*) in 5:1, translated "older man" by the NIV, can also be used to designate a person who is a leader in the church by virtue of his age, as in 5:17 where the plural form is translated "elders." It is quite unlikely, however, that Paul has only church leaders in mind in 5:1. To be sure, "elders" who were leaders would be included among the older persons Timothy is directed not to rebuke harshly, but the entire group of older persons would not be church leaders. This passage gives general advice on how to "exhort" or "encourage" (Gk. *parakaleo*) various age groups within the church.

Honor Widows in Need (5:3-16). The instruction to "properly recognize" and/or "help those widows who are really in need" opens and closes this lengthy section of 5:3-16. In this context, the mandate to "give proper recognition" (Gk. *timao*) or "help" (Gk. *eparkeo*) to those widows who are really in need (literally, "widows who are really widows") includes the idea of economic support (5: 3, 16; see also 5:17). In verses 4-8, Paul highlights the poverty and piety of the needy widows who are to be recognized by the church. Then in verses 9-15 he seems to provide a quite different set of criteria for "putting a widow on the list" (Gk. *katalego*, a technical term for placing a widow on a recognized list; see 5:9, 11). For this reason, and because the qualifications for putting a widow "on the list" are similar to those mentioned earlier for the overseer and deacons (3:2-3, 12), it has been suggested that widows who met the criteria of 5:9-10 held an official position in the church and were a distinct subgroup of widows within the larger category of "widows who are really in need." To be sure, later in the third century, an office of widows existed and this passage may have influenced the qualifications for that office. However, it is unlikely that Paul has a distinct group of official widows in mind; the entire passage is framed by a call to give proper recognition and help to "widows who are really in need" (5:3 & 16). Paul's instructions in 5: 4-10 contain no obvious literary break as in 5:11 with its clear reference to a subgroup called "younger widows." Thus, there is quite likely a single group of widows referred to either as "widows who are really in need" or "widows who have been put on the list." Of course, there are other widows in the church who do not qualify for the list (5:11), and hence are not members of this designated group.

To fully appreciate Paul's discussion of widows, it is essential to recall that the ancient world is not kind to unattached women unless they are wealthy. Women,

whether Jew or Greek, typically depend upon a male relative or husband for their social and economic status. Any
exceptions are confined to the upper classes. The churches associated with the Pastoral Letters give unattached
women some economic security as well as an opportunity for them to serve the Lord in specific ways, thereby
granting them the needed social status. As the years pass,
however, this group comes under criticism for two distinct yet interrelated reasons. First, the number of widows
appears to be increasing and straining the church's financial resources (5:16). The Christian responsibility to provide economic assistance for widows with inadequate
resources has its roots in Jewish custom and law. As the
most vulnerable members of a patriarchal society, widows
were under God's special care (Exodus 22:22-24) and the
more secure members of society were expected to be
God's agents by providing widows both food and justice
(Deuteronomy 24:19-22; Isaiah 1:17). There is ample evidence that the early church continues this practice of caring for widows (Acts 6:1; 9:36-41). But by the time Paul
writes to Timothy, this commitment, at least in Ephesus, is
becoming a financial burden on the church.

Perhaps the definition of "widow" has shifted,
increasing the number of women included in the group
and thus imposing a steep financial burden on the
church. In its most basic sense, the word "widow" (Gk.
chera) refers to a woman who lives without a husband
because her spouse is deceased. But in this passage, Paul
writes about a "pledge" (Gk. *pistis*) or solemn promise
that widows make, a pledge that would be violated if
they are to subsequently marry (5:11-12). Presumably, a
"widow" in the Ephesian church is one who makes a vow
of fidelity to Christ, analogous to a marriage vow. Christ
then becomes the male to whom they are attached.
Indeed, the entire passage suggests that celibacy, not the
death of a spouse, is the defining feature of this group.

Later, in an early first century letter, Ignatius writes to the Smyrneans, sending his greetings to "the virgins who are called widows" (Ignatius *Smyr.* 13.1). If something comparable exists in Ephesus, then the circle of widows not only includes women whose husbands have died, but also women who are virgins (1 Corinthians 7:25-38). All of these women have dedicated themselves to serve Christ in the context of the church. Perhaps membership in this group is appealing to women who want to escape the restrictions of a patriarchal marriage and live a life closer to the ideal articulated by Paul in 1 Corinthians 7:8 and Galatians 3:28.

Second, the younger widows are causing problems that are likely connected with the false teachers. If we have reconstructed the Ephesian situation accurately, then the widows live a celibate life similar to the false teachers (4:3). Paul's comment that some of the younger widows have "turned away to follow Satan" (5:15) may mean that they have become disciples of these false teachers. Moreover, the public behavior of these younger widows, who are castigated by Paul for "going about from house to house" (5:13), has the potential to embarrass the church. In the larger society, women are expected to pursue a more domestic and less visible pattern of behavior. The "enemy" that Paul fears will slander the church (5:14) is likely an outsider who has grown suspicious of the widows' behavior, especially the "younger widows" (see Titus 2:8). For these reasons then, Paul takes bold steps to address these problems. He introduces a strategy designed to reduce the financial burden on the church, minimize the oppositions' influence on this group of women, and prevent any criticism of the church by outsiders.

First, Paul insists that the widows' original families are responsible for them. Although it is an important part of Paul's instructions concerning widows, the meaning of

5:4 is disputed because of an inexplicable change in the sentence's grammatical structure. The first clause of the sentence has a singular subject: "But if a widow has children or grandchildren ..." (5:4a). The second clause has a plural subject: "these should learn (Gk. *manthanetosan*; literally, "they should learn") first of all to put their religion into practice ..." (5:4b). The plural verb may signal that the children and grandchildren mentioned in the first clause should learn or that the widows should learn. The latter interpretation is grammatically awkward, but not without precedent in this letter (see 2:15). Most commentators accept the former interpretation and argue that Paul wants to reduce the church's financial burden by encouraging Christian children and grandchildren to assume personal responsibility for their own widowed mothers and grandmothers. Paul's sharply worded denunciation of anyone who fails to care for his relatives as "worse than an unbeliever" is indicative of the gravity of the problem. Apparently, the children and grandchildren of widows are quite willing to let the church family, the household of God (3:15), assume the economic burden of caring for their needy female relatives. No wonder Paul reminds them that caring for one's parent is an opportunity "to put their religion into practice" (Gk. *eusebein*), a religious obligation rooted in the Decalogue (see Exodus 20:12).

Second, Paul endorses Christian women who support widows. He implores them to continue helping: "If any woman who is a believer has widows in her family, she should help them and not let the church be burdened with them..." (5:16). Unfortunately, the NIV translation of this verse is an interpretation, implying that a believing woman should help relatives who are widows. But the Greek text simply says, "Any believing woman who has widows, should help them..." (5:16). Christian women of considerable means often provide financial support—food, housing and clothing—to other widows in their congregation. Paul approves of such generous behavior by wealthy Christian women because it relieves the financial burden on the church. The story of Tabitha in Acts 9:36-42 is a likely antecedent to the kind of practice endorsed here by Paul.

Third, Paul limits membership in the group by carefully prescribing who may or may not be put on the list of widows. He depicts the "real" widow as a person who "puts her hope in God and continues night and day to pray and ask God for help" (5:5). This may be a reference to one of the duties of widows. A widow's constant supplication and prayers demonstrate that she has truly "put her hope in God" (5:5), whereas "the widow who lives for pleasure is dead even while she lives" (5:6). Although there is no indication here whether these prayers are performed alone or in the company of other widows, they are probably not part of the public worship service since women's participation is limited (2:8).

Additional criteria narrows the circle of widows on the list (5:9-10). Old age is a requirement: "No widow may be put on the list of widows unless she is over sixty" (5:9). The 60th year in antiquity marks the beginning of old age. It is also an age when marriage becomes an improbable option. To be put on the list, a woman must have been "faithful to her husband" (cf. 3:2) and "well known for her good deeds, such as bringing up children" (5:9-10). These requirements for membership in the group promote the Greco-Roman ideal of marriage and childbearing. Thus, a woman qualifies for membership in the group if she has led a life conforming to the expectations of Greco-Roman society. This lifestyle is antithetical to the demands of the celibate false teachers (see 4:3). Another set of criteria indicates that membership in the group is a reward for service to the church. Hospitality is widely encouraged as a Christian virtue (see 3:2; Titus 1:8). It reflects God's hospitable grace (Romans 12:13; 14:1; 15:7), nurtures relationships between Christian communities, and helps itinerant preachers of the gospel message. Washing the feet of visitors is customarily the task of a slave. In this church, however, women perform this service for other Christians as a demonstration of hospitality and a gesture of humility (cf. John 13).

Fourth, Paul excludes "younger widows" from membership in the group of widows placed on the list. He gives two reasons for their exclusion. First, they have failed to sustain the celibate life required of them. The language of 5:11-12 suggests that widows make a vow of fidelity to Christ, construed on the analogy of marriage. Christ becomes the male to whom they are attached. Thus, a "younger widow" who marries (deemed likely by Paul) violates her pledge to Christ, bringing judgment (Gk. *krima*) on herself. Since marriage is regarded positively in these letters, the judgment of younger widows who desire to marry indicates the gravity of their vow. Presumably this judgment comes from God (see 3:6; 1 Corinthians 11:29-34), not simply the community. Second, they have participated in activities deemed inappropriate for women in the church. Paul describes these younger women as "going about from house to house" (5:13a). This activity violates the prevailing social ideal of a secluded domestic life for women. Also, these younger women are "saying things they ought not to say" (5:13b), indicating that Paul has a problem with the content of their speech. A similar charge is leveled against the false teachers who "are ruining whole households by teaching things they ought not to teach" (Titus 1:11). If both groups live celibate lives, both may also be verbally promoting such. Thus, Paul excludes the "younger widows" from the list of widows and advises them to "marry" (5:14), thereby restoring them to a patriarchal household and to a non-celibate way of life (see also 2:15; Titus 2:4-5).

Honor Elders Who Rule Well (5:17-25). Paul shifts his focus to the third leadership group in the church, the elders (Gk. *presbuteroi*), who are the source of some difficulty. The precise nature of the problems associated with this group is not clear, nor is the relationship of these elders with other church leaders (overseer and deacons, 3:1-13) especially evident.

The antecedent of these elders is to be found among the synagogue leaders, a cluster of men who provided oversight of their Jewish community, particularly with respect to interpreting and teaching the law. Thus, leadership within the earliest Jewish Christian churches replicates, to some extent, the synagogue's leadership pattern. The book of Acts mentions elders who share leadership with the apostles in the Jerusalem church and who participate in the decision making process (see Acts 15:1-29; 16:4; 1 Peter 5:1). Although Paul never mentions elders in his other letters, Luke refers to them among the Pauline churches (see Acts 14:21-23; 20:17).

In his letter to Titus, Paul links elders (Gk. *presbuteroi*) with the bishop (Gk. *Episkopos*). In 1 Timothy the two positions are treated separately, although their respective functions overlap (Titus 1:5-9; cf. 1 Peter 5:1-2). A comparison of these two leadership positions indicates they both are expected to rule or manage the church well, to preach, and to teach (see 3:2, 5; 5:17; Titus 1:9). It is possible that all overseers are elders, but not all elders are overseers.

In this passage, Paul addresses the leadership issues of compensation and correction. Elders who "direct the affairs of the church well" (Gk. *proistemi*, "govern" or "rule") are to be given "double honor," which includes a financial honorarium as the scriptural warrants in verse 18 clearly indicate. But is the honorarium to be double what the widows receive (5:3), or double what other elders who do not preach and teach receive? With two groups of elders in mind, Paul, who assumes that all elders rule, proposes a double compensation for those who rule well, with a particular focus on teaching and preaching (5:17b). This is a clear contrast with the elders who not only rule poorly but have fallen into sin (5:19-20). Presumably the elders who have sinned are disqualified from any compensation and hence the standard of comparison is likely the widow's honorarium.

Paul cites two texts as a warrant for granting a double honor to elders who rule well: "For the Scripture says, 'Do not muzzle the ox while it is treading out the grain,' and 'The worker deserves his wages'" (5:18). The first quote is from Deuteronomy 25:4 which Paul also cites in 1 Corinthians 9:9 to support his argument that apostles have a right to receive payment for their work, although he himself refuses to take advantage of this right. The second scriptural warrant is a saying of Jesus, identical to the form found in Luke 10:7 (cf. Matthew 10:10). Paul also alludes to this saying as part of his argument in 1 Corinthians 9:14, but he does not quote it. Although Paul has a high regard for the Jewish scriptures (see 2 Timothy 3:16), 1 Timothy 5:18a is the only place in the Pastoral Letters where he cites them as "scripture" (Gk. *graphe*). Also, 5:18b is one of only two places in the entire New Testament where a Christian writing is cited as scripture (cf. 2 Peter 3:15-16). It is not until the late second century that the term "scripture" becomes widely used for the New Testament writings. It's use here is certainly not evidence for the early existence of a formal New Testament canon. In public worship, the Christian writings are likely read alongside the Jewish writings so that eventually the term "scripture" is applied to both.

Having addressed the matter of compensation, Paul now treats the procedures for correcting elders charged with unspecified sins, an issue that seems to be of great concern to him. At the outset, he protects the elders from irresponsible accusations: "Do not entertain an accusation against an elder unless it is brought by two or three witnesses" (5:19). Here Paul invokes the Old Testament norm of requiring two or three witnesses (see Deuteronomy 19:15; cf. Matthew 18:16; John 8:17; 2 Corinthians 13:1).

Next, Paul demands a public rebuke or exposure of elders who persist in sin (5:20). Although "elders" are not explicitly mentioned in verse 20, the context supports the assumption that Paul is still speaking about elders as a group. Admittedly, the exhortations in 5:20-25 are disjointed, but they acquire unity only by assuming them under the rubric of elders. Since the task of "rebuking" or "reprimanding" (Gk. *elengcho*) is elsewhere the responsibility of the overseer (see Titus 1:9; 2 Timothy 4:2), these guidelines for correcting erring elders are to be used by other church leaders. There is an apparent contradiction between 5:20 and 5:1 where Paul instructs Timothy to refrain from "rebuking" an older man, although a different verb is used (Gk. *epiplesso*). However, 5:17-25 likely represents Paul's qualification of his opening remarks in 5:1-2. Also, in 5:19-21 he places limits on correcting elders so as to avoid the kind of excessive harshness implied by 5:1. Further, in 5:20 he emphasizes the rebuke's pedagogical value (see also 2 Timothy 2:25), although the identity of "the others" instructed by the rebuke is not clear. Paul likely refers to "the other elders." Also, he does not list the kind of offenses that deserve a rebuke. These wayward elders are simply described as "sinning" (5:20; cf. 1:15; 2 Timothy 3:6; Titus 3:11). In the context of the Pastoral Letters it is possible the elders are "sinning" by joining ranks with the false teachers whom Paul castigates in 6:3-5. If so, this scenario may explain Paul's keen interest in rewarding elders who fulfill their teaching responsibilities well.

The next set of instructions to Timothy is introduced with an impressive vow: "I charge you, in the sight of

God and Christ Jesus and the elect angels..." (5:21). The reference to "elect angels" echoes Revelation 1:4-5, where the "seven spirits" are archangels (Revelation 8:2). The mention of angels in the triad is reminiscent of apocalyptic judgment (see Mark 13:26-27; Revelation 14:6-11), which seems appropriate to this specific warning. In this way, Paul's charge underscores the importance of avoiding prejudice and partiality, including excessive harshness as well as inappropriate leniency.

The action described in 5:22a does not refer to a penitent elder's restoration but to the initial appointment of an elder (see 4:14; 2 Timothy 1:6): "Do not be hasty in the laying on of hands..."). Given the problem of "sinful" elders, a period of testing or investigation is encouraged before appointing a church leader (3:10). The other two exhortations suggest that church leaders are in some way accountable for the sins committed by a person they have too hastily set apart for church leadership.

Paul's personal word to Timothy appears irrelevant to the immediate argument: "Stop drinking only water, and use a little wine because of your stomach and your frequent illnesses" (5:23). While it reflects the ideal of moderation, avoiding the extremes of total abstinence and drunkenness, it is difficult to determine its connection with Paul's argument here. Perhaps his reference to "purity" in 5:22 prompts Paul to caution against an overzealous purity. If the problem with the elders is linked to the ascetic tendencies of the false teachers, then this piece of advice may be a poke at his opponents' position of abstinence. In any case, a respect for wine's medicinal value is widespread (cf. Luke 10:34).

By way of conclusion, Paul cites an aphorism: "The sins of some men are obvious, reaching the place of judgment ahead of time; the sins of others trail behind them. In the same way, good deeds are obvious, and even those that are not cannot be hidden" (5:24). It speaks to the inevitable surfacing of sin and virtue, and places the exhortations about elders who sin within the final judgment's shadow. Also, the aphorism supports the injunction to avoid haste when laying hands on a person for it may take time for his sins to be exposed to the light of day.

Instructions for Slaves (6:1-2). At first sight, this brief set of instructions pertaining to "slaves" (Gk. *douloi*) seems, for several reasons, to be out of place. First, slaves are not an "official" group within the church like the "elders" and "widows" just described in 5:3-25. Second, the word "respect" or "honor" (Gk. *time*) is used here (6:1) without any financial nuance, in contrast to 5: 3 and 17 where the economic implications are obvious. Third, slaves as a category have no natural affinity to the various age groups treated in 5:1-3. The only connection between 6:1-2a and the preceding material is that slaves are another problematic group within the Ephesian church in need of specific instructions.

To appreciate Paul's instructions to slaves, it is important to remember that Christianity does not perceive itself as a revolutionary movement, although the gospel message certainly has clear racial, social and sexual implications. Both canonical and noncanonical Christian writings of the first and second century exhort slaves to obey their masters who are, in turn, instructed not to be harsh with their slaves (Ephesians 6:5-9; Colossians 3:22-4:1; 1 Peter 2:18-25; *Didache* 4:10; *Barnabas* 19:7).

Also, the Greco-Roman household management tradition is undoubtedly the background of this early Christian treatment of domestic responsibilities. The household's various members are given specific duties that define their functional relationship with each other, including the three key pairs—masters and slave, husband and wife, father and children. Wives, children and slaves are considered the subordinate members and owe their obedience to the household head. Adult males possess the natural right of authority in these relationships, although they are not to abuse this authority (see Balch 1981: 21-62). While most first century Greco-Roman organizations like clubs and guilds tend to be homogeneous, Christian gatherings are very heterogeneous, including within their ranks Jew and Greek, slave and free, male and female. Within the gathered Christian community, these social differences are deemed of no consequence (see Galatians 3:28) as all groups eat at table together and call each other "brother" and "sister" even though they may be master and slave outside the gathered faith community setting. This milieu of equality among God's people within the church gathered is in tension with their lives outside the church, especially in the setting of the extended family where relationships are defined hierarchically. Thus, this situation is a source of tension for Christians as they move between the social settings of home, church and society.

To exacerbate this situation, Roman magistrates tend to be quite suspicious of new religious movements or cults (and Christianity is considered one of them), suspecting that they disrupt proper social relationships and customs deemed normative by Roman society. Hence, the New Testament household codes often have an apologetic function (Balch 1981: 63-116). In an effort to silence criticism from outsiders and address tensions between social groupings within the church, Christian writers reinforce the normative patterns of social behavior that the wider society expects of its members to show that the Christian movement is not dangerous to the state's norms.

With this background in mind, it is not surprising that Paul instructs slaves to "honor" their masters: "All who are under the yoke of slavery should consider their masters worthy of full respect" (6:1a). Of course, this is not a reference to financial compensation (cf. 5:3, 17) but refers instead to the social disposition and conduct that governs a slave's relationship with his/her higher ranked master. Since respect and shame are the "pivotal values" of the Greco-Roman culture (Malina 1981: 25-50), Paul exhorts slaves to respect their masters.

It is noteworthy that this mandate to slaves is not accompanied by a corresponding exhortation for masters to treat slaves with fairness (see 1 Peter 2:18-25; Ephesians 5:9). Perhaps the best explanation for this omission is that Paul's concern here is primarily the effect that a slave's behavior and attitude has on the church, in particular on the church's perception by outsiders. Therefore, Paul instructs slaves together with elders and widows because the behavior of all three groups in the church is of great importance for its reputation among outsiders. Thus, the exhortation of 6:1 assumes that insubordinate behavior by Christian slaves calls into question the Christian message, whereas submissive behavior by the slaves makes the church attractive to outsiders (6:1b; Titus 2:9-10). Some things are more important than others and what matters most is the progress of the gospel message.

Next, Paul addresses the peculiar problem of slaves who have Christian masters and who feel the tension between their equality as fellow believers in God's household and their subordinate social status in the home and larger society: "Those who have believing masters are not to show less respect for them because they are brothers" (6:2a). Presumably slaves in the Ephesian church are expressing reluctance to serve their Christian "brothers" (Gk. *adelphoi*). Paul counters by using two other names for Christians: "faithful ones" (Gk. *pistoi)* and "beloved ones" (Gk. *agapetoi)*, or as the NIV translates, they are "believers and dear to them" (6:2b). Although not well developed here, Paul supports his argument with the rationale that since masters are faithful to God and beloved of God, slaves should similarly be faithful in their service to those masters who call them "brothers" and "sisters."

The NIV translation depicts these masters as "those who benefit from their (i.e., the slaves') service" (6:2b). But the final Greek clause of 6:2 refers to the masters, not the slaves, and supplies the motivation for the extra service due to the masters who are believers and dear ones (to God, Romans 11:28) "who devote themselves to good deeds." It is important to note that the Greek word translated "benefit" by the NIV (Gk. *euergesia*) typically defines the good service, good deed or benefit rendered by a superior to an inferior, not the other way around (see Rienecker/Rogers 1980: 633). In fact, Hellenistic rulers frequently adopt the title "Benefactor" (Gk. *Euergetes*) as a self-referent.

Paul's conservative social values are abundantly evident in this lengthy passage of 5:1 to 6:2. Younger widows are restricted to domestic roles and barred from participating in the widows' special ministry. Slaves are expected to serve their masters with full respect, even when their masters are fellow Christians. Paul undoubtedly fears that radical changes in the social status or conduct of women and slaves will bring shame upon the church and impede God's world mission through the church. Elsewhere Paul expresses his concern for the perception of outsiders and his desire that Christians win their respect (1 Thessalonians 4:11-12; 1 Corinthians 14:23-24). Paul's basic posture as an apostle is to give no offense to others. He encourages his churches to do likewise for his ultimate goal is to spread the gospel and convert outsiders (1 Corinthians 10:31-11:1). At the same time, Paul is convinced "this present world in its present form is passing away" (1 Corinthians 7:31). Thus, he sometimes endorses celibacy in spite of its negative social implications (1 Corinthians 7: 8), or delicately questions the compatibility of slavery with Christian love (see Philemon). But here in the Pastoral Letters Paul is battling with false teachers who espouse celibacy and outsiders who are suspicious of the Christian movement. Thus, he restricts the celibacy option (5:11-15) for Christian women who desire to be on the "widows list," even though it would free them from the limitations of a patriarchal marriage (a social arrangement closer to Paul's own ideal as expressed in 1 Corinthians 7:8 and Galatians 3:28) and free them to serve Christ by serving the Christian community (1 Timothy 5:10). Also, he advocates a conservative position on slavery, encouraging slaves to show full respect for their masters.

Slavery clearly drives the Roman Empire's economic systems. Surprisingly, the New Testament writers either actively endorse slavery or passively presuppose it. The rationales for supporting the institution of slavery vary within the New Testament. Sometimes Paul is quite stoical, maintaining that the external circumstance of slavery is of little real concern for persons who "belong to the Lord" (1 Corinthians 7:21-24). At other times, Paul supplies a theological rationale that encourages slaves to view service to their masters "as if (they) were serving the Lord" (Ephesians 6: 7; Colossians 3:23) or, as Peter argues, as a reflection of Christ's obedience (1 Peter 2:18-25). But in the Pastoral Letters, Paul's approach is missiological, arguing that a slave's obedience promotes the success of the Christian world mission. Since slavery is a pattern of conduct normative to Roman society, compliance with the social norms of the Greco-Roman world increases the Christian message's acceptability and thus promotes God's desire that everyone be saved (1 Timothy 2:4).

In the Pastoral Letters the extended patriarchal family is very much the norm for its many social exhortations. The household becomes the pattern for the church (3:15) with a great deal of interchange between church and family roles. For example, the qualifications for membership in the group of widows are a balance of deeds done in and for the family, and those done in and for the church. Also, since the Ephesian widow's familial position and responsibilities had grown to the point where they were eclipsed by their official status and role within the church (1 Timothy 5:11-15), Paul offers some correction for this situation (5:14). Again, the submissive attitude and conduct of slaves, although a domestic matter, is addressed in relationship to the church's mission; the entire church has a stake in the behavior of slaves.

Still, tension occasionally exists between the church as God's household and the individual households that comprise a typical congregation. In the setting of the gathered community, Christians are siblings, addressing each other as "brother" and "sister." But in the home context these same Christians assume different roles and positions as fathers, husbands and masters, or as children, wives and slaves. When conflict emerges between roles in the two different "households" (home and church), one system invariably prevails. In an earlier clash of "households," Paul drew heavily on Christian kinship language to persuade Philemon to modify his family headship role enough to embrace Onesimus, his runaway slave (Philemon 15-16), and even to set his "brother" free, the likely intent of Philemon 21. Paul takes a different approach in the Pastoral Letters. He essentially sidesteps the slaves' appeal to Christian kinship as a basis for modifying their servile social status and insists instead on obedient submission as a slave's Christian responsibility.

In the final analysis, Paul's mandates concerning slaves and women are provoked by a serious problem facing the Ephesian church as it seeks to make converts of outsiders: how to maintain the peculiar theological and social identity of the Christian community (which can appear offensive to outsiders) while simultaneously building bridges to the outside world so that conversion to Christ becomes a viable option. In these letters, Paul consistently chooses a missionary strategy.

Application, Teaching/Preaching Points

Admittedly, it is difficult to move from specific directives in the past to rules for the church today. Our social context is very different from Paul's of the first century. It is pretty much impossible now for a faith community to institute and maintain the sort of regulations Paul proposes to the Ephesian church. Yet this passage remains of vital importance to the church's life in every age.

Would You Put This Man in Charge? He's young, rural, insecure and has gastronomical problems. Why would Paul pin his hopes for the Ephesian project on such a dubious rookie? Timothy has many other strikes against him. His family is a mess, full of racial tensions (Jewish mother and Greek father) and religious conflict (Christian mother and pagan father). His hometown is Lystra—remote, mountainous, out of the Roman system. His identity is confused: Am I really Jewish? Am I too young for this assignment? Can I lead? How do these city folk think, anyway (surely not like down home). Was Dad right, or Mom? Will I fail Paul in this task? Conflict troubles Timothy; he personalizes it too much. Paul takes on his development. Timothy undergoes rites of acceptance by Jews (adult circumcision—ouch!) He interns on visits to other operations (Thessalonica, Corinth). He borrows Paul's files (2 Timothy 4:13). Yet Paul sees in him a person of great promise. Who else but a bi-cultural trainee from out of town could lead this diverse collection of beginners in the faith at Ephesus? All of this raises some pertinent questions for reflection: Where do leaders come from? What do they really look like? Are we biased against potential leaders who are not like us?

Who Should be Put on the List? To be put on the list is to be enrolled, a word used of soldiers in Greek. The church supports widows from the beginning but must be careful and selective. Paul lists the qualifications necessary for being included on the list. They include the following: over sixty, faithful to her husband, well known for her good deeds, raises her children well, hospitality, washing the feet of the saints, helping those in trouble, and helping other widows. Paul's list raises important questions for us today. In light of this passage, we may need to reconsider our reasons for not having elderly relatives living with us. This passage may challenge the church's priorities when it comes to nurturing the young or caring for the old. Also, our society has seen a great increase in the number of single parents (mostly mothers) raising children. What does this passage imply about our Christian responsibility to them? Are they responsible for their own welfare? Or should their families, the church or the state care for them? In what proportion? Finally, some churches treat marriage as the norm, leaving older single women to feel like the church has no place for them and no work for them to do. Do they feel marginalized and underemployed? Many churches place importance on "family services." How can single people be helped to feel a part of the larger family of God?

A Brief History of Widows in the Bible. The Bible says much about widows. In the Old Testament, Israel was told again and again to care for widows and orphans. There are 13 references to widows in the Law (Deuteronomy 10:18; 24:17). Elijah stayed with the widow of Zarephath, provided for her needs miraculously and healed her son (1 Kings 17:19ff.) The Book of Ruth tells us how three women reacted to widowhood: with bitterness, by remarrying and with patient waiting. The Lord is declared to be "the defender of widows" (Psalm 68:5) and he pleads "the cause of the widows" (Isaiah 1:17).

In the New Testament there are 26 references, nine in Luke's Gospel and nine in Paul's letters. Jesus condemns those who devour widow's houses (Matthew 23:14); commends the widow giving her mite (Mark 12:42); speaks of the widow to whom Elijah was sent (Luke 4:25); raises the widow's son at Nain (Luke 7:42). Acts 6:1 speaks of some widows being neglected. Mary, the mother of Jesus, is a widow. In Joppa there seems to be a distinct group (Acts 9:39, 41) blessed by Dorcas' good works. Widows could live lone lives—Anna (Luke 2:37) was widowed after seven years of marriage and lives alone at 84 years of age.

In the ancient world, men were more likely to die in warfare, and widowed men are more likely to remarry than women. Who provides for widows and orphans when the working man is dead? They are faced with the dangers of exploitation and prostitution. James 1:27 makes caring for widows and orphans (what today we call "single parents") a mark of true religion. Just as the early church rises to such social responsibilities, this issue remains relevant for the 21st century church. Even today, if you are a married female, the probability is that you will spend your later years as a widow.

Who is Obligated to Care for the Destitute? This chapter of 1 Timothy reminds us of the fundamental and unavoidable obligation we have as believers to support those without the means to support themselves. Paul confronts the issue of what falls to the individual families and what falls to the church. It is inconceivable to him to push the problem off on to the shoulders of the state. Justice requires that we care directly and appropriately for the needy among us. What would Paul think of us today as we lobby for social legislation but do not see the literal widows who devote themselves to prayer night and day in our own faith communities? What would Paul have said to those of us who betray the most elementary

demand of nature, not to mention the Ten Commandments, by leaving our parents' care to anonymous insti-
tutions because we simply cannot be bothered?

Sin, Failure, Justice and Holiness. Three short propositions related to our text can stimulate a process of reflection and lead to sermon construction. First, to be a church
and not a sect, a faith community must have ways of dealing with failure and even sin. A sect, defining itself in
terms of a realized perfection, has no other choice when
failure occurs than to divide itself again or to separate
itself from the failure or sin. But a church must find ways
to reveal and heal moral sickness within it. It must do this
even, or especially, when it is the community's leadership
that is diseased. Second, if a church is to live according to
the standards of "impartiality" mandated by scripture
and the Lord, then it must have just procedures for resolv-
ing these failures and sins. In the case of leaders, Paul
offers some helpful guidelines: the church cannot dismiss
its leaders on the basis of idiosyncratic complaints or
whispering campaigns. Charges must be openly stated
and supported "by two or three witnesses." On the other
hand, those who do wrong when in positions of leadership cannot be protected or camouflaged, for to do so is to
corrupt the church itself. Just as the charge against them
should be open, so should be their penalty: "Those who
sin should be rebuked publicly, so that the others may
take warning" (5:20). Third, if a church is to continue to be
a community of holiness and maintain its distinctive identity in the world, it must learn how to exercise judgment
within. Paul insists, in 1 Corinthians, that the community
is responsible for maintaining its own standards. When
wrongdoing or corruption in the community are not dealt
with "by the saints," then at some point they will be dealt
with by referral to outside authorities. When that happens, there is no more community; only a loose assem-
blage of litigants.

Comparing the Women of Chapters 2 and 5. There are many parallels between the women addressed in 1 Timothy 2:8-15 and the women addressed in 1 Timothy 5:3-16. The tone seems much the same, suggesting that the issues in the two chapters are somewhat related.

1 Timothy 2	1 Timothy 5
(9) "I want women to dress modestly with decency and propriety, not with braided hair or gold or pearls or expensive clothes."	(6) "The widow who lives for pleasure is dead even while she lives." (13) "they get into the habit of being idle."
(10) "but with good deeds, appropriate for women who profess to worship God."	(10) "well known for her good deeds ...all kinds of good deeds."
(11) "A woman should learn in quietness and full submission."	(13) "gossips and busy bodies, saying things they ought not to."
(12) "I do not permit a woman to teach or to have authority over a man; she must be silent."	
(14) "Adam was not the one deceived. It was the woman who was deceived (by Satan)."	(15) "Some have in fact already turned to follow Satan."
(15) "But the women will be saved through child-bearing if they continue in faith, love and holiness with propriety."	(14) "I counsel younger widows to have children."

Personal Reflection Questions

- Put your religion into practice by caring for your own family, says Paul. DISCUSS: Do you think it is appropriate to have elderly relatives living with you in your home? If not, provide a rationale. Is it more important for the church to care for the young or the old? Where should the church put its priority if it cannot do both?

- Caring for all people in the church is the major emphasis of this chapter. DISCUSS: Single parents (normally mothers) with children are increasing in numbers in North America. What should our Christian response be to this situation in light of this passage? Who is responsible for a person's welfare? Family? Church? State? In what proportion? Arrange these in order as a safety net for needy people.

- Marriage seems to be the norm in the Pauline churches. DISCUSS: If marriage is treated as the norm in the church, how are older single women affected? In what ways might they feel the church has no place/work for them? When and why might they feel marginalized and underemployed? How do single persons react to churches that emphasize "the family"? How can we include single persons as part of the church family?

- Paul holds preaching and teaching elders in high esteem. DISCUSS: How do we muzzle our church leaders? Does your church pay them enough and grant them the respect they deserve? Do you expect greater sacrifice from them than you ask of yourself?

- Elders who sin are to be rebuked publicly according to Paul. DISCUSS: If one of your church leaders were accused of moral failure, how would you apply these verses to the situation? How can you respond when a church is criticized and discredited by its leader's moral failures?

CHAPTER SIX

Guard the Gospel

The Text: 1 Timothy 6:3-21

If anyone teaches false doctrines and does not agree to the sound instruction of our Lord Jesus Christ and to godly teach-ing, [4] *he is conceited and understands nothing. He has an unhealthy interest in controversies and quarrels about words that result in envy, strife, malicious talk, evil suspicions* [5] *and constant friction between men of corrupt mind, who have been robbed of the truth and who think that godliness is a means to financial gain.* [6] *But godliness with contentment is great gain.* [7] *For we brought nothing into the world, and we can take noth-ing out of it.* [8] *But if we have food and clothing, we will be con-tent with that.* [9] *People who want to get rich fall into tempta-tion and a trap and into many foolish and harmful desires that plunge men into ruin and destruction.* [10] *For the love of money is a root of all kinds of evil. Some people, eager for money, have wandered from the faith and pierced themselves with many griefs.* [11] *But you, man of God, flee from all this, and pursue righteousness, godliness, faith, love, endurance and gentleness.* [12] *Fight the good fight of the faith. Take hold of the eternal life to which you were called when you made your good confession in the presence of many witnesses.* [13] *In the sight of God, who gives life to everything, and of Christ Jesus, who while testify-ing before Pontius Pilate made the good confession, I charge you* [14] *to keep this command without spot or blame until the appearing of our Lord Jesus Christ,* [15] *which God will bring about in his own time—God, the blessed and only Ruler, the King of kings and Lord of lords,* [16] *who alone is immortal and who lives in unapproachable light, whom no one has seen or can see. To him be honor and might forever. Amen.* [17] *Command those who are rich in this present world not to be arrogant nor to put their hope in wealth, which is so uncertain, but to put their hope in God, who richly provides us with everything for our enjoyment.* [18] *Command them to do good, to be rich in good deeds, and to be generous and willing to share.* [19] *In this way they will lay up treasure for themselves as a firm foundation for the coming age, so that they may take hold of the life that is truly life.* [20] *Timothy, guard what has been entrusted to your care. Turn away from godless chatter and the opposing ideas of what is falsely called knowledge,* [21] *which some have professed and in so doing have wandered from the faith. Grace be with you.*

The Flow and Form of the Text

The tone and content of the letter's concluding words (6:3-21) are similar to the opening words (1:3-20). Paul returns to the theme of the opposing teachers, giving his longest and most scathing polemic against them (vv. 3-5). Again he provides a portrait of the faithful leader by describing, through his instructions to Timothy, the key qualities of the "man of God" (6:11-16). These qualities are a sharp contrast to those of the false teachers. Numerous themes from the letter's opening chapter are revisited here, including the contrast between sound teaching and empty speculations or controversies (vv. 3-5; 1:4,10), vice lists (vv. 4-5; 1:9-10), doxologies (vv. 15-16; 1:17), recollections of Timothy's commissioning service (vv. 12-14; 1:18), and the theme of the good fight (v. 12; 1:18). There is also some fresh content, in particular the accusation that greed is the opponents' motivating factor. This leads to a set of instructions from Paul on the proper disposition of a church leader with respect to money. Between chapters 1 and 6, Paul has insisted that "widows who are really in need" and "elders who direct the affairs of the church well" be granted an honorarium (5:3,17). His scathing critique of the false teachers' greed serves simultaneously to curb the potential abuse by widows and elders of the church's generosity.

This chapter begins with a critique of the false teachers and its corresponding teaching on the dangers of greed (6:3-10). Then it shifts to instructions for Timothy with a corresponding reminder of his commissioning service (6:11-16). Although these two parts will be treated separately here, maximum benefit and warning is derived from reflecting on the contrasting portraits of false (vv. 3-10) and faithful (vv. 11-16) church leaders. Finally, Paul gives some advice to those who are wealthy (6:17-19) and concludes the chapter with a final charge to Timothy (6:20-21).

The Text Explained

Vices of the False Teachers (6:2b-10). Paul first exhorts Timothy: "These are the things (Gk. *tauta*, see also 3:14; 4:6, 11) you are to teach and urge on them" (6:2b), a reference to his preceding instructions in 5:1-6:2a, if not all of his instructions in this letter. Secondly, he warns against false teaching: "If anyone teaches false doctrines..." (Gk. *heterodidaskalein*, literally, "to teach something different"), a verb that recalls the initial warning of this letter where the same Greek verb is used (see 1:3). The exhortation (6:2b) and warning (6:3a) together signal the contrasts that are developed in the following verses (6:3-10). A glance at verses 3-5 reveals that much of the content repeats earlier warnings: the notion that correct teaching is "sound instruction" (1:10; see also 2 Timothy 1:13; 4:3; Titus 1:9; 2:1); the idea that the opponents lack understanding (1:7; see also Titus 1:15-16) and engage in senseless, speculative verbal disputes (1:4; see also 6:20; 2 Timothy 2:23; Titus 3:9); and a vice list depicting the moral consequences of their behavior (1:9-11; see also 2 Timothy 3:2-5).

Paul reiterates two of his key emphases in the Pastoral Letters. First, he perceives an inseparable link between "sound (Gk. *hugiaino*, literally, "healthy") instruction" and the moral way of life. Teaching that fosters "godliness" (Gk. *eusebeia*; see 2:2) is translated by the NIV as "godly teaching." Second, Paul sees a similar link between false teaching and a life of moral chaos (see 1:8-11; especially Titus 1:16).

The chaotic way of life fostered by "false doctrines" is described primarily in terms of antisocial behavior that destroys cohesion in the faith community (cf. Romans 1:29-31) by fostering "controversies," "quarrels," "envy, strife, malicious talk, evil suspicions, and constant friction." Paul dismisses the false teachers, with their different message, as persons who are "unhealthy" (Gk. *noseo*), "conceited" and "corrupt" (see Titus 3:11).

By contrast, "godly teaching" (literally, "teaching that is in accordance with godliness") is matched with "the sound instruction of our Lord Jesus Christ," although this latter phrase's exact meaning is disputed. It could refer to the basic Christian message in the sense of the gospel according to Jesus Christ, making the two phrases essentially the same (Fee 1988). However, in the Pastoral Letters, Paul prefers the singular "word" (see 2 Timothy 2:9; 4:2) for this meaning. Here he uses the plural form (Gk. *logoi*, literally "words"), a reference perhaps to Jesus' actual words known to Paul from oral tradition.

In the final analysis, the false teachers' actions are ultimately motivated by greed: "(they) think godliness is a means of gain" (6:5). This portrayal of the false teachers is characteristic of the Pastoral Letters. It is anticipated in the qualifications for the overseer and deacons (3:3, 8; see also Titus 1:7) and reiterated in subsequent attacks on the opponents (see 2 Timothy 3:2; Titus 1:11). If this is a valid accusation, how do the false teachers hope to "gain" (Gk. *porismos*) by means of "godliness" (Gk. *eusebeia*)? Presumably, they hope to gain by the church's willingness to support selected persons in their midst (see 5:3,17).

The balance of this passage develops legitimate and illegitimate gain. Paul focuses on the issue of "gain" (Gk. *porismos*) in his critique of the false teachers in 6:3-5. Thus, after warning the opposition of illegitimate gain (v. 5b),

Guard the Gospel

141

the meaning of legitimate gain is articulated and defended (vv. 6-8). Paul follows up with a graphic portrait of the consequences of illegitimate gain, or greed (vv. 9-10a), and ends by mentioning his opponents' greed and apostasy (v. 10b).

The gain that comes from godliness is not spelled-out by Paul, for he has already defined it as having value "for all things, holding promise for both the present life and the life to come" (4:8). Thus, godliness enhances the present life and leads to eternal life. But now he links "godliness" with "contentment" (Gk. *autarkeia,* 6:6), a word often translated "self sufficiency." A technical term in Greek philosophy, it denotes the wise person's independence of circumstances. However, Paul's strong awareness of God's grace (see 1:12-16) precludes the Stoic idea of total self-sufficiency. Thus, it is best to view Paul's idea here as "contentment" with one's current economic circumstances, as the subsequent argument demonstrates (cf. Philippians 4:11).

Paul undergirds his claim about contentment with two well-known maxims. The first (v. 7) is found in the book of Job: "Naked I came from my mother's womb, and naked shall I return there" (Job 1:21). This maxim is repeated elsewhere in Wisdom literature (see Ecclesiastes 5:15) and appears in Greco-Roman philosophical writings as well (see Seneca *Epistles* 102.25). The saying's specific form here is strange; for the two parts are connected by the Greek word *hoti,* meaning "because" (not "and," as the NIV translates v. 7). The second saying (v. 8) is also found in several other writings, including the sayings of Jesus (Matthew 6:25-34; also Hebrews 13:5), Israel's Wisdom literature (*Sirach* 29:21), and Hellenistic philosophy (Plutarch *Dinner of the Seven Wise Men* 12). This saying is striking in its rigor, limiting one's possessions to food and clothing. Elsewhere Paul attacks the ascetic tendencies of his opponents and celebrates instead the full enjoyment of God's creation gifts (4:4), including wine (5:23). Furthermore, a few verses later Paul advises the rich to be generous with their wealth, but he does not reduce their existence to food and clothing alone. Instead he invites them "to put their hope in God, who richly provides us with everything for our enjoyment" (6:17). Still, these verses clearly emphasize "godliness with contentment," not the absence of possessions. Paul wants church leaders to be characterized by an attitude of contentment in contrast to the greedy disposition that typifies the false teachers. After all, the qualifications for overseer and deacons assume the persons aspiring to these roles would have the resources to manage extended households and to grant hospitality to visitors. Thus, the two maxims quoted by Paul are not designed to encourage the rigors of self-denial as normative for church leaders. Rather, they are intended to encourage a disposition that sets a person free from greed's negative influences.

This text unit's concluding verses dramatize the fate of the person who is motivated by greed (6:9-10). They fall into a "trap," a favorite metaphor in the Pastoral Letters (see 3:7), and they "plunge" like a sinking ship into ruin and destruction which is undoubtedly not economic or even moral ruin, but eschatological destruction (see 1 Thessalonians 5:3). Paul again supports his description of the fate of the greedy by citing another maxim that effectively summarizes the greed's philosophical view: "For the love of money is a root of all kinds of evil" (6:10a). Finally, he returns to the actual situation of the false teachers, the obvious referent of the "some" of verse 10b: "Some people, eager for money, have wandered from the faith and pierced themselves with many griefs."

Virtues of the Faithful Teacher (6:11-16). Paul challenges Timothy to flee greed and pursue godliness. Some commentators see this text unit as an interruption of

Paul's instructions on the proper Christian attitude toward wealth, as articulated in verses 6-10 and 17-19, thus creating a disjointed conclusion to the letter. However, Paul consistently follows rebukes against the false teachers with direct words to Timothy, imploring him to live an exemplary life as a church leader. Thus, 6:11-16 complements Paul's diatribe against the false teachers, supplying a positive portrait of church leadership that stands in stark contrast to his opponents' negative behavior (see also 2 Timothy 3:14; 4:5; Titus 2:1). This positive portrait is expressed by means of a series of exhortations to Timothy: a virtue list replaces the list of vices which characterize the false teachers' lives, the promise of the reward of "eternal life" replaces the threat of ruin and destruction, and the "good confession" replaces greed as the motivation for behavior.

The language of this passage, especially verses 11-12, likely has its roots in a baptismal liturgy of the early church. The exhortation for Timothy to separate himself from sinful ways is fitting for the rite of baptism (see 1 Corinthians 6:9-11). So also is the invitation "to take hold of the eternal life" (6:12). The exhortation, "fight the good fight of faith" (6:12), pictures the rigors and possible persecution the newly baptized Christian faces in the world (see 2 Timothy 3:12). Here, and again in 2 Timothy 4:17, this image points to athletic competition, whereas the different wording of 1:18 conveys the image of hostile military engagement.

Although the language suggests baptism, the context here is actually Timothy's commission for ministry by the church. Paul intends to contrast the behavior and motives of "the man of God" with those of the false teachers (6:3). Since competing images of church leaders are envisioned here, an allusion to Timothy's commissioning service suits Paul's aim. The "man of God" epithet confirms this assumption. It is used in only one other place in the

Pastoral Letters: where the "man of God" (Gk. *anthropos theou*) is portrayed in the tasks of teaching, reproof, correction and training in righteousness (2 Timothy 3:16-17). These are, of course, tasks for the church leader, not the newly baptized (2 Timothy 2:24-25; Titus 1:9). Although the epithet in Greek is not as gender specific as the English translation implies, the NIV translation is appropriate because public teaching is almost exclusively reserved for men.

The "man of God" title has its most obvious background in the Old Testament. It puts Timothy in the noble company of a cluster of Israel's key leaders, including Moses (Deuteronomy 33:1), David (2 Chronicles 8:14), Samuel (1 Samuel 9:6) and various prophets (see 1 Samuel 2:7; 1 Kings 13:1). Linking this title with key leadership roles in ancient Israel implies a comparable link in 1 Timothy between the "man of God" and qualified and faithful leaders. Various phrases in this passage appear to support this implication. For example, the phrase "fight the good fight" appears three times in the Pastoral Letters and always in the context of a discussion of church leadership (1:18; 6:12; 2 Timothy 4:7). The mention of "witnesses" is used elsewhere to refer to those witnessing Timothy's commissioning service (see 2 Timothy 2:2; 1 Timothy 4:14). Of course, a baptism also has witnesses. But baptism is nowhere else referred to in these letters, whereas references to a community service commissioning leaders for ministry are frequent (1:18; 4:14; 5:22; 2 Timothy 1:6; 2:2).

Thus, Paul refers to Timothy's commissioning by the church for service in Christ's name. The wording of this passage has been shaped by the liturgy of such a service so that the "command" Timothy is exhorted to keep (6:14) relates specifically to the charge given to him at his commissioning service, not to the ethical demands of 6:11. While the language here implies the ceremony included elements of an earlier baptismal liturgy, the context focuses on the commissioning service that defined the public charge, the exemplary behavior, and the theological convictions of the one set apart to teach and lead the church.

The list of virtues mentioned in verse 11 does not describe behavior unique to church leaders, nor does it depict specific conduct contrasting with the false teachers. Instead, it names common Christian virtues that contrast in a general way with the opponents' vices (see also 2 Timothy 2:22, a virtue list that also begins with "righteousness"). In this context, "righteousness" refers to right conduct (cf. Matthew 3:15; 5:6; 1 Peter 3:14), not to God's gift of righteousness (Romans 4:5; 10:3-4). In Hellenistic Judaism and Greek philosophy as well as here, right conduct is linked with "godliness." Righteousness encompasses all behavior, including "right" conduct in one's relationship with other humans and God, or the gods. "Faith" (Gk. *pistis*), when paired with love and endurance, echoes the well-known Pauline triad (Romans 5:3-5; 1 Corinthians 13:13). Indeed, faith and love are always together as virtues in the Pastoral Letters (see 1:14; 2:15; 4:12; 2 Timothy 1:13). The quality of "gentleness" is of special importance in these letters (see 3:3; 2 Timothy 2:25; Titus 1:7).

The double acclamation of God's life-giving activity and Christ's good confession in verse 13 is undoubtedly rooted in a liturgical fragment of the early church. The reference to the activity of God, "who gives life to everything" (6:13a), echoes Paul's writing elsewhere (Romans 11:36; 1 Corinthians 8:6) as well as contemporary Greek philosophy (see Acts 17:28). However, Paul refers not only to God's creation activity but also to God's gift of eternal life, which is underscored in these writings (see 4:8; 6:12, 19). This acclaim will be developed shortly in the doxology of 6:15-16. The acclamation of Jesus centers

on his good confession before Pontius Pilate (6:13). Paul
does not mention the confession's content, but perhaps
he is thinking of something similar to John 18:33-37 (cf.
Matthew 27:11). What is likely emphasized is that Jesus
acted courageously, testifying to the truth in circumstances of real and imminent persecution and suffering.
At the same time, subsequent Christian confession centers on Jesus Christ as Lord (see 6:14; 1:2; Romans 10:9;
1 Corinthians 12:3).

Paul shifts from the confession of the earthly Jesus to
his return as Lord at his second coming, although he does
not use the normal term for this event (Gk. *parousia*).
Instead, he speaks of Christ's manifestation (Gk.
epiphaneia), introducing a characteristic emphasis of his
treatment of Christ in the Pastoral Letters. Indeed,
epiphany language is central to the christology of these
letters. Here, the second coming is called an epiphany
(see also 2 Timothy 4:8), underscoring that this event,
which also constitutes God's decisive intervention on
behalf of the faithful, reveals the risen Christ's glory
(Titus 2:13). Jesus' first appearance is also called an
epiphany, for God's salvific intentions for humanity are
made known through it (Titus 3:4-5). Christ will appear
in God's good time (see also 2:6). The nearness of that
time is not emphasized here (see Romans 13:11-12) for his
appearance will mean the fulfillment of the promise of
eternal life (6:12) and the confirmation of Timothy's good
confession (6:12). Meanwhile, Timothy's good confession
announces both Christ's glory and God's saving will. Of
course, God is the one who will bring about this
epiphany of our Lord Jesus Christ; he is the one who
gives life, both temporal and eternal, and from whom all
good things come (6:17).

After the mention of God as the source of Christ's
epiphany, Paul leaps into a doxology of praise to "God,
the blessed and only Ruler, the King of kings and Lord of

lords, who alone is immortal and who lives in unapproachable light, whom no one has seen or can see. To him be honor and might forever. Amen" (6:15-16). It contains several monotheistic emphases like "only Ruler," he " alone is immortal" (see 1:17; Romans 16:27) and biblical epithets like "Lord of lords" (Deuteronomy 10:17; Psalm 136:3). There is evidence that "King of kings" (Daniel 2:37) was a title used for eastern monarchs (Daniel 2:37), but then taken over for God in the Jewish synagogues (see 3rd Maccabees 5:35). Greeks and Romans posited immortality for their heroes and emperors. However, this doxology affirms that God alone is untouched by death. God's invisibility and inaccessibility have Hebrew and Greek roots (see Exodus 33:18-23; Pseudo-Aristotle *On the Cosmos* 399a). Like the first doxology of 1:17, this one focuses on God. God's total sovereignty is affirmed as the basis of Christian obedience and hope, and God's absolute inaccessibility is the precondition of the Christ-event's epiphany function. This doxology contrasts sharply with the philosophical maxims of 6:3-10, returning Paul's argument to its theological foundation.

If this portion of 1 Timothy is indeed a reflection of the theological themes associated with Timothy's commissioning ritual as suggested above, then Paul is really spelling out the Christian realities that motivate the "man of God": a call to faith and ministry (see also 1:18); a public confession that imitates Christ's own confession, pointing to hardship rather than greedy gain; a solemn commission; and a clear grasp that the second appearance of Christ will demand an accounting of how well the "man of God" has fulfilled his commission (2 Timothy 4:1-8). Thus, the true "gain" that comes from godliness will eventually be made manifest (6:6; 4:8). The doxology points to the theological power behind the commission. Its attributes for God contrast sharply with Paul's opponents' petty concerns (6:4-5).

Also, the attack on greed cannot be divorced from an issue that has plagued Christianity from its inception. The church quickly discovered that the necessity of giving financial compensation to her leaders brought with it the possibility of abuse (see Matthew 7:15; *Didache* 1.5-6; 11:6, 12). Even Paul faced such charges of greed in his dealings with the Corinthian church (see 2 Corinthians 8:20-21; 12:14-18). Thus, the issues addressed here reflect a widespread and recurring church concern.

Advice for Wealthy Christians (6:17-19). Following the doxology of verses 15-16, which functions as a fitting conclusion to the letter (see Romans 16:25-27; Jude 24-25), the return to exhortation is something of a surprise, if not a jolt. Some commentators view this text unit as continuing the earlier instructions on the love of money (6:9-10) following a digression in verses 11-16. However, as argued above, verses 11-16 complement verses 3-10. In addition, verses 17-19 do not continue the theme of the dangers of greed addressed in verses 3-10. Rather, they develop a new topic in the proper use of wealth. Some commentators think these verses are a later addition, but there is no textual evidence to support such an assumption. Nor is there any real evidence that these verses have been displaced from another position in the letter, such as after 6:1-2 or before 6:9-10. True, the transition to the proper use of wealth is rough, but the content of these exhortations fits the general tone and subject matter of this letter.

To understand Paul's thrust here it is important to remember that he has already treated a variety of management issues pertaining to God's household (3:15), including the following: instructions about gender appropriate behavior in public worship (2:1-15); qualifications for church leaders like the overseer and deacons (3:1-16); exhortations about various groups within the church and to groups like widows, elders and slaves (5:1-

6:2a); and instructions about the opposition of false teachers (4:1-16; 6:3-16). Since Paul understands the church as God's household (3:15), his instructions concerning its management are really an attempt to Christianize and embellish the common Greco-Roman household code and apply its many features to the church. The subject of money and property is a typical feature of these household management codes, especially the matter of how to acquire and use wealth for the household's support (Balch 1981: 40). Thus, it is not surprising that Paul should now treat the question of the proper use of wealth by members of God's household, the church.

There is nothing unusual about the form of this text unit (6:17-19). It simply consists of various commands of both a negative (v. 17a) and positive (vv. 17b-18) nature, together with their aim or result (v. 19). Its content also parallels Greco-Roman philosophy, Hebrew Wisdom literature, and the teachings of Jesus.

The word "rich" (Gk. *plousios*) holds all these exhortations together by means of an elaborate word play: "Command those who are rich... God, who richly provides... Command them to be rich in good deeds" (6:17-19). Thus, wealthy believers are warned not to put their confidence in riches but to trust in God who richly provides. They are to be rich in good deeds. The uncertainty of wealth is a pervasive motif in Israel's Wisdom literature and in the sayings of Jesus (Proverbs 11:28; Ecclesiastes 5:13-17; Luke 12:16-21), as is the perspective that God is a generous provider (Psalm 104:27-28; 145:15-16; Matthew 6:25-33). Paul focuses on the concept of God's generosity ("God, who richly provides us with everything for our enjoyment"), returning to the letter's basic anti-ascetic posture (see 4:4).

The theme of God's generosity supports Paul's exhortations concerning how to properly approach and use wealth. The rich are not asked to divest themselves of their wealth, but rather to divest themselves of their dependence upon it. They are to imitate God's rich generosity by being exceedingly generous themselves. Paul's admonition to the wealthy claims that the greatest benefit of wealth is the opportunity it affords "to be rich in good deeds." The greatest danger it holds is the power to corrupt a person's heart, especially to foster "arrogance" (6:17). Of course, when wealthy people follow God's example of generosity, there is potential for eschatological reward: "they will lay up treasure for themselves as a firm foundation for the coming age, so they may take hold of the life that is truly life" (6:19). Paul has likely been influenced here not only by Greco-Roman philosophical writings (Aristotle *Nicomachean Ethics* 4; Cicero *On Duties* 2.15), but also by Jewish piety with its emphasis on generosity through giving alms to the poor (*Tobit* 4:5-11).

Numerous comments in this letter imply Paul is addressing a congregation that includes at least some wealthy members (2:9; 3:2-7; 5:8, 16; 6:2). As he instructs them specifically, his restraint and moderation are remarkable. Paul views "greed" as "the root of all evil," yet he does not consider wealth *per se* as evil (cf. Matthew 6:19-21, 24; Luke 12:33-34; James 1:9-11). Nor does he insist that a person choose between God and "Mammon." By contrast, he views wealth as a vehicle for securing one's salvation. Thus, while the wealthy among us do indeed face certain ethical challenges, they are also given special opportunities for good deeds. Also, like the role of "benefactor" in Greco-Roman society, wealthy believers are encouraged to be benefactors with their reward for such generosity being eschatological rather than social. In a world where Greco-Roman benefactors use their wealth to cultivate significant social connections that essentially increase their power and wealth, the reward rich Christians will receive for their generosity in this life is "life that is really life" (6:19). Paul focuses on the ethical possibilities facing wealthy Christians. Again his conviction that God wants everyone to be saved (2:4, 15) seems to have influenced his admonition to them.

Final Charge to Timothy (6:20-21). Paul ends his letter where it began: with a warning about the activities of the false teachers (6:20b-21), together with an exhortation to "guard what has been entrusted to your care" (6:20a). The exhortation and warning essentially summarize the letter's thrust: to preserve the Pauline gospel in the face of the opposition's competing message. The typical personal greetings found at the conclusion of most of Paul's letters are omitted here (see 1 Corinthians 16:19-20; cf. Galatians 6:17-18). The letter ends with a brief benediction: "Grace be to you" (second person plural form of the Greek pronoun "you").

Aside from the opening salutation (1:2), this is only the second time Timothy is addressed by name in the letter. The first time occurs at the end of chapter one (1:18), which is part of the letter's opening or preface. Thus, the body of the letter is bracketed by these two direct references to Timothy.

The exhortation to "guard what has been entrusted to your care" is also found in a slightly modified form in 2 Timothy 1:14, illuminating its meaning here. There are several commands to "guard" or "keep" or "hold to" or "continue in" in the Pastoral Letters. However, this is the first time the object of the guarding or keeping is called "what has been entrusted to your care," the NIV translation of the Greek word, *paratheke* (literally, "something that is placed beside another, deposit, trust"). This term reflects the legal concept frequently found in the Greek, Roman and Jewish writings of the first century Mediterranean world: that of placing goods in the trust of another person's safe keeping (see Rienecker/Rogers 1980: 635). Although it is often applied to material goods, the concept is also widely used of less tangible treasures such as words, teachings and even spiritual goods (see Philo *Who Is the Heir* 103-8; Plutarch *Letter of Condolence to Apollonius* 28). In this instance, of course, Paul has left something for Timothy to guard. So what has Paul entrusted to Timothy?

We know that God entrusted Paul with the gospel (1:11), that is, the gospel message summed up in the opening remarks of this letter as "Christ Jesus came into the world to save sinners" (1:15). But what Paul now entrusts to Timothy are the Pauline traditions which not only encompass the gospel message as articulated by Paul, but also the Pauline teachings, including the contents of this letter. To support this interpretation of Paul's words here, it is only necessary to consider 2 Timothy 1:13-14 where two exhortations appear together. The first implores Timothy to "keep (what you have heard from me) as the pattern of sound teaching" (1:13). The second exhorts him, as in 1 Timothy 6:20, to "guard the good deposit that was entrusted to you" (1:14), the NIV translation of the same Greek term *paratheke,* modified only with the addition of "good."

Given this concept's legal roots, the instruction "to guard" implies preserving it unharmed and unchanged. In particular, the act of guarding has subsequent generations in mind. That is why Timothy is exhorted to identify faithful persons and to entrust to them "the things" he has heard from Paul (see 2 Timothy 2:2). In short, Timothy is to pass on the Pauline traditions to instruct and benefit other believers (see 1 Timothy 4:16). This task is especially urgent, given the presence of the false teachers whose message stands in sharp contrast to Paul's.

The phrase "what has been entrusted to you" (Gk. *paratheke*) is a very important term in the Pastoral Letters. Elsewhere Paul speaks of holding to the "traditions" (Gk. *paradosis*) and "passing them on" to others. He emphasizes the need for a reliable leader to transmit a body of teaching recognized and embraced as authoritative by the community (see 1 Corinthians 11:2; 15:3; Galatians 1:14). Here the concept of "guarding," while it includes the notion of reliability, underscores that someone (Paul) is handing over the tradition to a trustee (Timothy). In this way, our text accents the Pauline origins of the teaching preserved in these letters. Moreover, the recipient's faithfulness or reliability is an assumed dimension of this legal term. Hence, the use of the term *paratheke* in the letter's conclusion has the same effect as Paul's words about Timothy in the salutation when he refers to him as "my true (or "genuine") son in the faith," indicating that the apostolic traditions have been transmitted through faithful and reliable hands. In addition, it contains an implicit charge to the church to continue to hold to these traditions without distortion or modification until Christ's second coming. However, even as Paul interprets the gospel message to speak forthrightly to the issues facing the first century Ephesian church, so also it must be interpreted for subsequent generations.

The warning about the false teachers recalls elements mentioned earlier in the letter. Timothy is to literally "turn away from" Paul's opponents; he is not to engage them in discussion or debate (2 Timothy 2:16; 3:5; Titus 3:9). Paul dismisses their teaching as mere "godless chatter" (see 1:9; 4:7; 2 Timothy 2:16) that ultimately leads them away from the faith, not toward it. Here, as so often in the Pastoral Letters, the term "the faith" refers to the Christian message's basic content as articulated by Paul (3:9; 4:1; 5:8).

Apparently, the opponents believe they are teaching saving "knowledge" (6:20), a claim Paul repeatedly refutes (2 Timothy 3:7; Titus 1:16). He characterizes their so-called knowledge as "myths" and "contradictions." The false teachers mentioned here possibly represent a nascent form of a later Gnostic movement within Christianity, but they are not to be equated with this later heretical movement led by the second century heretic Marcion.

The final benediction, though typically Pauline, is abnormally brief. Although the letter is addressed to a single person (Timothy), the benediction is addressed to a group. The Greek pronoun "you" is plural. Paul likely assumes that God's people in Ephesus will hear his letter to Timothy.

Application, Teaching/Preaching Points

A repeated theme runs through all of Paul's instructions in this chapter, forming a basic challenge to much current thinking about human identity and value. Pulling the issues together here may help sharpen the question this text poses to us as 21st century Christians and provide the grist for building a sermon.

What is the Basis of Human Worth? Whether Paul addresses the rich or the slaves, the money-loving false teachers or the virtuously content person, the basic issue is that human worth does not depend upon possessions or social status. The person who is wealthy has no richer identity than the one who is poor; the master has no advantage over the slave. As Paul teaches elsewhere, Jews have no advantage over Gentiles, nor males over females (Galatians 3:28). God's kingdom does not consist of food and drink. You can marry or not marry. If you are a slave you are free; if you are free you are a slave. Hunger or plenty, these social categories make no difference in God's eyes. In this way, Paul eliminates the link between the human condition and human worth. Two implicates flow from this Pauline conviction. First, Paul's position does not demand affirmation of the status quo. In fact, his position legitimates the change of social structures precisely because the social structure is not ultimate. If it does not matter whether people are slaves or free, then we can dispense with slavery altogether. If both marriage and celibacy are gifts, we can choose either freely. If the worth of a woman is not determined by her role as head of the household, we are perfectly free to arrange things in our households so that she is at the head. Our ability as God's people to effect change comes precisely from understanding that no social order is equivalent to the kingdom of God or mandated by the gospel.

Second, much contemporary thought connects human dignity with human condition. If women are really degraded because they do not teach, then they must teach; they are not free to abstain. If a person's essential worth is deprived by slavery, then only when they are free does that person have worth. If economic inequality is itself essentially degrading, then only within a perfect community of equally distributed possessions is everyone just. When we connect our human condition with our fundamental identity, we make our worth dependent on the realization of those conditions. If poverty makes someone less than a person, then it becomes impossible to choose poverty as a voluntary witness. Both the woman who is completed only in childbirth and the woman who is real only because she carries a briefcase are in prison. Only when we insist with Paul that none of these differences matter will we be free to change them as well as to affirm them.

Who Are the Real Materialists? In larger measure, whether a person is a materialist or not depends on their attitude toward money and material goods. Here is one helpful distinction to keep in mind when discerning whether you are in the materialist's camp or not. If it is the mere possession of financial wealth that makes a person a materialist, then only the rich deserve this label. If materialism is a preoccupation with money and possessions, then the poor can also be materialists. Which camp does that place you in? Passages like 1 Timothy 6 encourage us to see all our material possessions in light of three checks and balances on our attitudes. First, do I experience contentment and express heart-felt appreciation to God for all my possessions (vv. 7-8)? Second, do I have a merciful, generous spirit in response to genuine need (v. 18)? Third, what "return on my assets" do I seek for God in my stewardship role (vv. 17,19)?

Another "Inconvenient Truth?" If there is uncertainty about our interpretation of 1 Timothy 2:11-15, there is no uncertainty about Paul's full-scale treatment of the dangers of wealth, especially for those who desire and misuse it (6:3-19). Paul is quite clear that these are real dangers against which Christians should be very vigilant. He is very serious about using income and possessions rightly and about the dangers of greed and envy. In our world, where many Christians earn relatively high incomes, where there are so many opportunities for lavish expenditure, and where a good many people are living in various degrees of poverty, the message of 1 Timothy 6 is another "inconvenient truth."

Are You Content with the Bare Necessities? "But godliness with contentment is great gain" (1 Timothy 6:6). Elsewhere Paul writes, "I have learned to be content whatever the circumstances" (Philippians 4:11). "Content" is a Stoic word for self-sufficiency, another New Testament teaching in passages like Luke 3:14 and Hebrews 13:5. When I hear the word "content," I am reminded of the Japanese samurai who picked his teeth even when he had not eaten for three days. If he was hungry he would not show it! In a similar manner, Paul suggests that we are to be content with whatever God chooses to provide. Perhaps it is not what we possess that matters most, but an inward attitude of heart that makes us content. This is not a very popular view today, especially among Christians with a little ambition flowing in the veins. It is especially unpopular among those with a "Health and Wealth Gospel." Yet Paul reminds us of Job 1:21 when he says, "For we brought nothing into the world and we can take nothing out of it" (1 Timothy 6:7). Jesus taught the simple lifestyle is made up of the basics like food and clothing (Matthew 6:25 and Luke 12:22; cf. Deuteronomy 10:18). Paul does not pull all of this out of his own head, but rather builds his teaching upon Scripture (see especially Ecclesiastes 5:10-20).

The Root of all Evil? An old popular song parodied 1 Timothy 6:10: "Money is the root of all evil, take it away, take it away!" But Paul does not blame money itself, but the love of money (literally, "love of silver," which is relevant in Ephesus, a city of silversmiths). Those who lust after profit and dedicate their energies to amassing capital throw themselves open to evil. The emphatic first word of this secular proverb is "root." It may mean "a root" or "the root" of all kinds of evil (and not the only root of all evil). The false teachers' love of money is mixed with Ephesian folk religion. All folk religions pursue health, wealth, good luck and general prosperity; they try to manipulate spiritual "powers" for personal gain. Bringing together Christian faith and moneymaking remains a danger today, especially in affluent nations.

Personal Reflection Questions

- Paul has blunt words for people who want to get rich. DISCUSS: What dangers face those who are determined to become rich? What positive attitude toward possessions is commanded for Christians? How do we prevent people from profiting financially from religion in our various communities?

- The text chides those who think that godliness is a means to financial gain. DISCUSS: What does this passage say to those who teach the so-called "prosperity gospel," the notion that God rewards his own children with riches in this life? What motivates us to serve Christ?

- Paul encourages the rich to be rich in good deeds. DISCUSS: How can we avoid arrogance and the tendency to despise those less fortunate whether by financial, social or other standards? Compare and contrast the two text units on exhortations to the rich (6:6-10 and 6:17-19). How do they help us to decide the proper use of our financial resources? To what extent should wealthy believers carry the financial burdens of the local church? What effect does a dependence on the wealthy have upon other members of a local church?

CHAPTER SEVEN

Confidence in the Gospel

The Text: 2 Timothy 1:1-17

Paul, an apostle of Christ Jesus by the will of God, according to the promise of life that is in Christ Jesus, [2] *To Timothy, my dear son: Grace, mercy and peace from God the Father and Christ Jesus our Lord.* [3] *I thank God, whom I serve, as my forefathers did, with a clear conscience, as night and day I constantly remember you in my prayers.* [4] *Recalling your tears, I long to see you, so that I may be filled with joy.* [5] *I have been reminded of your sincere faith, which first lived in your grandmother Lois and in your mother Eunice and, I am persuaded, now lives in you also.* [6] *For this reason I remind you to fan into flame the gift of God, which is in you through the laying on of my hands.* [7] *For God did not give us a spirit of timidity, but a spirit of power, of love and of self-discipline.* [8] *So do not be ashamed to testify about our Lord, or ashamed of me his prisoner. But join with me in suffering for the gospel, by the power of God,* [9] *who has saved us and called us to a holy life—not because of anything we have done but because of his own purpose and grace. This grace was given us in Christ Jesus before the beginning of time,* [10] *but it has now been revealed through the appearing of our Savior, Christ Jesus, who has destroyed death and has brought life and immortality to light through the gospel.* [11] *And of this gospel I was appointed a herald and an apostle and a teacher.* [12] *That is why I am suffering as I am. Yet I am not ashamed, because I know whom I have believed, and am convinced that he is able to guard what I have entrusted to him for that day.* [13] *What you heard from me, keep as the pattern of sound teaching, with faith and love in Christ Jesus.* [14] *Guard the good deposit that was entrusted to you— guard it with the help of the Holy Spirit who lives in us.* [15] *You know that everyone in the province of Asia has deserted me, including Phygelus and Hermogenes.* [16] *May the Lord show mercy to the household of Onesiphorus, because he often refreshed me and was not ashamed of my chains.* [17] *On the con-*

*trary, when he was in Rome, he searched hard for me until he
found me.*[18] *May the Lord grant that he will find mercy from the
Lord on that day! You know very well in how many ways he
helped me in Ephesus.*

The Flow and Form of the Text

Some scholars consider 2 Timothy to be an example of
testamentary literature, a kind of literature in which a
dying hero shares wisdom with his successors (see, for
example, Genesis 49:1-33). Others rightly argue that
2 Timothy has the classic marks of a *paraenetic* letter
(Johnson, 1987: 13). In this literary classification, the chief
protagonist assumes the role of a father who reminds his
son of traditional moral teaching in an effort to rekindle
his commitment to it. Such *paraenesis* addresses the individual rather than the community and is marked by three
major elements: memory, model and maxims. What is
typically remembered are the key figure's moral and
behavioral characteristics that function as a model for the
individual addressed in the letter. Moral maxims or
instructions dominate this kind of literature, taking the
form of "do this and avoid that." Thus, 2 Timothy is best
read as a *personal paraenaetic letter* as it exhibits these three
elements of memory, model and maxims.

Paul begins his second letter to Timothy with a salutation (1:1-2), followed by thanksgiving (1:3-5) in which
he speaks of his "clear conscience" and Timothy's "sincere faith." Then he shifts to a lengthy exhortation (1:6-
2:13), urging Timothy to suffer with him (Gk. *sygkakap-
athein*) for the gospel (1:8) like "a good soldier of Christ
Jesus" (2:3). To persuade Timothy to adopt his pattern of
living, Paul presents himself as a model of the conduct he
urges upon Timothy. Already suffering, Paul is not
ashamed because he knows the one in whom he puts his
trust: the God "who saved us and called us with a holy
calling, not according to our works but according to his

own purpose and grace" (1:9). For this reason, Timothy is not to be ashamed of the testimony about the Lord or of Paul, the Lord's prisoner.

In addition to his own example, Paul contrasts the behavior of the deserters Phygelus and Hermogenes with Onesiphorus, the one who is not ashamed of him and diligently searches for Paul in Rome (1:15-18). Paul and Onesiphorus are models for Timothy to imitate. As a soldier of Christ Jesus, Timothy can also learn from the conduct of a soldier who seeks to please his commanding officers, of an athlete who competes according to the rules, and of a farmer who cultivates a crop (2:3-7). Finally, Paul returns to the example of his suffering (1:8-13). He endures everything for the sake of the elect because he is confident that "If we have died with him, we will also live with him; if we endure, we will also reign with him" (2:11-12). The one for whom Paul suffers, Christ Jesus, will be faithful because he cannot deny himself. In this way, Paul's conduct in difficult circumstances provides Timothy with a model for moral and ethical behavior in similar circumstances.

The Text Explained

Salutation (1:1-2). Three features of this letter's salutation are common to ancient Greco-Roman letters: the sender's name, the recipient's name, and the formulaic greeting. Paul Christianizes each of these three features.

This salutation resembles those of 1 Timothy and Titus, but differs from them in several respects. Here Paul is not an apostle "by God's command" (see 1 Timothy 1:1) but "by the will of God." While there is no difference in meaning, this latter phrase is more characteristic of Paul, repeating verbatim the opening words of the salutations of 2 Corinthians, Ephesians and Colossians.

Another difference here is that Paul's apostleship is linked with "the promise of life," stating in more concise language the lengthier yet similar message of Titus 1:2 (cf. 1 Timothy 4:8). The Greek preposition (*kata*, translated by the NIV as "according to") may indicate the purpose or standard of Paul's apostleship. Perhaps both ideas are imbedded in this prepositional phrase. If so, "the promise of life" is both the standard by which God chose him and the intention of Paul's appointment: "to further, or make known, the promise of life." What is important is the clear link between Paul's apostolic message and life (i.e., eternal life). This life is depicted as being "in Christ Jesus," a prepositional phrase that appears frequently in this letter (1:9, 13; 2:1, 10; 3:12, 15). While the phrase may indicate the Pauline idea of mystical union with Christ (see Galatians 2:17-20; Philippians 3:17), it likely refers to Christ Jesus as the source of life (see 1:10), even as 2:1 indicates he is the source of grace.

A third difference is that Timothy is called Paul's "dear son" (Gk. *agapeton teknon,* literally "beloved child"), instead of his "true" son (1 Timothy 1:2; Titus 1:4). This greeting underscores Paul's warm relationship with Timothy, rather than Timothy's relationship to Paul. It also resembles the language of 1 Corinthians 4:17 ("I am sending to you Timothy, my son whom I love...") and points to the intimate bond between the apostle and his delegate, a bond that is reiterated throughout the letter (see 1:4; 2:1; 3:10-11; 4:9, 21).

The salutation conveys some significant ideas. First, Paul's apostleship and God's will are identified with the promise of eternal life. Here is a theme that will be revisited with variation throughout the letter, including Paul's role in preaching the message of life (1:10-11; 2:10-11) and his utter confidence in this promise of life (4:7-8). Second, by calling Timothy "my dear son" rather than "true son," Paul signals the letter's unique ethical focus. Timothy's behavior, not the conduct of various groups within the church, receives the center of attention. Paul's exhortations are based on his personal relationship with Timothy. Thus, Paul writes as an apostle to his delegate and like a father to a beloved child.

Thanksgiving to God (1:3-5). Unlike 1 Timothy and Titus, but like most of his other letters, Paul opens by expressing thanksgiving to God for Timothy's faith (vv. 3-5; Romans 1:18-15; 1 Corinthians 1:4-9). To convey his gratitude to God, Paul uses a Greek idiom (Gk. *charin echein*; literally, "to have gratitude"), instead of the more common New Testament practice of using the Greek verb *eucharisto* (see also I Timothy 1:12; Hebrews 12:28; Luke 17:9). While it is Timothy's faith that evokes Paul's gratitude (see 1:5), he first emphasizes the strong emotional bond between himself and Timothy. Employing the motif of memory, he says, "I constantly remember you in my prayers. Recalling your tears, I long to see you, so that I may be filled with joy" (1:3b-4). Except for the repetition of the word "memory," similar sentiments are found in other Pauline writings where thanksgiving invokes the memory of the recipients (Romans 1:9; Ephesians 1:16; Philippians 1:3; 1 Thessalonians 1:2). Timothy's tears likely reflect the consequent sadness of being separated from Paul (see Acts 20:37-38). They also hint that all is not well with Timothy, suggesting his fear and sorrow. The joy that accompanies Paul's anticipation of being reunited with his delegate is a stark contrast to Timothy's tears (see also 4:9, 21).

Paul claims that he not only worships (Gk. *latreuo*; literally "serves" or "worships") God with "a clear conscience" (see 1 Timothy 1:5, 19; 3:9), but also that his present Christian worship of God is continuous with his earlier worship as a Jew (1:3). Paul often highlights the discontinuity between his past in Judaism and his present Christian faith, especially in passages like Galatians 2:15-21 and Philippians 3:4-9. But here he underscores the continuity between the two forms of worship (see Luke's similar perspective in Acts 24:14-15; 26:6, 22); he does not acknowledge any differences between his worship of God in Judaism and his worship as a Christian. If anything, Paul emphasizes the antiquity of his faith.

Since Greco-Roman society tends to respect traditional forms of worship but is suspicious of new religious movements (Balch 1981), Paul's emphasis on the link between his Jewish heritage and Christian faith enables him to portray Christianity as a credible religion rooted in antiquity. The mention of the faith of Timothy's mother and grandmother has the same effect. Paul mentions Timothy's mother, Eunice, and grandmother, Lois, as followers of the Christian faith, intentionally locating Timothy's faith within the stream of earlier generations. Although the book of Acts does not name Timothy's mother, it does state that he is "the son of a Jewish woman who was a believer" (16:1). Thus, Paul highlights that Timothy's faith is rooted in antiquity. Meanwhile, Paul's opponents are characterized as members of a new religious movement whose activities undermine the established faith (see 3:1; 4:3).

Three Exhortations to Timothy (1:6-14). With Timothy's sincere faith in mind (1:6 "for this reason"), Paul exhorts Timothy with three interrelated reminders (1:6-7, 8-12 and 13-14). First (1:6-7), Paul reminds Timothy "to fan into flame the gift of God, which is in you through the laying on of my hands" (1:6). Paul is not necessarily censuring Timothy, implying that he had let God's gift expire. A fire is never a constant blaze of flames. Rather, it is kept alive by means of glowing coals or embers that are rekindled into flame by a bellows whenever the situation demands it. Likewise, Timothy's circumstances in Ephesus now demand that he "fan into flame the gift of God" (Gk. *anazopurein*; literally, "keep on fanning into flame"). Still, Timothy's tears (1:4) and timidity (1:7) suggest that his strength is flagging in the face of opposition.

So Paul fans the dying embers of Timothy's commitment with fresh memory so that his loyalty might once again blaze into flame.

According to an earlier text, God's gift is imparted to Timothy when the elders lay their hands on him (1 Timothy 4:14). However, Paul now underscores his personal role in the rite, a role that is consistent with this letter's emphasis on the intimate relationship between Paul and his delegate. Central to this rite was the imparting of God's ministry gift(s) to Timothy. It is not the Holy Spirit that is given during this rite of laying on hands, for the Spirit is bestowed on every believer at baptism (see Titus 3:5). Rather, God's gift (Gk. *charisma*) imparted by means of laying on hands is an aptitude for the special task of church leadership that includes "a spirit of power, of love, and of self-discipline" (1:7). While love is a characteristic Christian virtue in the Pastoral Letters (1:13; 1 Timothy 1:5), and self-discipline is undoubtedly linked with the self-control and moderation treasured by Greco-Roman society, of paramount importance in this instance is the "spirit of power" (Gk. *dynamis*) given to the church leader. It is the power of God at work in a leader, empowering him to discipline opponents (2:24-25), to preserve and proclaim the good news (4:2), and to endure the suffering that comes with the turf of being a Christ-follower (3:12) and a church leader (1:8).

In his second exhortation (1:8-12), Paul implores Timothy to eschew shame and recognize that God's power is present in the midst of personal suffering: "Do not be ashamed to testify about our Lord, or ashamed of me his prisoner. But join with me in suffering for the gospel, by the power of God" (1:8). If Timothy is indeed faltering under the opposition in Ephesus, Paul writes to bolster his confidence so that he can act appropriately as a church leader. Paul presents himself as an example for Timothy to follow, even as elsewhere he presents himself

as a model for his churches to follow (see 1 Corinthians
4:16; 11:1; Philippians 3:17; 2 Thessalonians 3:9). Here
Timothy is invited to follow Paul's example of "suffering
for the gospel" 1:8. Three interrelated themes are especially prominent from 1:8 to 2:13: "to be ashamed," "to
suffer," and "the gospel."

Paul does not state that Timothy is ashamed of the
gospel (Rienecker/Rogers 1980: 638); rather he writes to
encourage Timothy to proclaim the gospel boldly in spite
of the potentially shameful consequences of doing so.
Timothy preaches among an honor-sensitive people who
avoid shame at all costs. The gospel message of the crucified Christ and the low status of that gospel's herald,
Paul the prisoner, are the potential sources of shame for
Timothy. True, Paul does not develop this twofold connection here as he does elsewhere in 1 Corinthians 1:18-
2:5, where he argues that the foolishness of the crucifix-
ion message is reflected in his own unlikely role as its
herald. Indeed, Paul does not even mention the cross, the
source of the social stigma of Jesus' death and the theological meaning of Paul's suffering. Moreover, the sketch
of the gospel in verses 9-11 contains no "shameful" elements. Instead, encouraging Timothy towards bold
proclamation, Paul employs new categories that highlight the honor of preaching the good news: the herald's
role is a "holy life" (v. 9), the gospel brings "life and
immortality" (v. 10), and "the power of God" empowers
the herald to endure imprisonment together with its consequent suffering. Hence, he is encouraged to suffer for
the gospel.

Timothy is not invited to suffer with Christ, but with
Paul: "Join with me in suffering for the gospel, by the
power of God" (1:8b). God's power, rather than Timothy's
personal resources, will enable him to endure suffering,
especially God's power to rescue his herald from suffering
(3:11) or to provide him with help to endure it (see

2 Timothy 3:11; 4:7; 2 Corinthians 1:3-11; 4:7-12; 12:8-10; Philippians 1:30). What is left undeveloped is the usual Pauline link between Christian suffering and Christ's own suffering (see Romans 8:17; Philippians 3:7-11; Colossians 1:24; 1 Thessalonians 3:2-4).

The call to depend upon God's power is supported by summarizing God's demonstration of his power in the Christ-event (1:9-10). For the most part, this summary reflects Pauline thinking with a few nuances distinctive to the Pastoral Letters, including the frequently used epiphany language. This summary text is likely a fragment of early church liturgy (see 2:11-13; Titus 2:11-14; 3:4-7).

This liturgical fragment begins by focusing on salvation as a past event initiated by God's grace in Christ Jesus: "(God) who saved us and called us to a holy life— not because of anything we have done but because of his own purpose and grace. This grace was given to us in Christ Jesus before the beginning of time...." (1:9a). It is remarkably similar in content to Ephesians 2:8-9: "For it is by grace you have been saved, through faith—and this not from yourselves, it is the gift of God—not by works, so no one can boast" (see also Ephesians 1:11 with its stress on God's plan and purposes). The call to "a holy life" (Gk. *kalesantos klesei hagia*; literally, "called to a holy calling or vocation") is peculiar to these letters and contrasts with Paul's usual language, "called to be saints" (see 1 Corinthians 1:2). The immediate reference in this context is the call to church leadership. The wider reference is the vocation of all believers, namely, the call to live holy lives before God (Ephesians 4:1). "Grace" here refers to God's "before the beginning of time" desire to save us, not to his forgiveness of individual sins (Romans 3:24). God's saving will is revealed and accomplished by Jesus Christ who is appropriately called "Savior" (see Titus 1:4; 2:13; 3:6).

The term "Savior" is frequently applied to Jesus in the four Gospels. Only rarely is it applied to God apart from the Pastoral Letters (see 1 Timothy 1:1-2). A few people were termed "Savior" in the Old Testament time of the judges (Judges 3:9, 15; Nehemiah 9:27), but it was never a Messianic title in Judaism. Paul himself employs the title once for Jesus in a politically shaped passage (Philippians 3:20). It is, however, a frequent title for Hellenistic deities and rulers. Thus, Isis is depicted "as the greatest goddess, the mighty savior" and Ptolemy I is styled as "the savior and god." The appearance of the word "savior" in the later New Testament writings may be the result of this usage, although it is Christianized and given fresh content (Acts 5:31; 13:23; Ephesians 5:23; 2 Peter 1:1, 11; 2:20; 3:2, 18). Here, in 2 Timothy, "Savior" is linked with Christ's role in revealing God's salvific intentions for humanity: "This grace...has been revealed through the appearing of our Savior, Christ Jesus, who has destroyed death and has brought life and immortality to light through the gospel" (1:10).

It is important to note that Paul does not say Jesus brings about God's salvation by means of his atoning death. Instead, he speaks here of Jesus' appearance (Gk. *epiphaneia*; literally, "appearing"), a term frequently used to refer to his Parousia or Second Coming (1 Timothy 6:14; 2 Timothy 4:1; Titus 2:13). Before Christ's appearance, God's preexistent saving will was hidden. But now, with Christ's appearing, his salvific will is made known to humanity. Elsewhere in the Pastoral Letters, Paul speaks of the appearance of God's grace and loving-kindness without naming Christ as the agent of what is made known to us (see Titus 2:11; 3:4). There is also a clear emphasis on his intervening in human affairs so as to "destroy death," presumably by means of his own death and subsequent resurrection (see Romans 8:31-39; 1 Corinthians 15:35-57). The next phrase again underscores the revelatory nature of Christ's advent: "(he) brought life and immortality to light" (1:10). Although immortality is a quality peculiar to God (1 Timothy 1:17; 6:16), Jesus' resurrection announces that "eternal life," a form of immortality, is now the believer's hope (see Titus 1:2-3). True, Paul does not link the revelation of "life and immortality" to the resurrection, but to the gospel message about the death and resurrection (1:10). Today's heralds proclaim the resurrection as the hope and promise of eternal life. The act of proclamation generates the same hope as the original event itself.

Having established the importance of gospel proclamation, Paul speaks of his own role in proclaiming the gospel: "And of this gospel I was appointed a herald and an apostle and a teacher" (1:11). A parallel statement is found in 1 Timothy 2:7: "And for this purpose I was appointed a herald and an apostle—I am telling the truth, I am not lying—and a teacher of the true faith to the Gentiles." The only difference is that 2 Timothy 1:11 does not include a reference to Paul's Gentile mission. Although an overwhelming mass of manuscripts do include the words, "a teacher of the Gentiles," in 1:11, they are later manuscripts and represent a gloss introduced by copyists who were influenced by the parallel passage in 1 Timothy 2:7 (see Metzger 1971: 647). Also, 1 Timothy 2 focuses on God's universal saving will, whereas 2 Timothy 1:11 concentrates on Paul's willingness to suffer for the gospel for which he was given the triple appointment of herald, apostle and teacher. Hence, Paul essentially revisits the subject of shame, presenting himself as a model of confidence in God's ability "to guard what I have entrusted to him for that day" (1:12b).

This is an extraordinarily dense statement, the meaning of which is widely debated. The phrase "what I have entrusted to him" (Gk. *ten paratheken mou*) is understood by some translations as that which Paul has entrusted to

God (Paul's life in the face of opposition to the gospel message; see NRSV, NJB, NIV). Others view it as a reference to what God has entrusted to Paul (the gospel message; see NEB, REB, RSV, NAB). The first interpretation is supported by the argument of the preceding verses and by Paul's words in 2 Timothy 4:7-8. The second interpretation gains support from what follows, where Timothy is urged to guard the good treasure (Gk. *ten kalen paratheken*) entrusted to him and then to pass it on with care to others (1:14; 2:2). Since the careful preservation and transmission of the gospel message and the apostolic teachings are in focus here, verse 12b probably expresses Paul's confidence in God's ability to watch over that important process. To be sure, Paul's delegates have a responsibility to protect the gospel message, but they will do so "with the help of the Holy Spirit..." (1:14).

The third exhortation commands Timothy to adhere to the sound or healthy teaching (see 1 Timothy 1:10) he has received from Paul: "What you have heard from me, keep as the pattern of sound teaching, with faith and love in Christ Jesus. Guard the good deposit that was entrusted to you..." (1:13-14). Having fanned into flame the gift of God (1:6) and having conquered the potential shame associated with the gospel message (1:8), Timothy must cling to the sound or healthy teaching Paul has entrusted to him. Verse 14, including its promise of God's help and oversight ("guard it with the help of the Holy Spirit who lives in us") repeats the message of verse 12.

Confidence is a central theme in this portion of the letter. Initially, Paul expresses confidence in Timothy's faith (1:5). Then he invites Timothy to demonstrate his confidence in the gospel by eschewing shame. Finally, Paul expresses his own confidence in God (1:12). Thus, Timothy is called to join Paul in suffering for the gospel, confident of his eschatological reward (1:8-10); and to preserve the gospel, confident of God's help (1:11-14).

The liturgical fragment supports this theme of confidence by summarizing the gospel as a demonstration of God's power. The ultimate basis for confidence is God's grace and the abolition of death as revealed in Christ. Paul is confident in God's power and he invites Timothy to follow his example, especially in the arena of church leadership in Ephesus. Although Paul's exhortations have much relevance for every believer, they are particularly appropriate for church leaders. The gift of God, the holy calling, and the entrusted treasure pertain most directly to the church leader.

Another theme of considerable importance here is the meaning of suffering. Paul contends that suffering is inevitable for Christians and essential for church leaders. By means of suffering, a church leader identifies with Paul and thus reveals his confidence in the Christian promise of eternal life. Failure to suffer implies a lack of confidence in God's power to give endurance. Paul cannot imagine a situation free of the opportunity to suffer. Suffering may not involve imprisonment or persecution, but it does include a daily battle on behalf of the gospel, as 2:3-7 teaches. The ministry model promoted here is one of confidence in God's oversight and promise of eternal life (see 1 Corinthians 9:12-23; 2 Corinthians 11:21-12:10).

Examples of Shame and Confidence (1:15-18). Paul is not content to point to himself as an example so he presents other models for Timothy's imitation. First, he comments about the conduct of certain persons who are negative examples: "You know that everyone in the province of Asia has deserted me, including Phygelius and Hermogenes" (1:15). Comments of this nature are frequent in this letter (1:5; 2:17; 4:9-21), providing both negative and positive examples of behavior for Timothy. The persons named in this comment, Phygelius and Hermogenes, were ashamed of Paul; they desert him because they were embarrassed by his imprisonment in

Rome (1:17). Thus, this verse is a negative illustration of Paul's exhortation to Timothy in 1:8: "Do not be ashamed." By deserting Paul, these two men also demonstrated their lack of confidence in the gospel (see 1:8-9).

Desertion is a frequent motif in this letter (1:15; 4:10, 16). Here "everyone" in the province of Asia, including the city of Ephesus, abandons Paul. Presumably, the Asian believers fail to support Paul during his imprisonment in Rome. Or, if Paul is taken prisoner in Asia, they do not support him at the time of his arrest (see Philippians 2:25-30; 4:15-18 for a positive example). Although there is no support for either scenario in the book of Acts, what is important is the negative example of the Asians, particularly Phygelius and Hermogenes. Clearly, these people are ashamed of Paul, the Lord's prisoner (1:8).

In contrast to "everyone in the province of Asia" who deserts him, Paul presents Onesiphorus as a model of confidence: "May the Lord show mercy to the household of Onesiphorus, because he often refreshed me and was not ashamed of my chains. On the contrary, when he was in Rome, he searched hard for me until he found me" (1:16-17). The presence of this friend supplies a special tonic for the prisoner Paul who was repeatedly "refreshed" (Gk. *anapsuxo*; literally, "refresh, revive or cool again") by him. Although Paul is difficult to find in Rome, Onesiphorus diligently and energetically searches for him. He had even ministered (Gk. *diakoneo*) to Paul while he was still in Ephesus. Onesiphorus' behavior demonstrates that he "was not ashamed of (Paul's) chains" (1:16). Thus, he presents a positive illustration for Timothy of the message of 1:8, an example that is especially pertinent since Paul covets Timothy's presence in Rome (see 4:9, 21).

Since the focus of the first prayer is on mercy for Onesiphorus' household, not Onesiphorus himself, it gives the impression that Onesiphorus has died since he ministered to Paul in Rome. "May the Lord show mercy to the household of Onesiphorus..." (1:16). Also, the concluding prayer for Onesiphorus to find mercy on the day of judgment implies that he is dead: "May the Lord grant that he will find mercy from the Lord on that day!" (1:18; see also 4:19). However, there is no direct evidence of his death in these verses. What is clear is Onesiphorus' positive example of faithful discipleship; he is confident in the gospel and not ashamed of Paul's chains. Hence, just as Paul himself will be preserved by the Lord "until that day" (1:12), so Paul prays that Onesiphorus and his household will be shown mercy on that day by the God of mercy (1:2). In short, Onesiphorus' participation in Paul's suffering for the gospel has earned him an eschatological reward (see 4:8). How can Timothy miss the point?

In this brief passage, Paul supplies specific examples of what it means to be ashamed and not ashamed of himself and his gospel. Both cases involve not passivity, but clearly defined action. The negative example cites persons who actively turn away from Paul and desert him in his hour of need, thereby demonstrating their shame and lack of confidence in the gospel. In the positive example, Onesiphorus diligently searches for Paul in Rome, finds him, refreshes him and resumes the service he began while Paul was still in Ephesus, thereby modeling a shame-free confidence in the gospel.

Application, Teaching/Preaching Points

What do Paul's arguments in this chapter imply for the Christian community today? Several themes emerge with particular relevance for our day: the nature of prayer, the task of encouraging those who are discouraged among us, the value of models who embody truth, the Christian community's role in making the faith credible, and the gospel-shape of our Christian calling.

Memory and the Nature of Prayer. In the earlier verses of this chapter, Paul employs the motif of memory. He "remembers" Timothy constantly in his prayers (1:3), he "remembers" Timothy's tears (1:4), and he "remembers" the sincere faith of Timothy's grandmother and mother. Paul's use of memory is instructive of the nature of prayer. The memory Paul invokes is not simply recollecting information from the past. Rather, it recalls significant stories that shape Timothy's identity as an individual and as a member of Christ's community. "In this sort of memory," writes Johnson, "the past is made alive and powerful for the present. It can therefore help to shape the future" (1987: 15). Something comparable happens when we remember another person before the Lord in prayer. They are with us in the moment we present them to God. Thus, in recalling Timothy's tears, Paul indicates that he stands with him before God and identifies with his hurt.

Encouraging the Discouraged Among Us. Several things hint that all is not well with Paul's delegate, Timothy. First, Paul mentions Timothy's tears—a sure sign that he is emotionally challenged in his current assignment (1:4). Second, Paul recalls the sincere faith of Timothy's grandmother and mother (1:5) and then over-emphasizes his confidence in Timothy's continuing loyalty—a sign that Paul believes Timothy's faith is wavering. Third, as Paul seeks to bolster Timothy's courage (1:7), he contrasts "a spirit of timidity" with "a spirit of power"— a third sign that Timothy is faltering in the face of the opposition. Thus, Paul seeks to encourage his delegate by reminding him to "fan into flame the gift of God" that Timothy had received (1:6). Paul fans the dying embers of Timothy's commitment with fresh memories of his faith journey so that his loyalty might once again blaze into flame.

The Value of Models who Embody the Truth. Paul parades before Timothy a series of persons who are examples of the Christian faith: his grandmother, mother, Paul himself, and his fellow worker, Onesiphorus. He assumes that Timothy will learn the faith through real-life stories of virtuous people. A proposition or moral principle may tell us not to lie, but there is nothing as effective for learning the rigors of truth-telling as observing a real life truth-teller in action. Today we are reluctant to present ourselves as an example for others, perhaps because it implies a degree of virtue that makes us feel uncomfortable and presumptuous. Of course, there may be other reasons for our reluctance to present ourselves as models. Perhaps the consequent demand and responsibility to live the virtuous life is too much for us to bear. But surely Paul is correct in his approach. Johnson rightly argues, "people do learn their moral habits from the observation of role models rather than from propositions and maxims" (1987, 22). If such models are absent, where do young people learn their morals? Perhaps from the vice that is paraded before them in the media?

It Takes a Church to Raise a Christian. Early in the first chapter of 2 Timothy, Paul emphasizes the faith of Timothy's grandmother and mother. Also, he claims that his own worship of God is a continuation of his forefather's faith and obedience. Elsewhere, he says that Timothy's faith was learned "from infancy" (3:15). By implication, Paul suggests that faith takes shape in a human context where persons who believe and trust in God influence the disposition of faith in others. In other words, it takes a church (a faith community) to raise a Christian (see Bolsinger 2004). By contrast, we know that a social environment where the Christian faith is rejected or neglected is not the best preparation for hearing the gospel message. Hence, the New Testament emphasis on the church as the "household of God" or "family of God" is noteworthy in this regard. It takes a human community of faith, trust and acceptance to make credible the message of God's mercy and grace. The gospel message takes root best in the context of a whole "household" of persons who are faithful followers of Christ.

Suffering and the Call to a Holy Vocation. Paul insists Christians have been "called to a holy calling or vocation" (1:9). He speaks about the origin and nature of our Christian identity which has its source in God's grace, not our own accomplishments (1:9). In the Pastoral Letters context, the specific focus of "the call" is Timothy's ministry, given in Ephesus as Paul's apostolic delegate. Timothy has been gifted for church leadership (1:6-7). Indeed, Paul insists on the "gift" nature of his vocation or calling. Timothy serves not because of his own natural administrative abilities or inclinations. Rather, God gifts (1:6) those whom he calls (1:9). When Paul speaks of God's gift or grace, he also speaks of the Holy Spirit who lives among us (1:14). What is important is that Timothy's "calling"—or for that matter Paul's—is not reduced to a career or profession. It is defined by the gospel and the promise of life in Christ Jesus (1:10). Thus, the hope Paul and Timothy offer to others is based in God's own life, not on Timothy's human potential. For this reason, Paul can have hope even in his current difficult circumstances as a prisoner in Rome. He has learned that the path of those called by God follows the path of the one who calls. This perspective poses a challenge for us today. As Johnson asks, "If our understanding of life before God is one that does not encompass the depths of human suffering and sin, is our understanding in conformity to the gospel of the crucified Messiah?" (1987: 25). By implication, if the good news is proclaimed in a way that generates no suffering for those preaching or hearing it, we might ask whether it is really the good news that is being preached and heard.

Personal Reflection Questions

• Timothy's godly mother and grandmother influenced him. DISCUSS: Name the godly relatives in your life that are comparable to Timothy's grandmother and mother. How have they served you and inspired you in your faith?

• Paul suggests that faith takes shape in the crucible of the Christian community. DISCUSS: If we are intended to live in a faith community that surrounds us with a web of supportive relationships, in what ways are you helping to build such relationships in your congregation? How might we strengthen our community building efforts?

• Timothy is encouraged to fan into flame his God-given gift. DISCUSS: What gift has God given to you? What crisis is your faith community facing that begs you to fan into flame your God-given gift for the community's benefit?

• Christ has destroyed death and introduced life and immortality. DISCUSS: How does the promise of future resurrection enable you to cope with present suffering? What do you say to people who belittle your faith by accusing you of "pie in the sky when you die"?

• Some Christians abandoned Paul. DISCUSS: Have some Christians deserted you because of your distinctive brand of commitment to Christ? Or, have you abandoned other Christians because they have become too zealous about some aspect of the Christian faith?

CHAPTER EIGHT

Suffering for the Gospel

The Text: 2 Timothy 2:1-26

You then, my son, be strong in the grace that is in Christ Jesus. [2] *And the things you have heard me say in the presence of many witnesses entrust to reliable men who will also be qualified to teach others.* [3] *Endure hardship with us like a good soldier of Christ Jesus.* [4] *No one serving as a soldier gets involved in civilian affairs—he wants to please his commanding officer.* [5] *Similarly, if anyone competes as an athlete, he does not receive the victor's crown unless he competes according to the rules.* [6] *The hardworking farmer should be the first to receive a share of the crops.* [7] *Reflect on what I am saying, for the Lord will give you insight into all this.* [8] *Remember Jesus Christ, raised from the dead, descended from David. This is my gospel,* [9] *for which I am suffering even to the point of being chained like a criminal. But God's word is not chained.* [10] *Therefore I endure everything for the sake of the elect, that they too may obtain the salvation that is in Christ Jesus, with eternal glory.* [11] *Here is a trustworthy saying: If we died with him, we will also live with him;* [12] *if we endure, we will also reign with him. If we disown him, he will also disown us;* [13] *if we are faithless, he will remain faithful, for he cannot disown himself.* [14] *Keep reminding them of these things. Warn them before God against quarreling about words; it is of no value, and only ruins those who listen.* [15] *Do your best to present yourself to God as one approved, a workman who does not need to be ashamed and who correctly handles the word of truth.* [16] *Avoid godless chatter, because those who indulge in it will become more and more ungodly.* [17] *Their teaching will spread like gangrene. Among them are Hymenaeus and Philetus,* [18] *who have wandered away from the truth. They say that the resurrection has already taken place, and they destroy the faith of some.* [19] *Nevertheless, God's solid foundation stands firm, sealed with this inscription: "The Lord knows those who are his," and, "Everyone who confesses the name of the Lord must turn away from wickedness."* [20] *In a large house there are articles not only of gold and silver, but also of wood and clay; some are for noble purposes and some for ignoble.* [21] *If a man cleanses himself from the latter, he will be an instrument for noble purposes, made holy, useful to the Master and prepared to do any good work.* [22] *Flee the evil desires of youth, and pursue righteousness, faith, love and peace, along with those who call on the Lord out of a pure heart.* [23] *Don't have anything to do with foolish and stupid arguments, because you know they produce quarrels.* [24] *And the Lord's servant must not quarrel; instead, he must be kind to everyone, able to teach, not resentful.* [25] *Those who oppose him he must gently instruct, in the hope that God will grant them repentance leading them to a knowledge of the truth,* [26] *and that they will come to their senses and escape from the trap of the devil, who has taken them captive to do his will.*

The Flow and Form of the Text

Paul resumes his exhortations to Timothy in 2:1-13. He reiterates in verses 1-3 the substance of his three previous exhortations of 1:6-14 and emphasizes the call for Timothy to join him in hardship (2:3; see also 1:8). This call to endure hardship is supported by three classic examples for Timothy to imitate: the soldier, the athlete and the farmer (2:4-7). By using the literary device of ring construction (or *inclusio*), 2:1-7 is clearly identified as a literary unit for the beginning and end of the unit underscore what the Lord has given to Timothy, namely "grace" (2:1) and "insight" (2:7).

Next, a brief précis of the gospel leads Paul to acknowledge his own suffering for it (2:8-10; see also, 1:11-12), reciting a hymnic fragment that supplies the theological basis for his willingness to suffer (2:11-13). This liturgical fragment re-affirms the promise of eternal reward. It injects a note of warning, coupled with an affirmation of God's faithfulness.

The singular theme of suffering for the gospel dominates 2 Timothy 2:1-13. But Paul's argument consists of two parts. He first exhorts Timothy to endure hardship (2:1-7). Then he supports these exhortations by pointing to his own example of suffering for the gospel (2:8-10). Finally, he undergirds his three exhortations and personal example by reciting a liturgical fragment that emphasizes God's fidelity, the true source of Timothy's ability to endure hardship for the gospel's sake.

The balance of this chapter (2:14-26) focuses on the current threat to the church posed by Paul's opponents. This focus spills over into the next chapter (3:1-9). Paul's basic message remains constant throughout 2:14-26: that Timothy is to avoid these people and their controversies at all costs (see 2:14, 16, 22, 23). What emerges is a picture of a church seriously threatened by teachers who have embraced false teaching (2:18) and behaved inappropriately (3:6-7). The immediate passage (2:14-26) relates to the preceding call for Timothy to join Paul in enduring hardship for the gospel (1:3-2:13). It articulates how he is to fight for the gospel against the stiff opposition which comes from within the church.

The Text Explained
Second Challenge to Timothy (2:1-7). Paul begins this passage with the words "You then…" (Gk. *Sy oun*), inferring that the previous negative and positive examples (1:15-18) have implications for Timothy's present behavior. He is addressed as "my son" (Gk. *teknon mou*; literally, "my child"), recalling the intimate relationship between Paul and his delegate and supplying additional motivation for a suitable response from Timothy (see 1:2; 1 Timothy 1:2, 18). What follows are three exhortations coupled with three supporting maxims (2:1-7).

The first exhortation, to be "strong (Gk. *endynamou*) in the grace that is in Christ Jesus" (2:1), emphasizes God's empowering presence. The verb is in the present tense, indicating continuous action: "keep on being strong or strengthened" by God's grace. Paul does not suggest that Timothy is spiritually weak. Rather, with this exhortation, he creates a rhetorical foundation for the subsequent call to manifest this strength in hardship (see 2:3). The NIV translation assumes that grace is the sphere or locus within which Timothy is to be strong (1:9). But the preposition "in" (Grk. *en*) can also be instrumental, expressing "means." Timothy is to be strong by means of the grace that is in Christ Jesus. Timothy is to be strengthened by the grace that has its source in Christ Jesus, even as God's grace strengthened Paul (4:17; 1 Timothy 1:12). God's grace is an active source of power for Paul (see Titus 2:11-12). This first exhortation corresponds with 1:6 where Timothy is urged to keep on fanning God's gift into flame, including God's power or strength (Gk. *dynamis*).

The second exhortation, to entrust "the things you have heard me say" (2:2), develops the earlier exhortation of 1:13-14 where Paul urges Timothy to keep and guard "what you heard from me." Paul ensures the apostolic message's careful transmission, a feature of "keeping" and "guarding." What Timothy hears directly from Paul (see also 1:6; 3:10, 14), he hears "in the presence of many witnesses" (2:2). Some translations imply that Timothy receives this material from Paul indirectly, "through (Gk. *dia*) many witnesses" (see NRSV). However, the NIV translation is preferred here because the Greek preposition *dia* can also mean "in the presence of" or "before" (Zerwick 1979: 640). The many witnesses serve to corroborate the apostolic traditions Timothy hears directly from his teacher and mentor. Perhaps Paul has Timothy's commissioning service in mind, an occasion including many witnesses (1 Timothy 4:14; 6:12) and also a summary of the apostolic message (3:14).

Timothy is "to entrust" (Gk. *paratithemi*; literally, "to

place in another's trust" or "to commit for safekeeping") the apostolic traditions to persons who are "reliable" and "qualified to teach others" (2:2; see also 2:24; 1 Timothy 3:2, 9, 11; Titus 1:9). Shortly, Paul will develop the qualities of a reliable or trustworthy teacher (2:14-15, 24-25; 3:14-17; 4:2) and he will warn Timothy of other teachers whose doctrines and methods are the opposite of reliable teaching (2:14-3:9). But here, Timothy is exhorted to extend the apostolic mission by teaching others what Paul has taught him, thereby enabling them to teach still others.

The third exhortation, to "endure hardship with us" (2:3), echoes the injunction of 1:8 by using the same compound verb (Gk. *sygkakopatheson*; literally, "to suffer evil together," "to endure affliction together," or "to take one's share of rough treatment"). The force of this third exhortation is enhanced by means of three figures that model the meaning of "enduring hardship": the soldier, the athlete and the farmer. Timothy is urged to imitate specific aspects of these three figures, classic examples drawn from the repertoire of Hellenistic moral discourse. Elsewhere Paul uses these same figures as examples or metaphors, but for a different purpose (see 1 Corinthians 9:6-24; Philippians 2:25; Philemon 2).

First, a "soldier" refuses to be entangled or distracted by the affairs of daily life so that he might "please his commanding officer" (2:4). In this context, the image focuses on the soldier's devotion to his commanding officer. Since Paul defines "a good soldier of Christ Jesus" as someone who is willing to "endure hardship with us," there is no doubt that Christ Jesus is the commanding officer, and that the way to please him is by enduring hardship. The mention in Hebrews of Timothy's "release," presumably from prison, indicates that he experienced his own share of suffering for the gospel (see Hebrews 13:23).

Second, an "athlete... competes according to the rules" (2:5). Elsewhere Paul uses this same image to emphasize the prize or reward that awaits the athlete who wins the race (1 Corinthians 9:24-25; Philippians 3:12-14). The athlete's crown mentioned here (2:5) fore-shadows the eschatological rewards described in 2:10-13. However, the stress here is on competing according to "the rules"; the rules indicate that suffering and church leadership go together like hand and glove (see 1:8; 3:11-12; 4:5).

Third, a "farmer" ought to be the first to enjoy the fruit of his labors (see Deuteronomy 20:6; Proverbs 27:18; 1 Corinthians 9:7, 10). Paul emphasizes the farmer who is "hardworking" (Gk. *kopionta*; literally, "to work until one is exhausted"). Paul uses these three images elsewhere to emphasize the soldier's pay, the athlete's prize, or the farmer's share of the crop (see 1 Corinthians 9:6, 10, 24). But here he highlights the three images' common feature: namely, the hardship or suffering endured by the soldier, the athlete and the farmer in order to gain a reward.

When Paul tells Timothy to "reflect on what I am say-ing" (2:7), he undoubtedly wants Timothy to focus on what these three images have in common. He wants him to notice the struggle necessarily preceding the reward all three figures receive. In other words, he says, "Timothy you too must take your share of suffering before you can expect to receive the reward of life promised by the gospel." But this message must be teased out of these three examples, for Paul does not provide an explicit application to his argument as he does elsewhere (see 1 Corinthians 9:24-27). Indeed, the meaning of these three images, like the parables of Jesus, are in sufficient doubt so as to draw the mind into active thought. Timothy is promised some assistance with the task of interpreting these images for his particular situation. He is not with-out help: "for the Lord will give you insight into all this"

(2:7). Thus, both the understanding of what is to be done (2:7) and the strength to do it (2:1) come from the Lord Jesus Christ, but the decision to endure hardship for the gospel belongs to Timothy. By extension, it also belongs to us.

Paul's Example of Suffering (2:8-13). Paul challenges Timothy to endure hardship (2:3; 1:8). He supports his challenge with a cluster of persons who are not ashamed to endure hardship: Paul himself, Onesiphorus, the soldier, the athlete and the farmer. Now he reinforces his exhortations with the most important model of all: "Remember Jesus Christ, raised from the dead, descended from David" (2:8). The injunction to "remember" (Gk. *mnemoneuo*) picks up the theme of memory introduced in 1:3, 5, 15, and 18 where Paul recalls personal memories. Here he enjoins Timothy to recall the gospel tradition about Jesus Christ, a précis of the gospel that echoes Romans 1:3-4 but reverses its two key elements: resurrection and Davidic descent. While the resurrection easily supports Paul's focus here, it is more difficult to discern Paul's rationale for mentioning Jesus' royal lineage. The Pastoral Letters show no other interest in his "Davidic descent." If Paul wants Timothy to recall Jesus' humanity (cf. 1 Timothy 2:5; 3:16), it is a very indirect way of doing so. If he wants to convey Jesus' lowliness as somehow comparable to his own imprisonment, a reference to his "Davidic descent" fails to accomplish his goal. Perhaps it is best to see the reference to Christ's "Davidic descent" as a fixed element of the gospel tradition that has no immediate relevance for Paul's argument. It is the message of hope based on Jesus Christ's resurrection that supports Paul's call to endure hardship; it is the living, risen Lord who gives his life to the believer.

"This is *my* gospel," declares Paul (see also Romans 2:16; 16:25), meaning it is the gospel entrusted to him and "for which (he) is suffering even to the point of being

chained like a criminal" (2:8b-9; see also 2:11-12). Some
commentators argue (see Johnson, 1987: 20) that Paul
links his own suffering with the pattern of Christ's suffering and the message of the cross, even as he does elsewhere (1 Corinthians 2:2-5; 2 Corinthians 4:7-12;
Galatians 6:17; Philippians 3:10; Colossians 1:24). Here,
however, what is highlighted is the contrast between the
chained apostle and the unchained word (2:9), a contrast
that is remarkably similar to the argument of Philippians
1:12-14. Paul wants Timothy to understand that God is
able to guard and promote the gospel, even when those
entrusted with its proclamation are chained.

Indeed, in the next verse, Paul explicitly connects his
own apostolic suffering with the salvific power of God's
Word: "Therefore I endure everything for the sake of the
elect, that they too may obtain the salvation that is in
Christ Jesus, with eternal glory" (2:10). The salvation of
the elect is somehow directly linked with Paul's own suffering. So how does Paul's broadly defined endurance of
"everything" promote the elect's salvation? Numerous
suggestions have been made, including the idea that Paul
suffers in place of the elect, or that his suffering com-
pletes Christ's own atoning work (see Colossians 1:24), or
that Paul's suffering proclaims the cross's message by
embodying it. But the interpretation that seems to fit this
letter best is that the exhortation to endure hardship for
the gospel is essentially an invitation to work hard for the
gospel; to "fight the good fight of faith" (1 Timothy 6:12).
Paul's imprisonment is simply one of many ways to suffer for the gospel and God's power helps him deal with
his adversity (1:6-7, 14). The conviction that God's Word
is not chained encourages him to increase his efforts to
proclaim it (see 4:2). In this sense, Paul's willingness to
work hard—to "endure everything," including imprisonment if necessary—for the sake of proclaiming God's
Word, furthers the elect's salvation.

The benefactors of this hard work are "the elect" (Gk. *eklektoi*), an Old Testament term for Israel that was applied to Christians at an early stage to refer to their peculiar status before God (Psalm 105:6; Isaiah 43:20-21; Romans 8:33; Titus 1:1; 1 Peter 2:9). Here Paul calls Christians "the elect," thereby affirming their hope of salvation (see Matthew 22:11-14; Mark 13:20-27; Revelation 17:14). The concept of election is frequently linked with predestination (see Romans 8:28-33; Ephesians 1:4). However, that is not the case in this passage. Indeed, the "trustworthy saying" that follows (2:11-13) depicts salvation as a qualified hope, not a secure possession.

The expression, "Here is a trustworthy saying" (2:11; Gk. *pistos ho logos*), occurs four other times in the Pastoral Letters (see 1 Timothy 1:15; 3:1; 4:9-10; Titus 3:7-8). Here it refers almost certainly to the poetic passage that follows (2:11-13). The explanatory particle "for" (Gk. *gar*), omitted in the NIV translation, introduces the poetic passage and implies that it somehow ratifies the preceding saying's trustworthy nature. However, the gospel précis in 2:8 is an unlikely referent, as is the comment about the promise of salvation in 2:10b (although the motif of salvation appears to be the focus of all the "trustworthy sayings"). Perhaps it is best to consider the "for" of 2:11 as part of the quoted poetic passage rather than a feature of Paul's argument. If so, the NIV is correct in making the poetic passage of 2:11-13 the expression's referent, "Here is a trustworthy saying."

Since each line of the poetic passage (2:11b-13) is equal in length and parallel in structure, scholars are inclined to view it as a fragment of an early Christian hymn. It consists of four lines, each containing a conditional clause ("if...") followed by a result clause ("then..."), although the introductory particle "then" is unexpressed. Paul may have added 13b ("for Gk. *gar*) he cannot disown himself") to explain the meaning of the

surprising final line (13a). The conditional clauses of
Lines 1 and 2 emphasize forms of faithful human suffering; the result clauses focus on the consequent promise of
salvation. The conditional clause of Line 3 names the negative human action of denial (NIV, "disown"); the result
clause indicates "denial" as the corresponding divine
action. In Line 4, however, the conditional clause begins
in the same way as Line 3 by naming a negative human
action ("if we are faithless"). But then the result clause
breaks the symmetry of the poem by naming a positive
divine action ("he will remain faithful"). The interpretation of this poetic passage, especially Line 4 and its relationship to the rest of the poem, is widely disputed.

Another Trustworthy Saying

2 Timothy 2:11-13
Line 1: If we died with him, we will also live
        with him;
Line 2: If we endure, we will also reign with him.
Line 3: If we disown him, he will also disown us;
Line 4: If we are faithless, he will remain faithful,
        for he cannot disown himself.

In the first line, the NIV translation includes the personal pronoun "him," although it is omitted in the Greek
text which reads, literally: "if we have died together, we
will also live together" or "if we have died with (someone), we will also live with (someone)." Does the hymn
speak of dying and living *with Christ*, or dying and living
together? If the baptismal promise of Romans 6:8 supplies the original inspiration for this first line ("if we died
with Christ, we believe that we will also live with him"),
then it speaks of dying and living *with Christ*. Thus, Line
1 focuses on baptismal incorporation into Christ.
    Since Paul has just stated that salvation has its origins

"in Christ Jesus" (2:10), it is difficult to avoid a christo-logical interpretation of Line 1, especially if the explanatory word "for" (Gk. *gar*), omitted in the NIV translation but part of the Greek text, is reinstated. The past tense of the indicative verb, "to die with (someone)," indicates a past-completed action. This supports the metaphorical interpretation of dying as incorporation into Christ's death through baptism (Romans 6:3). Paul certainly views the new life that followed baptism to be the believer's present ongoing moral life as well as the future resurrection life (see Romans 6:4, 8, 11-14). But here, only the future resurrection life is mentioned, as the future tense of the verb "live" and the parallel claim in Line 2 ("we will reign with him") indicates.

In Line 2, the NIV translation includes the personal pronoun ("him") in the result clause but omits it in the conditional clause, as does the Greek text in both clauses of the line: "If we endure, we will also reign with him" (2:12a). Although the conditional clause of this line parallels its counterpart in Line 1, the verbal form emphasizes present tense enduring, rather than past tense dying. As a result, the message of Line 2's result clause shifts from the baptismal promise of salvation (Line 1) to the end-time reward for enduring hardship, perhaps particularly martyrdom (see Revelation 14:12-13; 20:4). If so, this line adds another meaning to the "dying" mentioned in Line 1. This interpretation, however, has its drawbacks, especially since Jesus' death is not directly addressed in these letters. To be sure, there are two references to his self-giving sacrifice (1 Timothy 2:6; Titus 2:14) and one to his resurrection from the dead (2:8). But the death of Jesus itself is not treated, and Jesus is not portrayed as "enduring" or "suffering" hardship.

Another interpretation of these two lines is worthy of consideration. It suggests that the text resembles a formula of friendship of the kind expressed by Paul in 2

Corinthians: "I have already said before that you have such a place in our hearts that we would live or die with you" (7:3; see also 2 Samuel 15:21). This friendship formula is commonly found in Greco-Roman literature: "I will choose to die or live with you" (see Euripides *Orestes* 307-8). It also fits this letter's scenario with its call for Timothy to join Paul in suffering or "dying" for the gospel. Paul has suffered and endured (2:10; 3:10-11). He faces the prospect of death (4:6-7) and anticipates the victor's crown (4:8). Thus, Timothy is exhorted to imitate Paul by suffering for the gospel.

The conditional clause of Line 3 describes a negative action, unlike the positive actions of Lines 1 & 2, and the result clause states what "he" (Gk. *ekeinos*; literally, "that one") will do: "If we disown him, he will also disown us" (2:12b). It is difficult to determine whether the antecedent of the pronoun "that one" is God or Jesus Christ, since the roles of God and Christ are not clearly distinguished in these letters (see, for example, 4:1,8; and 1:9). Also, Line 3 speaks of eschatological punishment ("… he will disown us"), while Lines 1 & 2 speak of eschatological reward ("we will also live with him" and "we will also reign with him"). This line may have been inspired by the saying tradition in Matthew 10:33 ("But whoever disowns me before men, I will disown him before the Father in heaven"). Both verbs of Line 3 are in the future tense and indicative mood, creating an element of contingency.

In Line 4, the conditional clause again describes a negative action like Line 3, but the result clause surprises with a positive divine response ("If we are faithless, he will remain faithful" (13a). This Line completely contradicts the message of Line 3! The connection between Lines 3 & 4 appears to depend on what it means for God—or Christ—to "remain faithful" (Gk. *pistos menei*). The concluding explanatory clause in 2:13b ("for (Gk. *gar*) he cannot disown himself") implies that the object of

God's faithfulness is God himself; that is, God's own nature or character. This begs the question: to what aspect of his character does God remain faithful?

Numerous interpretations have been proposed for the final line and concluding explanatory clause which break the poem's symmetry. For example, Line 4, together with its explanatory clause, may state that God's overall faithfulness to his people will not be overturned by the unfaithfulness of the few (see Romans 3:3-4). Or, it may accent God's grace, asserting that God's gracious nature overrides any inclination by him to punish the faithless. Or, it may state that God overrides our infidelity with his grace. Conversely, it may claim that God's faithfulness is best understood as faithfulness to his own just character, which requires the punishment spelled-out in Line 3's result clause: "he will also disown us" if we disown him (see Romans 2:2). The primary weakness with these interpretations is that they move outside of the Pastoral Letters' literary context for their basic understanding of God's faithfulness. Moreover, the poem's literary structure itself demands that Lines 3 and 4 be interpreted together, even as Lines 1 and 2 are interpreted as a unit.

In the verses preceding this poem, Paul has exhorted Timothy to "not be ashamed to testify about our Lord, or ashamed of me his prisoner" (1:8; 2:3). Line 3 supports this Pauline injunction, for it speaks about "disowning" or "denying" Christ, an action associated with feeling shame as the Gospel tradition makes clear (see Mark 8:38). In the verses following the poem, Paul warns Timothy about other people whose behavior and teaching are essentially expressions of denial and faithlessness to the truth (2:14-19; 3:5-8; and Titus 1:16). Paul's description of God's response to these people who deny him thusly exposes his understanding of what God's faithfulness means in the poem's concluding line. God's faithfulness is a complex reality, as revealed by Paul's description of God's response to the Ephesian situation in the first century. First, God's treatment of the gospel's opponents reveals something of his ongoing faithful commitment to his promise of life for all people (1 Timothy 2:4). Specifically, Timothy is encouraged to be "kind to everyone," and to "gently instruct" these opponents "in the hope that they will come to their senses and escape the trap of the devil, who has taken them captive to do his will" (2 Timothy 2:24-26). Second, God's treatment of the elect who are being disturbed by the opponents' teaching also reveals his fidelity to them. If the opponents "destroy the faith of some," Paul reassures those upset believers in Ephesus that God's faithfulness to "those who are his" is a "solid foundation" in times of doubt and uncertainty. Third, God's treatment of his messengers who suffer from a lack of resolve and even shame, reveals his faithfulness to the gospel, including his fidelity to its preservation and transmission. Specifically, Paul assures Timothy of "the help of the Holy Spirit" (1:14) as he seeks to "guard the good deposit that was entrusted" to him (1:14). He assures Timothy that, although he (Paul) is chained like a criminal, "God's word is not" (2:9). Finally, God's treatment of those who deny him reveals that his faithfulness does not preclude rejection. Specifically, if God recognizes "those who are his," by implication he also denies those who are not (2:19).

Human suffering for the sake of the gospel is a major theme of this passage. The primary exhortation to Timothy is not to "suffer with Christ," but to share with Paul in suffering for the gospel. Co-suffering with Paul is the dominant motif. Also, the suffering of Paul and Timothy as church leaders seems to be of primary concern here, not the suffering common to all baptized Christians. Specifically, the letter calls church leaders to actively proclaim and teach the gospel message. Christ Jesus is not the model for such suffering, but rather the source of strength for engaging in such hard work.

Timothy's calling to endure hardship speaks most directly to church leaders rather than the church as a whole. Even if the poetic passage was originally intended for baptismal candidates, in its present context it poses a challenge for church leaders to endure hardship for the sake of the gospel. They are to work hard to proclaim it daily, thereby demonstrating their confidence in, and faithfulness to, the gospel. Thus, Paul's invitation for Timothy to join him in suffering for the gospel (1:8; 2:3) is a call to proclaim the gospel confidently in the face of tough opposition (4:5; see also 1 Timothy 4:10). This, of course, may lead to persecution (3:10-12), but in this case from insiders, not outsiders. In other words, Paul's primary struggle is not with the Roman Empire but with coworkers who are ashamed, opponents who are faithless, and a church that is unresponsive. While Paul's Roman imprisonment forms the backdrop for this message, it is more of a metaphor for the struggle and endurance to which he calls Timothy than a dominant aspect of his message. Nothing that happens to Paul or Timothy can "chain" God's word. In short, Paul's message is an expression of confidence in God.

Exhortation to Avoid Controversies (2:14-26). Paul instructs Timothy to avoid arguments with his opponents whose teaching is depicted as "quarreling over words" (14), "godless chatter" (16), and "foolish and stupid arguments" (23). He juxtaposes the opponents' destructive behavior with the constructive behavior that should characterize Timothy as he engages in more profitable actions like correctly handling the word of truth (15), pursuing righteousness (22), being kind to everyone (24), and gently instructing his opponents (25). These instructions to Timothy, which constitute the heart of this passage, are supported by Scriptural quotes (19). They are also enriched by the concrete negative examples of

Hymenaeus & Philetus (17-18) as well as the image of the "large house" (20-21). If Timothy acts appropriately, he will present himself as a church leader who is approved by God, a worker with no reason to feel ashamed before God.

Paul begins his exhortation with a transitional remark: "Keep on reminding them of these things..." (2:14). The memory motif that introduced the preceding pericope (2:8, "Remember Jesus Christ...") reappears at the outset of this pericope's pastoral exhortation to Timothy. He is to remember (2:8) and remind (2:14; Gk. *hypomimnesko*; literally, "keep on reminding someone of something"). Unusual for this letter, Paul appears to address a larger audience here than simply Timothy. However, the Greek text lacks the pronoun ("them"), the expected indirect object of the verb. The NIV translation, like many others, supplies it. Presumably, Timothy is to remind the "faithful people" who have been entrusted with the gospel (2:2), that is, other church leaders rather than the entire community or "the elect" (2:10). "These things" (Gk. *tauta*) is a cipher in the Pastoral Letters for the Pauline tradition that Timothy is to entrust to other faithful people. In this context, "these things" refers specifically to the liturgical fragment introduced with the words, "Here is a trustworthy saying" (2:11-13). However, the connection between the following exhortations (2:14-26) and the preceding examples of enduring hardship for the gospel (2:3-7), especially Paul's example, should be included within the purview of what Timothy is to recall.

With the addition of the clause, "warn them before God against quarreling about words..." (2:14), Paul describes one of the opponents' activities (Gk. *logomachein*; sole occurrence in the NT; literally, "fighting or battling over words") and gives Timothy's role the aura of a witness in a courtroom drama with God as the presiding judge. The battle image is picked up again in verses 23-24 with reference to arguments that produce "quarrels" (Gk. *machas*, a word frequently used of military battles) and to the directive for the Lord's servant not to quarrel (Gk. *machesthai*). These exhortations clarify the nature of Timothy's struggle. In spite of the battle imagery (see also 2:3-4), Timothy and the faithful people with whom he has entrusted the gospel are not to engage in verbal warfare; they are to avoid verbal battles that destroy the people along with the arguments.

Paul's exhortation to refrain from quarreling about words is supported by two complimentary statements. The first states that waging word wars "is of no value" (NIV translation) and "serves no useful purpose" (Zerwick 1979: 641), a characteristic measure of Paul's pragmatism in these letters (1 Timothy 4:8; Titus 3:8-9). The second reason for not engaging in disputes over words is that it "only ruins those who listen" (NIV translation) and "serves only to upset the listeners" (Zerwick 1979: 641), eventually "destroying their faith" (2:18), particularly if it is weak (3:7). Thus, Paul reminds Timothy of the long-term consequences of his conduct as a teacher. He needs to remember that he teaches in the presence of God. Also, if he fails to teach appropriately, there will be disastrous consequences for his listeners: namely, their eschatological destruction (see also 1 Timothy 4:16).

Paul balances this negative exhortation (2:14) with a positive one (2:15). Timothy is to present himself as a qualified worker who has no reason to feel ashamed before God. "Worker" (Gk. *ergates*) is a technical term for church leader in the Pauline churches, including persons actively engaged in proclaiming or evangelizing (see 2 Corinthians 11:13; Philippians 3:2; 1 Timothy 5:18; Romans 16:3, 6, 9). Timothy is to do his best (Gk. *spoudazo*; literally, "be eager or zealous") to present himself to God as an "approved" (Gk. *dokimos;* literally, "approved after testing") worker. He will have no reason to feel shame (Gk. *anapaischuntos*; literally, "having nothing to be ashamed of") before God if he performs his duties appropriately (Marshall 1999: 748). Specifically, he must teach the word of truth without deviation (Gk. *orthotomounta*; literally, "cut something straight," here a metaphor for "teaching the word of truth without dilution;" sole occurrence in the NT). Thus, Timothy must not get sidetracked as a teacher, engaging in "quarrels about words" (2:14) and "godless chatter" (2:16) like the opponents. Instead, he is to teach the Christian message to profit rather than destroy his hearers. In effect, Paul gives Timothy his "job description."

In the next verse, Paul reiterates the message of 2:14, emphasizing the empty content of his opponent's teaching: "Avoid godless chatter, because those who indulge in it will become more and more ungodly" (2:16). If virtue is the natural companion of sound teaching, then empty or vain talking will result in ungodly behavior (1 Timothy 6:4, 11; Titus 3:8-9). In the ancient world, useless talking was rooted in a sickness of the soul; it manifested itself in speech patterns lacking in quality (see Rienecker/Rogers 1980: 642). Thus, Paul reminds Timothy that "godless chatter" only enables people to progress further in ungodliness.

Paul describes the situation in Ephesus in more detail, naming two opponents whose godless chatter spreads like gangrene and subverts the faith of some community members (2:17-18). Hymenaeus is also mentioned in 1 Timothy 1:20 as one who scuttled the faith and was handed over to Satan. Philetus is otherwise unknown to us. Presumably, the Ephesian community knows both of them. The metaphor of "gangrene" (Gk. *gangraina*; literally, "cancer, spreading ulcer") illustrates false teaching's insidious nature. Like cancer, it initially attacks one part of the body, quickly spreads to other parts, and finally eats away at the bones. The image of gangrene suggests that Hymenaeus and Philetus pose a serious threat to the church's health. Paul uses similar medical imagery elsewhere to develop the opposite image of the church as the locus of "healthy" or "sound" teaching (1:13; 4:3; 1 Timothy 1:10; 6:3; Titus 1:9, 13; 2:1).

Hymenaeus and Philetus have "wandered away" (Gk. *estocheo*; literally, "to miss the mark, to go astray") from the truth (2:18; see also 1 Timothy 1:6; 6:21). Specifically, this deviant message involves teaching that "the resurrection has already taken place" (2:18). It is not Paul's habit to reveal the content of his opponent's teaching (see 1 Timothy 4:3). Indeed, this is the only time in the Pastoral Letters that he divulges their theology. Paul does not specify how they understand the resurrection. If they teach that it has already occurred, then they do not deny the possibility of the resurrection (see 1 Corinthians 15:12-13). Rather, they indulge in some form of over-realized eschatology, teaching that "resurrection" is a metaphor for conversion. If so, such a spiritualized reinterpretation of the resurrection is tantamount to denying the reality of the future, bodily resurrection (2:8, 10; see also 1 Corinthians 15:35-55). Elsewhere Paul is careful to interpret the baptized Christian's new life as a new moral life of obedience that carries the promise of future resurrection (Romans 6:3-11; see also 2 Timothy 2:11-12; Titus 2:11-13; 3:6-7). Perhaps his opponents in Ephesus fail to make this important distinction, teaching instead that the resurrection is a past—purely spiritual—event. If so, they may embrace the spirit-body dualism that fosters this view, promoting an ascetic life similar to the one Paul encountered in Corinth (see 1 Timothy 4:3; cf. 1 Corinthians 7:1-16).

While it is impossible to determine with accuracy the nature and source of Hymenaeus and Philetus's deviation from the truth, they have clearly experienced some

success, as Paul focuses on some of the consequences: "…
they destroy (Gk. *anatrepousin*) the faith of some" (2:18).
Titus 1:11 uses this same verb in a figurative sense to
mean "subverting" or "undermining" whole households
for the sake of money. "Destroy" has the same figurative
sense here so that these two false teachers are subverting
or undermining "the faith" of some. In the Pastoral
Letters "faith" refers to the content of Christian belief
rather than to a personal relationship with Christ Jesus.
Indeed, 2 Timothy virtually equates "the faith" (Gk. *ten
pistin*, 2:18) with Paul's gospel (2:8), the word of God
(2:9), the trustworthy saying (2:11), and the message of
the truth (2:15). Thus, it is the faith's content that is being
distorted by such characters as Hymenaeus and Philetus.
By their false teaching about the resurrection, they skew
the basic message of the Christian faith.

Against the cancerous spread of defections from the
truth, Paul offers some reassurance: "Nevertheless, God's
solid foundation stands firm…" (2:19). The solid nature
of the foundation is emphasized with the verb "stand"
(Gk. *histemi*) and the adjective "firm" (Gk. *stereos*; literally, "solid, strong, hard"). This image of a building con-
structed on a solid foundation is drawn from Isaiah 28:16
and is applied to Christ in the New Testament (Romans
9:33; 1 Corinthians 3:10-12; 1 Peter 2:6). Elsewhere, Paul
uses this image as a metaphor for the local church
(Romans 15:20; 1 Corinthians 3:10-12), the probable referent here. Paul emphasizes the church's stability and the
reliability of its message in the face of defections from,
and distortions of, the faith.

Paul goes on to makes two points, one about the foundation (2:19) and another about the building (2:20-21).
First, he draws the reader's attention to the two
epigraphs on the foundation: "The Lord knows those
who are his." This first quotation is drawn verbatim from
the Septuagint (LXX) version of Numbers 16:5, with

"Lord" replacing "God" in the original. While it appears nowhere else in the New Testament, it comes from a passage that describes a revolt against the leadership of Moses and Aaron. This has an obvious application to the Ephesian church, given the fact that some community members are turning away from the faith because of Hymenaeus and Philetus. This saying ("the Lord knows those who are his") points either to those within the church who are not influenced by the opponents' teaching, or to the church leaders who "correctly handle the word of truth."

The second epigraph on the foundation, "Everyone who confesses the name of the Lord must turn away from wickedness" (2:19c), is a freely composed saying based somewhat loosely on the wording of two or three texts (see Job 36:10; Isaiah 26:13; 52:1; Sirach 17:26). The words "turn from wrongdoing" echo the call to repentance of Sirach 17:25-26, but the Greek verb (*apostrophe*) has been replaced by a verb in the past tense (*aposteto*), implying a conversion experience. The phrase, "everyone who confesses the name of the Lord," comes from a lengthy prayer for deliverance found in Isaiah 26:1-27:1. The first portion of the prayer is the people's declaration of their loyalty to the one God after having sinned by acknowledging other gods. In effect, this quotation warns the Ephesian community not to follow the path taken by Hymenaeus and Philetus; it summons the community to turn away from the wickedness promoted and exemplified by the opposing teachers. If anyone calls on the name of the Lord but does not live accordingly, that person should know that God is not fooled (see Matthew 7:21-22; Luke 6:46; 13:25-27). God knows those who really belong to him, for they demonstrate their belonging by the way they chose to live.

Paul turns his attention from the foundation to the building (a metaphor for the church) by introducing the image of a "large house" (2:20). It is a relatively large structure containing utensils made from a wide variety of material and used for cooking, lighting and eating. If Paul had been thinking of the homes of the poor, he would not have mentioned utensils made of gold and silver. The reference to the large house may indicate something of the faith community's affluent social status. But it does not necessarily imply that all members in the Ephesian church are affluent. The majority of people in a typical Hellenistic city like Ephesus are slaves who are familiar with the various utensils used by their masters, especially if they are household managers (Gk. *oikonomos*). Indeed, slaves are responsible for using and maintaining these utensils.

The description of the utensils creates a twofold distinction: Paul distinguishes the materials from which the vessels are created from the uses to which they are put. Concerning the materials, a further distinction is made between those utensils made from precious metals (gold and silver) and those made from ordinary material (wood and clay). Concerning their use, some are used for noble purposes (Gk. *eis timen*) and others for ignoble purposes (Gk. *eis atimian*). Utensils used for less noble purposes, like chamber pots or garbage buckets, are made of the least valuable materials (wood and clay). On the other hand, if the distinction is simply between ignoble and noble uses of the utensils, Paul may be suggesting that gold and silver plates and utensils are used for special events, whereas wood and clay utensils are used for everyday events.

In 2:21, Paul exhorts: "If a man cleanses himself from the latter, he will be an instrument for noble purposes, made holy, useful to the Master and prepared to do any good work." This inference is drawn from the metaphor of a large house and its various utensils. Paul does not speak of "washing" the utensils so they can be used again for another purpose. Rather, he speaks of a person who washes himself or herself. Thus, a person is a like a utensil insofar as both have to be clean in order to be useful. A person must cleanse himself "from these things" or "from these persons" (Gk. *apo touton*, can mean either). The only possible referent is the "wickedness" of 2:19 (cf. Sir 17:26, "turn from wrongdoing"), which is supported by the thought development in 2:23 and indicates that Paul has activities in mind. The goal of the cleansing—to produce utensils "useful to the owner"—reflects this letter's interest in shaping Timothy as a useful church leader who struggles for the gospel (2:3-4, 15; 3:16-17). Thus, the two kinds of utensils seem to represent, on the one hand, the "approved worker" (2:15) or "Lord's servant" (2:24) and, on the other hand, the opposing teachers (3:2-9).

Paul now returns to direct exhortation (see 2:14), especially underscoring how the leader Timothy is to behave before his opponents. The initial exhortation has two parts that are accentuated by juxtaposing the verbs "flee" and "pursue" (see also 1 Timothy 6:11). First, Paul admonishes Timothy to flee (Gk. *pheugo*; literally, "shun, flee") "evil desires" (2:22). The Greek text lacks the term "evil" which is supplied in the NIV translation, presumably because the Pastoral Letters display a consistent aversion to "desires" (Gk. *epithumia*; literally, "passion, strong desire") which connote sexual urges and desires (see also 1 Corinthians 6:18). Paul describes the passions Timothy is to flee as "youthful" (Gk. *neoterikas*; see also 1 Timothy 4:12), which adds a pejorative meaning since young persons are often portrayed as being unable to control their passions (see Titus 2:6). By contrast, church leaders like Timothy are presumed to be mature persons who choose to control their passions (see 1 Timothy 5:1, 2, 17, 19; Titus 1:5). Perhaps Paul alludes to tendencies in the church that his delegate is to combat rather than to

Timothy's own conduct (Marshall 1999: 764).

Having enjoined him to flee evil desires, Paul urges Timothy to "pursue" (Gk. *dioke*) a litany of virtues, including "righteousness, faith, love and peace" (see 3:10; 1 Timothy 4:12; 6:11). Such lists, a common literary form in the Hellenistic world, are frequently found in Paul's writings (see 2 Corinthians 6:6-7a; Galatians 5:22-23; Philippians 4:8). As is the case here, they are primarily used to describe the characteristics of persons in leadership. "Faith and love" is a frequent description of the Christian life in Paul's writings (see 1 Thessalonians 3:6; Galatians 5:6); "faith" points to one's relationship with God, and "love" expresses one's relationship with other people. By contrast, "righteousness" (Gk. *dikaiosynen*) is rarely found in these virtue lists (see Philippians 4:8; 1 Timothy 6:11). It is a desirable ethical characteristic of the person who is in correct relationship with others and hence in a right relationship with God. Here in the Pastoral Letters, righteousness does not have the rich theological nuance that it does in other Pauline writings like Romans and Galatians. The final item on the list, "peace," is exceptional since this is the only time it appears in the body of any of the Pastoral Letters (see 1:2; 1 Timothy 1:2; Titus 1:4). Among other New Testament virtue lists, peace is cited only in the list of Galatians 5:22. Hellenistic virtue lists portray peace in the negative sense, that is, the absence of armed conflict or pain. By contrast, in the New Testament peace is a positive virtue that points to the biblical idea of *shalom* and God's full covenant blessings to his people (Romans 14:17).

In the NIV, as in most other translations, the concluding prepositional phrase is attached to the verb "pursue." Thus, Timothy is urged to pursue the four virtues "along with (together with) those who call on the Lord out of a pure heart" (2:22). This expression recalls what Christians do when they gather together for corporate worship (see

1 Timothy 2:8-10). It is a Christian designation with roots
in the Old Testament (1 Samuel 12:1f; 2 Samuel 22:7). The
phrase "a pure heart" (see 1 Timothy 1:5) reflects the
Semitic way of expressing "a clear conscience" since
Hebrew lacks the word "conscience" (Marshall 1999:
765). It also recalls Paul's opening remark that, like his
ancestors, he serves God with "a clear conscience" (1:3).

In his third and final exhortation to avoid arguments
with the opponents (2:23; see also 2:14, 16), Paul dismisses his opponents' discussions as "foolish" (Gk. *moros*)
and "stupid" (Gk. *apaideutos*; literally, "without discipline, without training, uninstructed;" see also 1 Timothy
1:6-7; 6:4; Titus 3:9), highlighting the contentious and
quarrelsome (2:23) nature of their discussions. Having
described his opponents' combative and disruptive
nature, Paul shifts to a description of "the Lord's servant"
who promotes peace (2:24; see also 2:15; Titus 1:1). Most
of the ideal church leader's characteristics parallel the
requirements expected of the bishop (1 Timothy 3:2-3),
although here the focus is on the required gentleness: "in
the hope that God will grant them repentance... (2:25).
This hope is deeply rooted in the conviction that God
desires the salvation of all persons (1 Timothy 2:4; Titus
1:13) and it is assumed that the gentleness of the Lord's
servant will give God a window of opportunity, so to
speak, to draw the opponents toward repentance. The
first stage of this repentance is described in terms of
"leading them to a knowledge of the truth" (2:25). This is
a technical term in the Pastoral Letters to designate the
community's understanding of the truth (see 3:7;
1 Timothy 2:4). The second stage of repentance is
expressed as an "escape from the trap of the devil" (2:26;
see also 1 Timothy 1:20; 3:6-7), which is predicated on the
hope that "they will come to their senses" (Gk. *ananepho*;
literally, "to sober up, to return to sobriety, to return to
one's senses"). This metaphor implies that the devil's

strategy is to numb the conscience and paralyze the will (Rienecker/Rogers 1980: 644). If so, the devil's "trap" is to delude God's people in Ephesus by means of myths and wordy debates (see also 1 Timothy 3:6-7).

The balance of this chapter's concluding verse is widely debated: "who has taken them captive to do his will" (2:26). The NIV translation fails to do justice to the Greek text, which uses two different pronouns: "captive by *him* (Gk. *autou*) to do *his* (Gk. *ekeinou*, literally, "that one's) will." This has prompted some theologians to infer that two different agents are involved: namely, the devil and God. If the two pronouns refer to the same agent, then it is appropriate to ask: is God or Satan the agent of this activity? Also, the unusual Greek word *zogreo*, translated "has taken them captive" by the NIV, means "to capture *alive*" or "to capture and *keep alive*." If we focus on the positive notion of "keep alive," the agent may well be God. However, the preceding reference to "the trap of the devil" seems to emphasize "capture," making Satan the most likely agent. Hence, the opponents have been trapped and captured by the devil. If so, they are his slaves, forced to do his will. It is interesting to note that the term "will" (Gk. *thelema*) is only used twice in the Pastoral Letters: here it refers to the devil's will, but in 1:1 it refers to God's will. To summarize, repentance is a gift of God. It is depicted here as a form of redemption because it liberates a person from the devil and sets them free for God. In the process, one's allegiance shifts from the devil to the Lord.

Application, Teaching/Preaching Points

In the "Text Explained" section of this chapter, I have already tried to start the process of reflection necessary for enabling the text to speak to us today. Here, I want to speak more directly on several aspects which could be developed into sermons.

Wanted: Gentle Teachers and Leaders. This chapter paints a pretty grim picture of the social dynamics within the Ephesian church community. At least two factions struggle for influence over God's people: Hymenaeus and Philetus represent one group while Timothy represents the other. The strong imagery ("spreading gangrene") and the harsh language Paul uses to critique his opponents (2:14, 16, 23) suggest that the opposing faction has been quite influential. Still, he is confident they will not prevail (3:9). What is fascinating to notice is that both factions exist within the church yet Paul does not advocate the expulsion of the opponents. By implication, the Lord's house (2:20) has both useful and disreputable utensils: leaders who correctly explain the word of truth and others who do not even know it; those who are the Lord's servants and others who do the devil's bidding. Both factions continue to exist side-by-side, even when they disagree on key theological matters like the resurrection. Paul's primary concern is not with theory, but with praxis, especially debating and arguing. He repeatedly exhorts Timothy to avoid such activities (see also 1 Timothy 6:3-5, 11, 20; Titus 3:9). Indeed, engaging in such debate is considered harmful to the church. Timothy is to pay attention to his own teaching style (2:15) and actions (2:22), assured that God knows what is going on (2:19) and will reward the faithful (2:12). All of this suggests a radical form of suffering for the gospel as a church leader. The godly leader endures the presence of opponents inside the community, tolerating even their short-term gains; he refrains from hostile debate with opponents, but gently corrects them since they are "utensils" which may have some use in God's household. At the same time, since "the Lord knows those who are his" (2:19), a godly leader remains patient and hopeful that even the disruptive opponents belong to God. Thus, everyone is to be treated with kindness and benevolence

(2:24), knowing that God is a God of mercy (1:18; 2:25). In short, God's desire for the salvation of all (1 Timothy 2:4; 4:10; Titus 3:11), God's evident mercy (1 Timothy 1:16), and God's goodness and loving-kindness (Titus 3:4-5) are best promoted by church leaders who embody these traits in their own words and deeds.

Who Are We to Teach? Regarding Paul's gospel message, the NIV and AV translations say "entrust to reliable men" undoubtedly because Paul uses a Greek word (*anthropoi*) that often means "men" (1 Corinthians 7:1; Matthew 19:5 and Ephesians 5:31). But the basic concept behind the Gk. word *anthropoi* is that of generic man. In this general sense, men and women can be subsumed under the one overall term that means "persons" of either gender. Therefore, it is sometimes argued that if Paul intends to ban any woman from teaching on any subject at any time, he has a great opportunity to do it here by using *aner*, the clear, exclusive Greek word for "males." However, I think the NIV got it right. Paul probably has only males in mind, given the cultural setting where women are limited primarily to domestic roles. But this reading of the text does not mean we should limit the teaching role to men, for we serve in an egalitarian cultural context (North America) where women are free to teach in public settings. Paul's primary point here is that the gospel message must be passed on to faithful persons who are capable of teaching others. Like the four laps of a relay race, each person must pass on what they have learned to the next runner. Unfortunately, today we have many church leaders who insist on doing it all alone. But surely, the secret of being an effective missionary like Paul is training up others to continue and expand the church's teaching ministry.

Personal Reflection Questions

- Timothy is exhorted to teach others what he has learned from Paul. DISCUSS: To whom have you passed on your gifts and insights? How do you encourage others to employ their gifts for kingdom work?

- The text implies that only "men" are to be entrusted with the task of teaching. DISCUSS: Does your faith community tend to slot men into certain tasks and women into others? Or are all roles in the church open to anyone, irrespective of gender? According to this passage how should enlightened church leaders function? Is such a policy also applicable even in church planting situations?

- Consider the three images of soldier, athlete and farmer. DISCUSS: Which image do you prefer? Why? What can we learn from each comparison? How do you reconcile Paul's call for hard work with the old maxim "to let go and let God"?

- Timothy is encouraged to be strong in the grace that is in Christ Jesus. DISCUSS: What is the "grace" in which Timothy is to be strong and for what purpose has it been given to him (see especially 2:2, 15, 24, 25)? Who in your faith community possesses this "grace?" How can this grace become more plentiful?

- Consider the hymn of 2:11-13. DISCUSS: How would the words of this hymn encourage someone who is doubting or wavering in their commitment to Christ, especially in the face of opposition or persecution?

CHAPTER NINE

Charge to the Lord's Servant

The Text: 2 Timothy 3:1-17

*But mark this: There will be terrible times in the last days.
² People will be lovers of themselves, lovers of money, boastful,
proud, abusive, disobedient to their parents, ungrateful,
unholy, ³ without love, unforgiving, slanderous, without self-
control, brutal, not lovers of the good, ⁴ treacherous, rash, conceited, lovers of pleasure rather than lovers of God—⁵ having a
form of godliness but denying its power. Have nothing to do
with them. ⁶ They are the kind who worm their way into homes
and gain control over weak-willed women, who are loaded
down with sins and are swayed by all kinds of evil desires, ⁷
always learning but never able to acknowledge the truth. ⁸ Just
as Jannes and Jambres opposed Moses, so also these men oppose
the truth— men of depraved minds, who, as far as the faith is
concerned, are rejected. ⁹ But they will not get very far because,
as in the case of those men, their folly will be clear to everyone.
¹⁰ You, however, know all about my teaching, my way of life, my
purpose, faith, patience, love, endurance, ¹¹ persecutions, sufferings—what kinds of things happened to me in Antioch,
Iconium and Lystra, the persecutions I endured. Yet the Lord
rescued me from all of them. ¹² In fact, everyone who wants to
live a godly life in Christ Jesus will be persecuted, ¹³ while evil
men and impostors will go from bad to worse, deceiving and
being deceived. ¹⁴ But as for you, continue in what you have
learned and have become convinced of, because you know those
from whom you learned it, ¹⁵ and how from infancy you have
known the holy Scriptures, which are able to make you wise for
salvation through faith in Christ Jesus. ¹⁶ All Scripture is God-
breathed and is useful for teaching, rebuking, correcting and
training in righteousness, ¹⁷ so that the man of God may be
thoroughly equipped for every good work.*

The Flow and Form of the Text

The focus on the opposing teachers within the church, which begins in 2:14, continues in the first unit of this chapter (3:1-9). A major portion of it is a lengthy list of eighteen vices (vv. 2-4), the second longest in the New Testament and exceeded only by the twenty one vices in Romans 1:29-31 (see also Romans 13:13; 1 Corinthians 5:10-11; 6:9-10; 2 Corinthians 12:20-21; Galatians 5:19-21). It portrays the moral decadence that characterizes the "last days" (3:1). In contrast to the gentle and upright behavior exemplified by the "the Lord's servant" (2:22-26) and the apostle Paul (3:10-11), the final days are pictured in terms of violence and moral rebellion. Thus, they are difficult days for the church. Of course, no individual is presumed to have each and every one of the eighteen vices; they describe various forms of social and antisocial behavior. The vice list is designed to make a global impression by the accumulation of terms. A single exhortation is inserted into Paul's description of these depraved persons: "Have nothing to do with them" (3:5), connecting the present passage with the previous exhortations of 2:14-26, especially 2:16, 22, 23. The injunction of 3:5 also indicates a shift from the prediction of future distress to the present dangers that mark the balance of 3:1-9.

In the next section (3:10-13), Paul holds up his own life and ministry as a foil to the portrait of the opposing teachers given in the preceding passage. The contrast is especially sharp if the virtue list of 3:10 is compared with the vice list of 3:2-4. Also, the Pauline example of 3:10-13 supports the exhortations of 3:14-17 that extend to 4:8. Indeed, 3:10-4:8 forms a coherent literary unit.

Many of the exhortations to Timothy (3:14; 4:2, 5) reiterate earlier exhortations to him (1:6, 8, 13). References to the opponents described in 2:14-3:9 also supply the motivation for several of the exhortations to Timothy, especially 3:13; 4:3-4. Finally, as in 1:6-2:13, Paul is presented as an example for Timothy to emulate (3:10-11; 4:6-8), with 3:10-11 pointing to the model of the suffering Apostle (see also 1:15-16; 2:9-10) and 4:6-8 promising the eschatological reward (see also 2:11-12).

The entire unit of 3:1-4:8 contains a wide assortment of literary forms, including exhortations, recollections of Paul's life and ministry, vice and virtue lists, a theological statement about Scripture, and predictions of future challenges. The pattern of argument is once again a series of contrasts and comparisons involving the opposing teachers, Timothy and Paul. The text is highlighted by phrases like "But mark this," "You, however," "But as for you," and "But you," (3:1,10, 14; 4:5, 6).

The Text Explained

The Chaos of "the last days" (3:1-9). The conjunction in the NIV translation, "But mark this" (Gk. *de*), connects and contrasts the exhortations to Timothy in 2:22-26 with the announcement of future moral decay in 3:1-9. The immorality depicted here is not directly linked with the opponents of chapter 2. Rather, the prediction of moral chaos supplies the larger context within which these opponents are to be understood—the chaos of "the last days." If apocalyptic literature identifies the chaos in cosmic and ethical terms, the attention here is exclusively on moral decay minus cosmic features. Indeed, this passage resembles the testamentary literature of Hellenistic Judaism where a dying patriarch exhorts his successors, often in conjunction with predictions of forthcoming immorality and the rise of dangerous opponents (see Testament of Moses 5-9; Daniel 5:1-6; Acts 20:18-35; 2 Peter 2:1-3; 3:3-10). In similar fashion, Paul exhorts Timothy and predicts widespread immorality in the last days, but with no apocalyptic cosmic fanfare. While 2 Timothy has several references to "that day" (1:12, 18; 4:8), the letter does not focus primarily on the end of the world but on the end of Paul's suffering. References to the last days are primarily an interpretive device, situating the opponents' beliefs and behaviors within the "terrible times of the last days" (3:1). In this way, Paul heightens the gravity of the letter's warnings and exhortations.

The lengthy list of vices opens and closes with similar categories: "lovers of themselves" (3:2; Gk. *philautoi*; literally, "lovers of self") and "lovers of God" (3:4; Gk. *philotheoi*). The description of these evildoers as "disobedient to their parents" (3:2) begins a series of five vices characterized by alliteration. Each term begins with the Greek letter *alpha* (the equivalent of the negative prefix "un-"), or the *alpha* privative. Six of the eighteen words on the list are not found elsewhere in the New Testament. Four are also found in Romans 1:9-31, the longest vice list in the New Testament and a passage that may have inspired this list. There are similar lists in the Greco-Roman writings of philosophers like Philo that also contrast love of self with love of God (see *On Flight and Finding* 81).

Many of the words on this list allude to themes developed elsewhere in the Pastoral Letters. For example, the term "lovers of money" matches the criticism of the opponents in passages like 1 Timothy 6:5-10 and Titus 1:11 and contrasts with the absence of greed that should characterize church leaders (1 Timothy 3:3, 8; Titus 1:7). Likewise, terms like "abusive," "without love," "unforgiving," "brutal" and "treacherous" are consistent with the battle imagery used in the Pastoral Letters to describe the opponents' behavior (see 2 Timothy 2:14, 23; 1 Timothy 6:5; Titus 1:10). Finally, the charge of "disobedience to their parents" suggests a lack of respect for the social order that is at the core of several exhortations in 1 Timothy and Titus (1 Timothy 3:4, 12; 5:1-2; 6:1; Titus 1:6; 2:5, 9; 3:1) and contrasts with the behavior expected of Timothy as Paul's "dear son" (1:2).

In conclusion, the list suggests that people who are characterized by these vices are not "God-lovers" (3:4). They are not authentic lovers of God, as Paul explains in 3:5. He uses two contrasting participles "having" and "denying" to distinguish a sham religiosity from the kind of love of God that empowers a true believer's everyday life. Godliness (Gk. *eusebeia*) includes a reverence for God as well as a reverent life-style. Thus, Paul exhorts Timothy to "have nothing to do with them" (3:5); he must "turn away from" (Gk. *apotrepou*) them.

The balance of this passage (3:6-9) addresses the problems posed by Paul's opponents in Ephesus whose behavior is rooted in "the terrible times of the last days" (3:1). After exhorting Timothy to avoid these people (3:5), Paul describes their activities as a way of belittling them (3:6-7); he compares them with two Old Testament figures (3:8) and assures Timothy of their eventual defeat (3:9).

Paul's opponents are engaged in a type of clandestine operation where they "worm their way into homes and gain control over weak-willed women" (3:9). They enter (Gk. *endynein*; literally, "creep in, or slip in") into houses where they take complete possession (Gk. *aichmalotizein*; literally, "to hold captive") of women with their deceptive words (3:13) and false teaching (4:3-4). Paul denigrates the teachers by denigrating the women who are attracted to their teaching, describing them as "little women" (Gk. *gynaikaria*; the diminutive of the Greek word *gyne;* literally, "silly or idle women;" sole occurrence in the NT). These women are "loaded down with sins" and "swayed by all kinds of evil desires" (3:6), creating a very negative image. Although the NIV translation implies sensual appetites (see James 4:3-4; 2 Peter 2:13-14), that is not necessarily the Greek text's connotation. To be "swayed by all kinds of evil desires" is simply the opposite of the temperate, godly, dignified and contented life Paul holds up as the Christian ideal (1 Timothy 2:2; 6:6). The final description of these women indicates that while they can learn (see 1 Timothy 2:11-12) and they can be taught, they are "never able to acknowledge the truth" (3:7). Paul employs a cultural stereotype to portray the Ephesian women in verses 6-7 in order to discredit his opponents as teachers who can only persuade persons incapable of recognizing the truth.

Apocalyptic literature characteristically refers to the past as a way to unlock the future (see Mark 13:14). To illustrate the corrupt nature of these end-time agents who undermine the faith, Paul cites the case of Jannes and Jambres (3:8), the names given in some extracanonical writings to the magicians who opposed Moses and Aaron at the time of the Exodus (Exodus 7:11-8:19). They are said to have hindered the work of Moses and Aaron when Israel passed through the Red Sea. Indeed, they are even blamed for instigating Israel's apostasy in the golden calf incident of Exodus 32. Here Paul suggests the false teachers of the final days also oppose the truth, even as Jannes and Jambres opposed God's servants at a decisive moment in history. The false teachers are simply the contemporary example of a recurring pattern of opposition that has its roots deep in the history of God's people. Thus, the difficulties that Timothy experiences with false teachers in Ephesus are nothing new. In every era, there are those who oppose the word of truth.

These false teachers are described as people whose minds are thoroughly corrupt (Gk. *anthropoi katephtharmenoi ton noun*). They are simply unqualified (Gk. *a-dokimos*; literally, "failing the test, disqualified after the test") with regard to understanding the faith. Timothy is also to find strength and reassurance in this history lesson which includes the opponents' inevitable defeat: "But they will not get very far because, as in the case of those men, their folly will be clear to everyone" (3:9). Jannes and Jambres were defeated in their confrontation with Moses (see Exodus 8:18-19; 19:11) and the same fate awaits the opposing teachers of Timothy's situation.

On the surface, the message of 2:14-3:7 is crystal clear: avoid evil people. But at a deeper level, it aims to promote apt teaching by means of contrasting portraits of "the Lord's servant" (2:24-26) and Paul (3:10-16) on the one hand with the successors of Jannes and Jambres on the other. The ideal Christian teacher is to avoid arguing with his opponents, but he should not avoid the opponents themselves. On the contrary, he is to be gentle, patient, kind and to always act out of hope for their redemption. The opposing teachers depicted in 3:1-9 are associated with abuse, arrogance and self-love. They use deceitful tactics and capture their students rather than instruct them. This portrait of godlessness reinforces Paul's picture of the ideal Christian teacher by depicting its opposite.

Paul's Example of Suffering (3:10-17). Paul now offers his own life and ministry as a sharp contrast to the portrait of the opposing teachers given in the preceding passage. This positive Pauline example of 3:10-13 forms the basis for the final exhortation of 3:14-17. Unlike the false teachers of the last days ("You, however"), Timothy "closely and actively followed" (Gk. *parekolouthesas*) various aspects of Paul's life (3:10; 1 Timothy 4:6). He grasps and follows the truth as it is embodied in Paul's life. Indeed, the triad "my teaching, my way of life, my purpose" (3:10) means Timothy is familiar with the qualities and circumstances of Paul's life (see 1 Timothy 4:6; Luke 1:3). First, he closely follows the apostle's teaching (Gk. *didaskalia*). The singular form of the noun "teaching" is almost a technical term for "apostolic or Christian teaching." The Pastoral Letters consistently distinguish between authentic and false teaching by using, respectively, either the singular (Gk. *didaskalia*) or plural (Gk.

didaskaliai) form of the noun. This letter repeatedly indicates how much and how faithfully Timothy has learned from Paul (see 1:13-14; 2:2, 8-9, 11-13). Second, Timothy closely follows Paul's way or manner of life (3:10; Gk. *agoge*; literally, "way of life"). In these letters, teaching and conduct go together like hand and glove. Although Paul's manner of life is not described here, the four virtues that follow name its characteristic qualities. Faith and love are fundamental Christian virtues (see 1 Timothy 1:5, 14; 2:15; 1 Corinthians 13:13). Here they are enriched with patience (2:24; 4:2) and endurance, virtues repeatedly extolled in the surrounding exhortations (see 2:10, 12; Titus 2:2). Third, Timothy observes Paul's purpose (Gk. *prothesis*; literally, "resolve or aim"), which is consonant with God's purpose in choosing Paul for the apostolic work (1:9).

The focus now shifts to Paul's sufferings, which are described for the first time in this letter as "persecutions" (3:11; see also 2 Corinthians 4:9; 12:10; Galatians 5:11; 6:12; Acts 13:50). The language of 3:11 makes it appear as if hardship and difficulty are normative for a servant of the Lord. The references here to Paul's persecution in the three cities of Antioch, Iconium and Lystra in south central Asia Minor fit the narrative's pattern of Paul's travels as reported in Acts 13-14. The emphasis on Paul's suffering and endurance has a twofold message. First, it highlights the apostle's perseverance. He continues his ministry regardless of any and all difficulties. No obstacle prevents him from preaching the gospel. Second, it underscores the power of the gospel message. God empowers his messengers to spread his word in spite of difficulties. Thus, although the apostle's endurance of suffering and persecution is emphasized, the motif of deliverance surfaces in the final clause of verse 11: "Yes the Lord rescued me from all of them" (see Psalm 34:7, 17, 19). This theme of God's deliverance, which reappears with even greater emphasis in 4:17-18, recalls the initial exhortation to rely on God's power (1:8).

Persecution is also presented as part of a general pattern: "In fact, everyone who wants to live a godly life in Christ Jesus will be persecuted..." (3:12). However, Paul does not indicate the source of this general persecution of faithful Christians. Although Rome holds him prisoner at the time of this letter's writing and Jews are responsible for his persecution in the three cities of Asia Minor, Paul does not associate either Romans or Jews with the persecution common to God's faithful. Instead, he links the general pattern of persecution to opposition that arises from *within* the church.

The remark that "evil men and imposters will go from bad to worse, deceiving and being deceived" (3:13) echoes the traditional apocalyptic expectation that evil will gain momentum in the "last days" (see 3:1). Also, it indirectly predicts the success of Paul's opponents in Ephesus. Still, Paul is not pessimistic because their transformation from "bad to worse" and from "deceiving to being deceived" signals their own eventual demise. By calling them "imposters" (Gk. *goes*; literally, "magicians, charlatans, swindlers, cheats"), Paul underscores the connection between these "evil men" and the magicians Jannes and Jambres, all the while hinting at their treacherous and deceitful methods (3:6-8; 2:26; see also 1 Timothy 1:7; 6:5). Momentarily, Paul will exhort Timothy to live by an alternative set of values.

Final Charge to Timothy (3:14-17). The opening phrase of 3:14 in the NIV translation, "But as for you" (Gk. *sy de*), continues the basic pattern of contrast (see 3:10; 4:5). The "progress" of the evil men who go from bad to worse contrasts with the constancy of the Lord's servant: "Continue (Gk. *mene*) in what you have learned and have become convinced of" (3:14). Timothy is to model constant and continual habits based on the sound teaching he has learned and embraced (see 1:13; 4:3). The sound teaching refers to the gospel preserved and protected by the church as its tradition or "deposit" (see 1:14; 1 Timothy 6:20). The "one from whom" Timothy learned the gospel message must be Paul, who is called his instructor throughout these letters (see 1:13; 2:2; 1 Timothy 1:18). Since the pronoun "whom" is plural (Gk. *tinon*), Eunice and Lois are also included as sources "from whom (he) learned it" (3:14). Indeed, the reference to his childhood in 3:15 supports this hypothesis. Thus, while Paul is Timothy's primary instructor of the gospel message, others are included as those through whom, or with whom, Paul transmitted the deposit of faith (2:2).

If knowledge of the one from whom he learned the gospel message provides one reason for Timothy's confidence, another reason is his firm grounding in the Scripture from infancy (3:15). "The holy Scriptures" (Gk. *ta hiera grammata*; the definite article "the" (Gk. *ta*) is missing in some manuscripts, but that does not affect the meaning) is a technical term used by Greek speaking Jews for the Jewish Old Testament. Indeed, Timothy has only been instructed in Jewish Scriptures, not Christian ones, from babyhood (Gk. *apo brephous*) since the Christian writings were not yet in circulation. Still, Paul assures Timothy that these Jewish Scriptures "are able to make you wise for salvation through faith in Christ Jesus" (3:15; see also Romans 1:2; 15:4; Galatians 4:21-31). This last clause invites Timothy to respect his forefathers' tradition in a way that is decidedly Christian, for they have salvific value. Paul asserts that the sacred writings in which Timothy had been instructed since his youth explain salvation in light of their message about Christ Jesus.

Paul now digresses briefly to discuss the Scripture's usefulness: "All Scripture is God-breathed and is useful for teaching, rebuking, correcting and training in righteousness..." (3:16). The Greek word "scripture" in the NIV translation of verse 16 is different from the word in verse 15 (the singular noun, *graphe,* instead of the plural one, *grammata*). Although the Greek term, *graphe,* can mean "writing," it is generally a technical term for Scripture in Jewish and Christian contexts (see Romans 4:3; Galatians 4:30) and should be understood here as such.

The next term that the NIV translates as "God-breathed" (Gk. *theopneustos;* literally, "God-breathed, breathed into by God, inspired by God"), has spawned the most vigorous debate. The word recalls the account of Genesis 2, which describes the creative, life-giving power of God's breath (2:7; see also Job 33:4; Psalm 33:6). This Greek verbal adjective, *theopneustos* (sole occurrence in the NT) can have either an attributive or predicative relationship with its subject, "all Scripture." If attributive, then the text reads, "All Scripture inspired by God is also useful for ..." (so REB; NEB; NJB). If predicative, then it reads, "All Scripture is inspired by God and useful for ..." (so NIV, RSV, NRSV). The first reading implies that there are writings or scriptures that are not inspired and hence are not useful for the four purposes listed. The second reading suggests an opposite meaning: that all Scripture or every Scripture text is inspired and hence useful. Grammatically, both readings are sound. But in neither case does Paul develop a theory of inspiration (see 2 Peter 1:19-21). Paul assumes the inspiration of Scripture and mentions it here to highlight Scripture's origins and inherent authority, all of which complement its proven usefulness for ministry.

The thrust of Paul's statement is undoubtedly the usefulness (Gk. *ophelimos*) of Scripture (see also 1 Timothy 4:8; Titus 3:8). This contrasts sharply with his opponents' myths that simply "tickle the ears" (see 4:3-4). It is also possible that the phrase "all Scripture" is a polemic against the opponents who may deem only certain parts of Scripture as authoritative. In any case, the first practical use of Scripture relates to teaching, emphasized here by placing it first on the list of four activities mentioned (see 3:10; 4:2-3). The other activities—rebuking, correcting and training in righteousness—are highlighted in the Pastoral Letters especially, but not exclusively, in discussions that pertain to the opponents (see 2:25; 4:2; 1 Timothy 5:20; 6:11; Titus 1:9, 13; 2:12, 15).

The relationship between verse 17 and the preceding verse about Scripture's usefulness is quite clear in the NIV translation: "so that the man of God may be thoroughly equipped for every good work." The Greek text speaks of "the man of God" (Gk. *ho tou theou anthropos*) as the benefactor of Scripture's usefulness, not "everyone who belongs to God" (so NRSV's translation). This same phrase appears in 1 Timothy 6:11 where it refers to Timothy in his role as church leader. Considering that the thrust of the whole of the second letter to Timothy addresses the role of the church leader, Paul likely has the church leader and his ministry in mind (see also 2:21). Scripture, says Paul, is an inspired and useful resource to the church leader, especially as he instructs, rebukes, corrects and trains his opponents.

Application, Teaching/Preaching Points

Several very important contemporary messages for the church flow from this chapter of 2 Timothy. Let me mention a few of them here.

Do Virtues & Morals Really Matter? Paul unleashes a major attack against his opponents, accusing them of immoral behavior (3:2-9, 13). He assumes that bad ideas lead to bad morals. By condemning his opponents' morals, he simultaneously rules their ideas out of court. One often gets the impression today that the life of faith is divorced from this matter of virtues and vices. Indeed, some commentators are almost embarrassed by Paul's injunction to Timothy, urging him to pursue righteousness, faith, love and peace (2:22). They suggest that "righteousness" in this context somewhat perverts the pure gospel which emphasizes God's forensic declaration concerning humans. But Paul willingly speaks of righteousness as a virtue elsewhere too (see Romans 6:13, 19; 14:17). Indeed, virtues represent one's life habits and are consonant with faith in God. Authentic Christians exhibit a peculiar "character," a pattern of life shaped by the choices they make in daily life. This character, in turn, influences all of their subsequent choices. Thus, if the dominant pattern of a person's life is self-centered, hostile and deceitful (3:2-5), then such a person is not embodying the gospel message. However, if peace, love, righteousness and justice dominate a person's life, then such a pattern of living reflects the direct influence of God's good news. In short, it behooves us as God's people to cultivate patterns of behavior that truly embody the faith. We should ask: What are our habits of the heart? Virtues enable and facilitate our choice of the good.

Kingdom Mentoring: A Better Way. Paul reminds Timothy of the many factors that equip a person "for every good work" (3:17): a godly family heritage, Bible study, the example of godly men and women, and hands-on ministry experience. Like Jesus' disciples (John 14:12), Timothy is encouraged to do greater works than his mentor. Sadly, Timothy suffers from a lack of confidence. Happily, kingdom mentoring is designed to restore confidence in God's people so they can serve others in the style of their Lord. Kingdom mentoring is a bit like parenting. But unlike parenting, it is negotiated. Both parenting and mentoring are similar to leadership. Unfortunately, leadership is often structured and imposed, whereas kingdom mentoring is not. Both are similar to training; but kingdom mentoring is *high touch*, while training is often more *high tech*. This difference can be seen by studying Barnabas with Saul (see Acts 9:27; 11:22-30), Priscilla and Aquila with Apollos (Acts 18:24-28), and Paul with Timothy. Such mentoring is an intimate partnership between two strugglers in the Christian faith. Today's "Timothys" are more interested in our life experiences and life habits than in our ideas and rhetoric. Today's Timothys are over-exposed to the problems of dysfunctional families and to the breakdown of values, especially as portrayed on TV and the WEB. They are under-exposed to meaningful relationships with adults who embody the faith. Your Timothy in the marketplace could be any emerging worker who confesses Christ and who needs to be mentored by someone who has been following Christ a little longer. No doubt, there is a Timothy willing to follow in your footsteps—if you are available.

All of Scripture Has Value for Christians. This chapter of 2 Timothy underscores Scripture's value and usefulness for the Christian community. It employs the only biblical use of the Greek term *theopneustos*, "breathed by God" (3:16), which is applied to "all" or "every" (passage of) Scripture. There is no reference to the Holy Spirit here in our text as there is, for example, in 2 Peter 1:21. Nor do we have the suggestion here that God "played" on the human writers like a musician playing on an instrument. The message of our text is quite straightforward: Scripture teaches understanding of salvation and provides whatever believers need for instruction in the Christian way of life. The implication is that any and every passage of Scripture may have value for the Christian. Since "all Scripture" originates with God, it has authority, truthfulness and usefulness. The habit of applying this text of 2 Timothy 3:16-17 to the New Testament is justified. Indeed, some early Christian writings were already being regarded as Scripture by the time 2 Timothy was penned.

Personal Reflection Questions

• Paul paints a pretty negative picture of the last days. DISCUSS: The expression "lovers of" occurs four times in verses 1-4. Look at each one carefully. Do any of them apply to us? What do we really love most? What should a congregation do about the prevalence of vices within the church as described in 3:2-5?

• Paul suffered for the sake of the gospel. DISCUSS: Do we suffer from persecution today? Do we suffer "from" other people because of our commitment to the gospel or because of our insensitivity to them?

• The text teaches that Scripture equips us for daily life. DISCUSS: Is reading, studying and reflecting on Scripture the primary way God equips us for ministry? If not, list other vehicles God uses to prepare us for ministry in his name. How can we encourage our children, friends or fellow-Christians to value Bible reading in a TV- and computer-dominated society?

CHAPTER TEN

Faithful Church Leadership

The Text: 2 Timothy 4:1-22

In the presence of God and of Christ Jesus, who will judge the living and the dead, and in view of his appearing and his kingdom, I give you this charge: [2] *Preach the Word; be prepared in season and out of season; correct, rebuke and encourage— with great patience and careful instruction.* [3] *For the time will come when men will not put up with sound doctrine. Instead, to suit their own desires, they will gather around them a great number of teachers to say what their itching ears want to hear.* [4] *They will turn their ears away from the truth and turn aside to myths.* [5] *But you, keep your head in all situations, endure hardship, do the work of an evangelist, discharge all the duties of your ministry.* [6] *For I am already being poured out like a drink offering, and the time has come for my departure.* [7] *I have fought the good fight, I have finished the race, I have kept the faith.* [8] *Now there is in store for me the crown of righteousness, which the Lord, the righteous Judge, will award to me on that day—and not only to me, but also to all who have longed for his appearing.* [9] *Do your best to come to me quickly,* [10] *for Demas, because he loved this world, has deserted me and has gone to Thessalonica. Crescens has gone to Galatia, and Titus to Dalmatia.* [11] *Only Luke is with me. Get Mark and bring him with you, because he is helpful to me in my ministry.* [12] *I sent Tychicus to Ephesus.* [13] *When you come, bring the cloak that I left with Carpus at Troas, and my scrolls, especially the parchments.* [14] *Alexander the metalworker did me a great deal of harm. The Lord will repay him for what he has done.* [15] *You too should be on your guard against him, because he strongly opposed our message.* [16] *At my first defense, no one came to my support, but everyone deserted me. May it not be held against them.* [17] *But the Lord stood at my side and gave me strength, so that through me the message might be fully proclaimed and all the Gentiles might hear it. And I was delivered from the lion's mouth.* [18] *The Lord will rescue me from every evil attack and*

*will bring me safely to his heavenly kingdom. To him be glory
for ever and ever. Amen.* [19] *Greet Priscilla and Aquila and the
household of Onesiphorus.* [20] *Erastus stayed in Corinth, and I
left Trophimus sick in Miletus.* [21] *Do your best to get here before
winter. Eubulus greets you, and so do Pudens, Linus, Claudia
and all the brothers.* [22] *The Lord be with your spirit. Grace be
with you.*

The Flow and Form of the Text

Before announcing his imminent departure (4:6-8),
Paul delivers a five-point charge (4:1-5). He employs the
image of a solemn courtroom ceremony as he outlines the
charge to Timothy (see also 1 Timothy 5:21; 6:13), his suc-
cessor in the ministry of evangelizing and teaching. As he
follows Paul's example, especially as a preacher, Timothy
should expect to suffer even as Paul has suffered. The
motif of Christ's appearance ("his appearing" - 4:1 and 8)
frames this chapter's opening paragraph and defines it as
a discrete literary unit. By framing the charge within a
greater eschatological perspective that includes the final
judgment of all people (4:1), Christ's appearance to render that judgment, and Christ's heavenly kingdom promised for the righteous (4:8, 18), Paul injects a note of
urgency and importance to the charge. He continues to
maintain the two-stage eschatology with its distinction
between the "last days" (see 3:1) and "that day" (see 4:8).
Paul's departure and the last times precede "that day,"
the day of Christ's appearance. During the last days, people will prove to be dilettantes and skeptics, amassing
around them a plethora of teachers to tickle their ears.
But on "that day," a crown of righteousness will be given
to those who stand fast in their longing for Christ's
appearance.

Paul ends most of his letters with personal greetings
and travel plans. Second Timothy is no exception to the
rule (Romans 15:22-16:23; 1 Corinthians 16:5-24; Phile-

mon 22-25; Titus 3:12-15). Thus, the letter's conclusion includes personal greetings information about various co-workers, greetings and a final benediction (4:9-22). Throughout this passage, there are repeated requests for Timothy to come to Paul (4:9, 11, 13, 21). Also, the greetings and instructions are very detailed and quite ordinary, supporting the case for Pauline authorship.

The passage contains four distinct parts: instructions to Timothy interspersed with information about Paul's co-workers (4:9-15); a recollection of the early stages of Paul's trial, concluding with a formal word of praise to God (4:16-18); greetings to and from various persons (4:19-21); and a final benediction (4:22).

The Text Explained

Paul's Final Charge (4:1-5). The charge begins with a formula that echoes a solemn oath ("In the presence of God;" Gk. *enopion tou theou*) which recalls the biblical expression "before the Lord" (see 1 Samuel 7:6; Psalm 56:13; 61:7; 68:3), a formula frequently used with respect to judgment. Paul links the name of Christ Jesus with that of God (see also 1 Timothy 5:21), but depicts Christ Jesus alone as the one "who will judge the living and the dead" (4:1). By naming Christ Jesus as judge, Paul counters the claim that one of the gods or the emperor is the judge. Indeed, Paul's words are similar to Peter's speech in the house of Cornelius (Acts 10:39-43). However, unlike Peter's speech, Paul makes no explicit reference to Jesus' death and resurrection. Also, the formula here lacks the "subordination" of Luke's account where God, as the principal agent of judgment, appoints Christ as the judge of the living and dead. This nuance of the relationship between God and Jesus is absent here, for Paul juxtaposes God and Christ Jesus and attributes the judiciary role to Christ Jesus. Furthermore, Paul's favorite christological title, Lord (Gk. *kyrios*), is noticeably lacking in his reference here to Christ's judicial function, unlike Peter's speech where Peter says he is "Lord of all" (see Acts 10:36).

Paul believes in the imminent parousia of Jesus as Lord. Indeed, at one point in his ministry, he believes it will happen during his own lifetime (see 1 Thessalonians 4:15, 17). During the course of his ministry, however, that expectation seems to have waned and thus, his later writings do not suggest that the parousia is on the immediate horizon. The NIV translation, "who will judge the living and the dead" (4:1), fails to recognize the note of imminence signaled by the Greek text of 4:1, where Paul uses the participial expression "about to" (Gk. *tou mellontos*; literally, "who is about to judge ..."). The earlier idea that judgment is right around the corner has a lingering influence here. The expression, "the living and the dead" (4:1), is an example of the literary device called *merism,* where antithetical expressions are used to mean "all" (see 4:2). Christ Jesus will judge *all* people although, as Paul often states, not all will be dead at the moment of the parousia (see 1 Corinthians 15:51; 1 Thessalonians 4:15-17).

Paul uses a word of judicial vocabulary when he says, "I give you this charge" (Gk. *dia-martyromai*). Technically, it means "I call as witness" (see Deuteronomy 4:26; 8:19; 30:19; 31:28), which explains the abrupt transition from the two nouns in the genitive case ("God" and "Christ Jesus") to the pair of nouns in the accusative case ("appearing" and "kingdom"). Jewish tradition required a pair of witnesses in a judicial procedure (see Deuteronomy 17:6; 19:15). In biblical tradition, inanimate beings like "heaven" and "earth" were often called as witnesses. Traditional "kingdom" language, with its New Testament roots in the teaching and preaching of Jesus (see Mark 1:15), is rare in the Pauline writings (14 times); it appears only twice in the Pastoral Letters (2 Timothy 4:1, 18). To the more familiar language of "appearance" (Gk. *epiphaneia*), Paul adds "kingdom" language in 4:1.

The presence in the text of the initial "and" (Gk. *kai*) supports the NIV translation: "*and* in view of the appearing *and* his kingdom," suggesting a "both … and" understanding of these two themes. Christ's appearing refers to the parousia, and his kingdom's full manifestation is associated with it. Thus, "Timothy is being urged to do his work in a way that will lead to recognition and reward at the final judgment when Christ visibly rules" (Marshall 1999: 799).

The solemn charge to Timothy consists of five imperatives that enumerate his duties, with an additional four imperatives in 4:5. The imperatives focus on Timothy's faithful proclamation of the Christian message, with the corresponding discipline of people who are tempted not to listen. Timothy is to preach the word, be ready at all times, correct, rebuke and encourage (4:2; see also 3:16). "Preach the Word" (Gk. *keryxon ton logon;* see also 1 Timothy 2:7), a phrase that does not occur elsewhere, sums up the mission of evangelization, proclaiming the truth and refuting error. Mark characterizes Jesus' ministry as one of preaching (Mark 1:14). Thereafter, Mark, followed by Matthew and Luke (nine times each) describe Jesus as engaged in the task of preaching. What Jesus preached, however, was the "good news," "the gospel" (Gk. *to euangelion;* Mark 13:10; 14:9; 16:15). In Acts, Luke summarizes Paul's ministry as "preaching the kingdom" (see Acts 20:25; 28:31). But when Paul commissions Timothy, he charges him to preach "the Word" (4:2), not "the gospel" or "the kingdom." In the Pastoral Letters, "the Word" is used as a cipher for the Christian message. It is the word of God (2:9; 1 Timothy 4:5; Titus 1:3; 2:5), the message of truth (2:15), and the words of faith (1 Timothy 4:6). Five times this "word" is summarized in the so-called "trustworthy sayings." Thus, when Timothy is charged to preach "the Word," he is mandated to preach Paul's gospel message.

Timothy must be prepared (Gk. *epistethi*) to preach the
Word no matter what the circumstances; in good times
and in bad (Gk. *eukaioros akairos*). The *merism* is quite
intense because it lacks a conjoining particle in the Greek
text. Paul places two antithetical terms side by side to
speak about all times. Timothy is well aware that bad
times lie ahead (3:1-9, 12), for the opposition's teaching is
already causing problems in the community. After this
charge in 4:1-5, Paul reminds Timothy of the "good
times" that lie ahead (4:8).

The next three words challenge Timothy to correct,
rebuke and encourage (see 3:16). The Lord's servant must
correct people by noting moral and intellectual error,
rebuke them so as to diminish their evil deeds or prevent
it altogether, and encourage them to conduct themselves
in a way that is appropriate to their calling as God's people (1 Thessalonians 2:12). In doing this, Timothy is to
emulate Paul's patience and careful instruction (4:2; see
also 3:10). Earlier, Timothy was warned about how to
deal with his opponents; he is to treat them with gentleness (2:24-25).

Although presented as a description of the future (see
also 3:1; 1 Timothy 4:1), 4:3-4 actually describes the situation in Paul's time. It is an unfavorable time in the church
for the kind of sound teaching that is to characterize
Timothy's ministry (4:2). Here, as in 3:6-7, Paul places a
large part of the responsibility for these difficult times on
the hearers, rather than on the teachers, of the opposing
doctrines. The metaphor of being tickled in reference to
their hearing (Gk. *knethomenoi ten akoen*) alludes to a
curiosity that looks for interesting and spicy bits of information. This itching is scratched by the new teachers who
dabble in speculations, myths and debates (2:16; 3:7;
1 Timothy 1:4; 6:4-5; Titus 1:14; 3:9). These verses portray
a rather large-scale defection within the Ephesian church
to the opposing teachers (see also 1:15; 2:17; 3:13).

Presumably, people have no patience for sound and familiar doctrines. They prefer to heap up or amass (Gk. *episoreusousin*) "a great number of teachers to say what their itching ears want to hear" and "they will turn away from the truth and turn aside to myths" (4:3-4; see also 2:18; Titus 1:4). This picture of abandonment is reinforced on a personal level in the concluding section of this letter as Paul names the people who have deserted him (4:10, 14, 16).

In contrast to the opponents' negative behavior (Gk. *sy de*; literally, "but you;" 4:5), Paul calls Timothy to "keep (his) head in all situations" (4:5). This is a call to remain clear-sighted and prudent in spite of the challenges posed by a fickle congregation and the opposition's competing claims. Also, Timothy is to "endure hardship" (4:5), a reference to enduring the opposition presented by the new teachers. In this context, it goes hand in hand with doing "the work of an evangelist" (4:5). This last phrase does not refer to a special office within the church (see also Acts 21:8), but to the fundamental task of proclaiming and teaching the gospel. By way of summary, Timothy is "to discharge all the duties of (his) ministry" (4:5).

Paul's Imminent Departure (4:6-8). The example of Paul's life (3:10-11 and 4:6-8) frames the exhortations of this final section. In addition to supplying Timothy with a model for the behavior demanded of him, these verses hint strongly at Paul's imminent death. In effect, Timothy is not only called to imitate Paul, but serve in his place.

The exhortations of 4:1-5 are now grounded (Gk. *gar*; literally, "for") in the statements about Paul's imminent departure: "For I am already being poured out like a drink offering…" (4:6). The emphatic "I" (Gk. *ego*; literally, "as for me") contrasts with the equally emphatic "as for you" of 4:5 (Gk. *sy de*). With these words, Paul sharply contrasts his own struggles, which are completed, with

Timothy's, which continue. The cultic image of "being poured out like a drink offering" (Gk. *spendomai*) is a metaphor for death. The drink offering is a libation poured out, often on the ground or around the altar, in honor of a god (see Numbers 15:5; 28:7; 2 Kings 16:13; Jeremiah 7:18; Hosea 9:4). Elsewhere, Paul uses this same metaphor to refer to his death (Philippians 2:17), giving his final suffering a religious quality and a sign of his total dedication to God. Having set the stage by using a cultic metaphor for death, Paul makes his announcement: "... and the time has come for my departure" (4:6). This reference to his departure (Gk. *analysis*) echoes Philippians 1:23 where it also refers to his death.

Paul speaks about his ministry's completion in three ways. First, he has "fought the good fight" (Gk. *ton kalon agona egonismai*), a familiar image drawn from an athletic contest, not the battlefield (see also 2:5; 1 Timothy 4:7-10; 6:11-12; cf. 1 Timothy 1:18). It emphasizes an untiring struggle (see also Philippians 1:30; Colossians 2:1; 1 Thessalonians 2:2). Second, Paul has "finished the race" (4:7), a metaphor for life (Gk. *ton dromon teteleka*) frequently found in Paul's letters (see 1 Corinthians 9:24; Galatians 2:2; Philippians 2:16; 3:13-14). The same words found here are ascribed to him in Acts 20:24, although there the completion of the race is a future hope rather than an accomplished event. Third, he has "kept the faith" (4:7). This final clause speaks directly of Paul's fidelity to the truth, drawing on the peculiar use of the words "the faith" in these letters where they refer to the Christian message. All three clauses together portray Paul as having completed what the letter asks Timothy and other church leaders to do (see 1:13-14; 2:3-5, 15; 4:5). In other words, Paul's life and ministry epitomize the ideal church leader.

The image of the athletic games resumes in verse 8: "Now this is in store for me...." The expression "now"

(Gk. *loipon*) introduces a description of what is to happen to Paul, now that he has completed his assigned tasks. To the victor belongs the spoil. Paul is to receive "the crown of righteousness," the gift (see Philippians 3:9) that will be bestowed on him by the Lord, "the righteous Judge," on "that day," that is, on the day of judgment (see 1:12, 18). "That day" is also the day of the Lord's appearing or epiphany (see 4:1; 1 Timothy 6:14; Titus 2:13). The righteous Judge will award the crown of righteousness. The link between the quality of the crown and the quality of the judge is apparent: The righteous (*dikaios*) Judge will reward Paul with a metaphorical and righteous crown (Gk. *dikaiosynes*), symbolizing the reward for a life lived in proper relationship with the Lord and his people.

Paul carefully states that he is not the only one who will receive the victor's crown. Unlike the athletic games where there is only one winner (1 Corinthians 9:24), all who long for that day (Gk. *tois egapekosi*; literally, "those who love" it) will receive a similar crown (2:11-12; see also Titus 1:2; 2:13). In this way, Paul affirms the solidarity Christians share in salvation (see also 1:10). In the imagery of 4:8, the Lord our Savior presides over the ultimate games, giving a reward to all who long for his appearance. His "appearing" is God's ultimate gift: the Christian hope fulfilled and salvation realized.

Paul's life and ministry are a model for Timothy and thus, for all church leaders. But a warning accompanies this model, for the promises of God are conditional. The trustworthy saying of 2:11-13 establishes this point with clarity: "If we endure, we will also reign with him." Paul reinforces this point by exhorting Timothy in the shadow of the final judgment (4:1, 8). Since Paul faithfully completed his ministry assignment, he can face the final judgment with confidence (4:8). Timothy should conduct his ministry with full awareness of the eschatological consequences of faithful and/or faithless service.

Over the years, theological interest in this passage has been focused almost entirely on the nature and purpose of Scripture. For Paul, however, the primary issue is to foster faithful church leadership in a crisis situation. Paul provides the example for it; Scriptures provide a resource for it; the final judgment provides the motivation for it.

Personal Instructions to Timothy (4:9-15). This letter opens with Paul stating that he longs to see Timothy (1:4) and it closes with Paul asking for Timothy to come to him "quickly" (4:9). Four times (4:9, 11, 13, 21) Timothy is urged to come. Indeed, he is to make every effort (Gk. *spoudason*; literally, "be eager to") to come to Paul. Clearly, Paul is unable to visit Timothy (cf. Philippians 2:24; Philemon 24). If Timothy does as he is instructed, he will prove to be as faithful to Paul as Onesiphorus (1:15-18), and presumably Luke (see 4:11). The preceding references to Paul's imminent death (4:6-8) add a note of urgency to Paul's request. However, the major reason for Timothy's requested presence seems to be Paul's loss of companions and co-workers, not his imminent death. The theme of abandonment is stressed in this passage (4:10, 11, 16), picking up a theme introduced earlier in conjunction with Onesiphorus. Since Paul is in circumstances identical to what Timothy will encounter if, or when, the prediction of 4:3-4 is fulfilled, Paul's conduct serves as an example for Timothy and later church leaders to follow.

Paul supports his invitation to Timothy with a series of informative statements about his absentee co-workers and companions. Six of Paul's seven companions are, for a variety of reasons, no longer with him; "only Luke is with (him)" (4:11). Paul's remarks about these absentee companions are sandwiched between two requests that Timothy come to visit (4:9 and 21), creating the impression of a lonely apostle.

Demas is mentioned elsewhere in Paul's letters (Colossians 4:14; Philemon 24), with no hint of criticism. Here, he is presented as being in love with "this world" (Gk. *ton nyn aiona*), a comment that reflects an apocalyptic worldview in which the present age, deemed to be evil, is contrasted with the coming age (see 1 Corinthians 1:20; 2:6, 8; 3:18; 2 Corinthians 4:4; Galatians 1:4; Ephesians 1:21). Demas's attitude stands in sharp contrast to the disposition praised in 4:8 (love for Christ's appearing). In this context, love for "this world" probably connotes a reluctance to embrace the suffering and persecution that accompanies the gospel's proclamation. Crescens (sole occurrence in the NT) and Titus (presumably the same one addressed in the letter to Titus) are mentioned alongside Demas, giving one the impression that they too have abandoned Paul. But the text does not indicate the motivation for their departure. Perhaps their absence is mentioned to heighten the solitude of the apostle. "Only Luke is with me," writes Paul (see Colossians 4:14; Philemon 24). Luke, like Onesiphorus (1:16), is an exception to the rule.

Timothy is told to "get Mark and bring him with you, because he is helpful to me (Gk. *emoi euchreston*; literally, "useful to me;" see Philemon 11) in my ministry" (4:11). Mark, whom tradition reveres as the author of one of the canonical Gospels, is Paul's companion from his first missionary journey (see Acts 12:25; 15:37-39). The references to Luke and Mark imply that the authors, and perhaps the texts, of two of the canonical Gospels are with Paul. Thus, two pillars of early Christianity are closely identified with Paul.

Paul sends Tychicus to Ephesus, perhaps to replace Timothy when he departs to join Paul. Tychicus is closely identified with the Pauline mission (Acts 20:4; Ephesians 6:21; Colossians 4:7; Titus 3:12), although details about the nature of his ministry are not provided.

However, if Paul intends that Tychicus replace Timothy, then he would continue the Ephesian ministry begun by Timothy and mandated by this letter (2:15, 23-25; 3:14; 4:2-5).

Paul's request for his cloak, scrolls and parchments is an intriguing aspect of this letter (4:13), raising numerous questions. The first item on the list, "the cloak" (Gk. *phailone*), is associated by some commentators with the mantle of authority, recalling Elisha's succession to Elijah's prophetic office (see 2 Kings 2:13). The second and third items, "my scrolls (Gk. *ta biblia*), especially my parchments" (4:13), are frequently identified as the sacred Scriptures (see 3:15), or at least copies of Paul's own letters. However, the Greek term for parchments (*membranes*) is a common word meaning "notebooks" (see the REB and NEB translations). Also, the word translated in the NIV as "especially" (Gk. *malista*; literally, "above all") identifies the scrolls with the notebooks. Thus, Paul is simply requesting his personal notebooks, which he left at Troas in the care of Carpus (see Acts 20:7-12).

Alexander is likely the same person mentioned in 1 Timothy 1:20, but his identification as the Jew who was involved in the silversmiths' riot in Ephesus (see Acts 19:33) is less certain. In any case, he harmed Paul by speaking against him and the gospel, and the effects of Alexander's opposition linger on. Timothy is warned about him, implying that those who follow Paul in ministry can expect to follow him in persecution as well (3:12).

The reference to God's retribution picks up the earlier note of eschatological triumph: "The Lord will repay him for what he has done" (4:14; see 4:6-8; cf. Psalm 62:12; 28:4; cf. Romans 2:6). The conviction that God rewards the faithful (2:11-12a) finds its corollary in the conviction that God punishes the faithless (2:12b). But it is God's reward to the faithful that dominates the next passage.

Paul's First Defense (4:16-18). The theme of Paul's isolation continues with the words, "At my first defense, no one came to my support, but everyone deserted me" (4:16). The expression, "my first defense," (Gk. *prote mou apologia*) evokes an image of the judicial hearing that will have preceded Paul's imprisonment. It suggests a second hearing or trial that will lead to his anticipated death (see 4:6-8). However, if this is a reference to Paul's first Roman trial and imprisonment (see Acts 28), then it resulted in his release (2 Timothy 4:17), subsequent mission work including his work in Crete and Ephesus, and then finally a second arrest and imprisonment in Rome. In these letters, there is no other reference to an earlier Roman imprisonment, even when the context encourages it (see 3:10-11). Thus, it is likely that 4:16 refers to an earlier stage of the same trial described in Acts 23:1-11; 24:1-21; and 26:1-23. At the time of Paul's first trial, no one stands by him. Everyone leaves him in the lurch, underscoring his sense of isolation. The expressions, however, are hyperbolic, recalling the charge of 1:15. In reality, only Demas has deserted him (4:10) and Luke is still with him (4:11).

Paul emphasizes the strength, support and rescue that the Lord provides (4:17). Paul's experiences provide his delegate with an object lesson, for Timothy has been urged to rely on God's power and strength (see 1:8; 2:1). The message's proclamation to the Gentiles implies Paul's release. The statement that Paul was rescued "from the lion's mouth" should not be taken literally. Rather, it is a metaphor that celebrates Paul's rescue from the jaws of death, echoing the language of Psalm 22:21 (see also Psalm 7:2; 17:12; Daniel 6:20-22, 27) and expressing confidence in future rescues as well.

Admittedly, there is an apparent tension between this confident expectation of "rescue" (4:18) and the intimations of imminent death (4:6-8). However, the rescue operation described here is a rescue for "his heavenly kingdom," not necessarily a rescue for life "in the flesh" (cf. Philippians 1:22-26). Still, several comments in these final verses imply an ongoing ministry of some sort: the request that Mark (4:11) and the notebooks (4:13) be brought to him. Furthermore, the primary motive for Timothy's haste is not Paul's imminent death, but the onset of winter when sea travel becomes more difficult (4:21). In any case, the language of 4:18 reflects that of the psalms, especially with its petitions for and trust in God's deliverance (see especially Psalm 31:2, 22; 71:2, 4, 23; 144: 2, 7, 11). This passage is full of confidence and trust, concluding appropriately with words of praise that undoubtedly reflect the church's liturgy (see also 1 Timothy 1:17; 6:15-16).

Final Greetings and Benediction (4:19-22). Personal greetings are characteristic of Paul's letters. They portray the bonds of friendship and affection that link the Pauline churches to one another. Many of the persons named here are known from other New Testament writings. Priscilla and Aquila, for example, join Paul in planting the Ephesian church (see Acts 18:18-19, 24-25; cf. Romans 16:3; 1 Corinthians 16:19). Onesiphorus is mentioned earlier in the letter (1:16) as an example of a faithful Pauline companion. The reference to his household implies that he has died. Erastus is identified with Timothy in Acts 19:22 and as a resident of Corinth in Romans 16:23. Trophimus is mentioned, albeit briefly, in Acts 20:4 and 21:29. The people who send their greetings (Pudens, Linus, Claudia) are unknown, but their large number tends to modify the earlier portrait of the apostle's solitude and abandonment.

These concluding verses of 2 Timothy support the letter's fundamental theological message with its call to suffer hardship for the promise of eschatological reward. Paul is in prison. He is alone, abandoned by some and opposed by others. In sum, he suffers for the gospel (1:8). Yet there is no sign of weakness or regret. Although he awaits death, Paul energetically directs the work of proclaiming the gospel message (4:11-2). Even more: he professes his utter confidence in God's strengthening presence, faithful support and promised heavenly reward. In this way, he exemplifies the behavior and disposition he demands of Timothy.

The request for Timothy to come to Paul is likely a test for him to prove his loyalty. A reunion between them would demonstrate Timothy's lack of shame at Paul's circumstances and the gospel. In effect, Timothy is being asked to imitate the much-praised Onesiphorus (1:16-18). All subsequent generations demonstrate their loyalty and lack of shame when they do not abandon the Pauline standard of sound teaching; even when they are abandoned and reviled by others.

People like Demas demonstrate that deserting a co-worker in the faith is equal to the failure to endure hardship in ministry; it reveals a dangerous preference for this world over the appearing of Christ and the kingdom he brings. The example of Alexander suggests that opposing the Pauline message is tantamount to betraying Paul himself (4:11-12), thereby equating those who oppose him with those who persecute him (3:11).

At the same time, the many companions and co-workers—Crescens, Titus, Luke, Mark, Tychicus, Carpus, Priscilla, Aquila, Erastus, Pudens, Linus, Claudia, and even Timothy—demonstrate that the Pauline churches, the Pauline tradition and the Pauline gospel will survive the death of the apostle. The struggle will continue (3:1, 12; 4:3) and the Lord will remain faithful (2:13).

Application, Teaching/Preaching Points

Three features of this chapter require some comment and application to the contemporary church scene.

Knitting Networks for Kingdom Work. No one really works alone! Many co-workers and teams of people are needed for effective faithful ministry today. Other people cover weaknesses, blind spots, ego needs and abuses of authority that could ruin the good results God covets for our ministries. Paul is no different. He is no superman or solo operator. He is a network builder, as highlighted here (see also Romans 16). Among those he knits together in Ephesus are Luke, historian and beloved physician; Timothy, former trainee and now chief delegate in Ephesus; Tychicus, co-author and special courier; and Priscilla (Roman) and Aquila (Jewish), business partners and co-founders of the Ephesian church. Others are released for ministry elsewhere: Crescens to Galatia, Titus to Dalmatia, Erastus to Corinth, Carpus in Troas, and Trophimus in Miletus. Some fall along the way: including Demas who loves "this world" more than the gospel; Alexander who harms Paul by opposing his message; and Trophimus who takes sick in Miletus. Still others are restored to the ministry team, including John Mark who once dropped out when the going got tough (see Acts 13; 15:36-41) but ultimately proves useful to Paul in Rome (see Colossians 4:10; Philemon 24). Kingdom work requires network, teamwork and patchwork so that we can be knit together with God. God calls us to himself to be part of a well-knit team of people who partner with him in his world ministry. Are you growing in your ability to partner with God and others in kingdom work?

Shaped by the Language of the Faith. Paul frequently uses athletic language ("I have fought the good fight, I have finished the race"). But more often than not, he uses the language of his faith tradition to depict his circumstances. For example, instead of saying he is lonely, he claims he has been "abandoned." He does not say the Emperor will rescue him, but "the Lord will rescue me."

He does not say I have worked hard, but "I have kept the faith." Today, many of us resist such language as pious nonsense. We deplore people who use it because we believe they are hiding behind it or that they are out of touch with their real feelings. We believe such persons require linguistic therapy to unpack what they really want. But maybe, just maybe, this negative reaction to the use of our faith language together with its symbolic system, is just that, a cynical reaction. To be sure, we cannot simply imbibe the language of Paul and the Gospels, forcing our experience to match it. But neither can we abandon the language of the faith in favor of other linguistic systems like psychotherapy for it changes our identity as God's people. Language not only describes reality, it constitutes it. After all, there is a difference between "gut feeling" and "conscience." There is a difference between "error" and "sin." A great chasm separates "I'm OK, you're OK" from "the grace of God in Christ Jesus." The symbols and stories of our religious tradition not only identify us as God's people, they shape us and form us, and help us to perceive our lives in a unique way. We cannot eliminate our linguistic heritage as Christians. There is no simplistic solution to our problem. "It demands," writes Johnson, "the willingness of pastors and preachers and theologians and laypeople to exercise the asceticism of attentiveness in their use of language" (1987: 47). As we speak of our important life experiences, we need to employ the symbols and stories of our biblical and historical heritage to see how they fit our experiences and how our experiences fit them. Sometimes the "clothes" will not fit because they are too large or too small. Or maybe they won't fit because our faith in God has become too flabby, too meager.

On the Perseverance of the Saints. The Christian life is empowered and guaranteed by God. This is the unanimous conviction of most Christians with whom I am familiar. But most of my friends would be quick to add that the Christian life also depends on the individual believer's faith and commitment being supported by the Christian community. In the Pastoral Letters, these two dimensions of the Christian life seem to be placed side by side without ever suggesting that the believer is automatically carried safely through every danger and temptation to a heavenly reward, or that everything depends on the believer's personal commitment and effort. Thus, in contrast to some Christians like Demas (4:10), who fell away, there is the deep conviction of the Apostle Paul. Perseverance to the end is expressed as trust in God's faithfulness.

Personal Reflection Questions

• This chapter begins with the words "in the presence of God." DISCUSS: Do we "welcome" God to join our services of worship? Or, does God call and invite us to join in his work in the world? What difference does your answer make to the way you approach and celebrate in corporate Christian worship?

• Paul describes a time when people turn their ears away from the truth. DISCUSS: In what ways is our situation today similar to the one described in 4:3-4? How can we apply the remedies of 4:1-2 to our situation? Should there be any qualifications?

• "I have kept the faith," says Paul. DISCUSS: How important is human example for Timothy to understand the kind of ministry he should pursue? Which people—biblical, historical, contemporary—have been examples for you?

• The expression "his appearing" occurs twice in these verses. DISCUSS: What importance does Christ's future appearance have for our day-to-day lives? What did Christ's parousia mean to Paul? What do you think will happen to you on "that day"? Write your own epitaph as Paul does here. If your small group is a "safe place," share the results with one another.

- Paul says Demas loved this world. DISCUSS: What do you think it means in today's terms to "love this world"? What aspects of "this world" compete with following Christ?

- Paul had a large team of co-workers. DISCUSS: Do we do "ministry" in like fashion today? If not, what hinders our ability to do "team ministry?"

CHAPTER ELEVEN

The Need for Sound Teaching

The Text: Titus 1:1-16

Paul, a servant of God and an apostle of Jesus Christ for the faith of God's elect and the knowledge of the truth that leads to godliness—[2] *a faith and knowledge resting on the hope of eternal life, which God, who does not lie, promised before the beginning of time,*[3] *and at his appointed season he brought his word to light through the preaching entrusted to me by the command of God our Savior,*[4] *To Titus, my true son in our common faith: Grace and peace from God the Father and Christ Jesus our Savior.*[5] *The reason I left you in Crete was that you might straighten out what was left unfinished and appoint elders in every town, as I directed you.*[6] *An elder must be blameless, the husband of but one wife, a man whose children believe and are not open to the charge of being wild and disobedient.*[7] *Since an overseer is entrusted with God's work, he must be blameless— not overbearing, not quick-tempered, not given to drunkenness, not violent, not pursuing dishonest gain.*[8] *Rather he must be hospitable, one who loves what is good, who is self-controlled, upright, holy and disciplined.*[9] *He must hold firmly to the trustworthy message as it has been taught, so that he can encourage others by sound doctrine and refute those who oppose it.*[10] *For there are many rebellious people, mere talkers and deceivers, especially those of the circumcision group.*[11] *They must be silenced, because they are ruining whole households by teaching things they ought not to teach—and that for the sake of dishonest gain.*[12] *Even one of their own prophets has said, "Cretans are always liars, evil brutes, lazy gluttons."*[13] *This testimony is true. Therefore, rebuke them sharply, so that they will be sound in the faith*[14] *and will pay no attention to Jewish myths or to the commands of those who reject the truth.* [15] *To the pure, all things are pure, but to those who are corrupted and do not believe, nothing is pure. In fact, both their minds and consciences are corrupted.* [16] *They claim to know*

God, but by their actions they deny him. They are detestable, disobedient and unfit for doing anything good.

The Flow and Form of the Text

After a lengthy salutation (1:1-4), Paul launches into an explanation of his letter's purpose, omitting entirely his usual expressions of thanksgiving. Titus has been left on the island of Crete to "straighten out what was left unfinished," specifically to "appoint elders in every town" (1:5). This opening chapter lists the qualifications of elders (1:5-9). It includes a warning about "rebellious people," whom the elders are charged to rebuke and refute (1:10-16).

Paul insists that elders be "blameless" (Gk. *anegkletos*; 1:6, 7) and "hold firmly to the trustworthy message... so that he can encourage others by sound doctrine and refute those who oppose it" (1:9). With a list of vices to be avoided and virtues to be cultivated (1:6-9), Paul explains what he means by "blameless." In short, one who is blameless has a firm grasp of the gospel message and exhibits self-control along with control over his house-hold.

The character of the "rebellious people" is diametri-cally opposite to that of the elders'. The false teachers ruin entire households (1:11), demonstrating by their actions that the saying is true: "Cretans are always liars, evil brutes, lazy gluttons" (1:12). More importantly, they are not sound in the faith and their minds and con-sciences are corrupt (1:13, 15). The bottom line is that they are "unfit for doing anything good" (1:16). This motif of doing good works will be developed in the remainder of the letter. In sum, the false teachers are incapable of liv-ing moral lives or of teaching others to do so. Thus, Titus must appoint "blameless" leaders so that others can learn to live a virtuous life. After all, cultivating a people who live morally good lives depends upon sound teaching.

The Text Explained

The Salutation (1:1-4). The salutation of Titus (sixty-five words!) is longer than that of most other Pauline salutations, including those of 1 & 2 Timothy (thirty-two and twenty-nine words respectively). Only the salutations of Romans and Galatians are longer and more complex. Here, the length is due to the description of Paul's apostleship, explaining the goal and basis of Paul's assignment. As in 1 Timothy, this salutation refers to God's command, to hope, to God as Savior, and to its recipient as a "true son" in the faith.

Paul claims two titles for himself: the familiar "apostle of Jesus Christ" and the new "servant of God." Elsewhere Paul refers to himself as a servant or slave (Gk. *doulos*) of Jesus Christ (see Romans 1:1; Galatians 1:10; Philippians 1:1), thereby indicating the lordship of the one he serves. Also, he knows that all believers are enslaved to God (Romans 6:22) in the sense that they are committed to a life of obedience to him (see Romans 6:18). However, elsewhere he does not apply the title "servant of God" to himself or others even though it is frequently used in the Old Testament to refer to persons who served God in various leadership roles within Israel. Hence, by means of this ancient title, Paul identifies himself with the likes of David, Abraham, Moses and the prophets (2 Samuel 7:5; Psalm 105:42; Joshua 1:1-2; Jeremiah 25:4; Amos 3:7). In this way, Paul is situated within the history of God's people as one of God's agents, speaking and acting in his name and at his command (1:3; see also 2 Timothy 2:24).

The goal of Paul's apostleship is indicated by the word "for" in the NIV translation (Gk. *kata*; literally, "with a view to" or "for the furtherance of"): "for the faith … and… the truth." In the Pastoral Letters, these two terms are almost synonymous, although "knowledge of the truth" highlights the rational aspect of faith (see 1 Timothy

4:3b; also 2:4; 2 Timothy 2:25). While the term "truth" in this context includes the basic Christian message (see 1 Timothy 3:15-16; 4:3-4; 2 Timothy 2:18), nowhere does this letter spell out the precise content of the term. However, what is clear is that Paul's opponents reject the "truth" (1:14; 2 Timothy 3:8). Indeed, their message is nothing more than a "myth" (see 1:14). By contrast, "truth," one of the twin goals of Paul's apostleship, is "the truth that leads to godliness" (Gk. *aletheia kat'eusebeian*). It is truth based on, or leading to, genuine godliness; that is, it is the kind of truth that leads to a life of piety and reverence for God (see 1 Timothy 6:3-10; 2:2). In other words, correct belief is inseparably linked with appropriate behavior.

The NIV translation, "a faith and knowledge resting on (Gk. *epi*; literally, "based upon") the hope of eternal life" (1:2), makes "the hope of eternal life" the basis of "faith and knowledge" (these last two terms are not found in the Greek text of verse 2a). However, it is not grammatically clear whether "the hope of eternal life" further defines the aim of Paul's apostleship, the nature of godliness, or the basis of faith and knowledge of the truth. The phrase leads naturally to the next point concerning the revelation of God's previously hidden plan. The terms of verses 2b-3 are unique and the syntax is awkward. But the theme is familiar Pauline teaching (see Romans 16:25-26; 1 Corinthians 2:7-10; Colossians 1:25-26). The basic contrast is between a promise made "before the beginning of time" (Gk. *pro chronon aionion*; literally, "before eternal times") and its revelation through the event of preaching the gospel. The text, quite literally, speaks of a revelation of God's word (Gk. *ton logon autou*; literally, "his word") in "its own appointed times" (see 1 Timothy 6:15; 2:6), in contrast to the NIV translation: "at his appointed season" 1:3a). In the Greek text, the plural "times" (Gk. *kairois*) indicates that every apostolic proclamation reveals God's promise of salvation. Thus, the "word" is the gospel message (see 2 Timothy 2:9), which unveils the eternal promise whenever it is proclaimed by Paul, by Titus (3:8), or by any other appointed church leader (1:9).

Since God's promise of salvation anchors the gospel's proclamation, it is appropriate to call God "Savior" (1:3b). However, in the next verse, Christ is also called "Savior" (1:4b), probably because it is only through Christ that the promise of salvation can be realized, as 2:13-14 and 3:6-7 make clear.

Like Timothy, Titus is greeted as Paul's "true son" (1:4a). Here, Paul includes an additional reference to "our common faith" (Gk. *kata koinen pistin*; literally, "according to the common faith"), meaning the faith shared by all authentic Christians (1:1; see also 1 Timothy 1:3-5). However, in this context it refers specifically to the shared faith of Paul and Titus. Hence, when the opponents are mentioned later in the letter, the contrast with Titus is evident; they do not share Paul's faith (1:13, 16; 3:11) and are therefore not his legitimate heirs.

One of the distinctive features of the Pastoral Letters is the emphasis on Jesus' coming as an epiphany; that is, a revelation of God's salvific intentions. Frequently, the Christ-event is viewed globally and compressed into a single revelatory moment (see 2 Timothy 1:8-10; Titus 3:4; 1 Timothy 2:3-6). No attempt is made to link this revelatory moment with earlier revelations of God's saving nature, such as the Exodus from Egypt, the covenant at Sinai or the promises to David. In other words, there is no sense of "salvation history" in the Pastoral Letters, just God's plan of salvation revealed through an isolated and singular Christ-event.

A unique feature of revelation does, however, emerge in this salutation. Instead of emphasizing earlier revelations of God's salvation plan, subsequent revelations of God's plan occur as the gospel message is proclaimed by

Paul and his successors (2 Timothy 1:10b), thereby creating multiple revelatory moments. The Christ-event is the primary revelation, but every subsequent apostolic proclamation of the gospel is a revelatory moment in as much as the word proclaimed reveals God's saving intentions for humanity. Indeed, even Paul's own life story reveals God's saving grace (see 1 Timothy 1:13-16), and local church leaders whose lives embody the gospel message reveal the transforming power of God's grace (1 Timothy 4:11-16). Given this emphasis on God's saving nature, the Pastoral Letters contribute to the ongoing revelation of God's salvific character and will.

Qualifications for Church Leaders (1:5-9). The opening verse of this passage sets the stage for the letter by referring to Paul's ministry on the island of Crete. Presumably, this visit to Crete occurs after Paul's release from Roman imprisonment as described in Acts 28:16-31. However, there is no supporting evidence in Paul's letters or in the book of Acts for such a mission, apart from the fact that Paul's ship lands at Crete while on his way to Rome (see Acts 27:7-13). Crete, a Mediterranean island, has a sizeable Jewish population, making the reference to the "circumcision group" plausible (1:10). Its seaports provide pirates with a safe haven and its inhabitants are widely known for their excesses, especially their incurable love of lies (1:12).

The instructions to Titus are broadly defined: "The reason I left you in Crete was that you might straighten out what was left unfinished…" (1:5). Apart from the appointing of elders, it is difficult to determine what other matters are "left unfinished," especially since the balance of the letter consists of basic ethical exhortations.

The qualifications for church leaders seem to be presented in two parts: the first to an "elder" (1:5, 6; Gk. *presbuteros*) and the second to an "overseer" (1:7-9; *episkopos*). If so, the same basic qualification applies to both an elder and an overseer: "blameless" (1:6, 7; Gk. *anegkletos*; literally, "above reproach, without indictment"). Some interpreters assume that the two terms, elder and overseer, are interchangeable and refer to the same leadership position. However, the information supplied by 1 Timothy suggests two distinct roles and positions within the community. For example, an overseer is expected to exercise a teaching role (1:9; 1 Timothy 3:2), but only some elders serve as teachers according to 1 Timothy 5:17. It is likely that all overseers are elders, but not every elder is an overseer. An overseer is probably chosen from among the ranks of the elders as a leader over them and over the church in a specific locale (see 1 Timothy 3:1-7). Hence, the qualifications for an overseer and elder seem to overlap, although the positions are distinct. Paul's focus, however, is not on the leadership positions *per se*, but on the qualifications for these roles within the community. The qualifications are essentially an edifying list of virtues that stand in stark contrast to the "rebellious people" whom the overseer is expected to refute.

The two-part list of qualifications corresponds to a similar list in 1 Timothy 3:1-7. The stipulation that an elder's children not be "open to the charge of being wild and disobedient" (1:6) seems to be framed with the "rebellious people" of 1:10-16 in mind. These children are to be "believers" (Gk. *pista*), requiring not only that the children be Christians (see also 1 Timothy 6:2), but also that they exhibit a pattern of loyalty that is the opposite of rebellion. Paul seems to indicate that an elder's ability to prevent rebellion in his own household bodes well for successfully dealing with instances of disloyalty in the church. This link between family management and church leadership is not as explicit as in 1 Timothy where the church is identified as "God's household" (1 Timothy 3:15), but the definition of an overseer as one who is "entrusted with God's work" makes the same point. The final item on the list for an overseer seems important since Paul elaborates upon it (1:9). It reflects Paul's concern for sound or healthy teaching; that is, teaching that does not deviate from the received tradition (see 2:1; 1 Timothy 1:10-11; 4:6; 2 Timothy 1:13; 2:24-25). If 1 Timothy 3:2 reflects a concern for an overseer's ability to teach, here it reflects a concern for his knowledge and understanding of the church's sound doctrine. This knowledge is to be the basis of an overseer's exhortations (Gk. *parakalein*; NIV: "encourage") of the faithful, and his correction (Gk. *elegchein*; NIV: "refute") of the opponents.

Warning about Rebellious People (1:10-16). The troublemakers in the Christian community on the island of Crete are called "rebellious people" (Gk. *anhypotaktoi*), a charge that stands out from the more generic items that follow. This charge is anticipated in verse 6 where one of the requirements of an elder is the ability to quash this sort of behavior. The Greek word, formed by adding a negative prefix ("*an*") to a word meaning "subordinate," describes an unruly independent spirit that refuses to show respect and proper submission to persons in authority. The issue with these people is framed initially, not in moral or theological terms, but in social categories. To be sure, the following verses indicate that these people also rebel against the truth. Still, given the insubordinate nature of these troublemakers, the threat clearly comes from among the ranks of God's people on the island of Crete. Thus, some believers within the church are rejecting the established leadership together with its message. This may explain the letter's concern for wives to be submissive to husbands (2:5), slaves to masters (2:9), and the whole community to be subject to rulers and authorities (3:1). That is, there is a general concern for maintaining the social order.

The concluding verse of this chapter levels a string of charges against these rebellious people. First, they are described as "detestable" (Gk. *bdelyktoi*; literally, "loathsome or abominable"), a very harsh term used elsewhere in the New Testament of the temple's desecration that would signal the final days of this age (see Matthew 24:15; Mark 13:14). It is also a word with ethical overtones, as seen in its application to the "whore of Babylon" in the canonical Apocalypse (Revelation 17:5; Leviticus 18:26-30). This ethical nuance prevails in Titus. The next two charges focus on the rebellious people's behavior: they are "disobedient" and "unfit for doing anything good" (1:16). The same ideas resurface in positive form in the letter's concluding exhortations: "Remind the people … to be obedient, to be ready to do whatever is good" (3:1). Indeed, the call to do "good works" is a recurring theme in this letter (2:7, 14; 3:1, 8, 14).

This passage also reveals some concrete facts about the rebellious group within the community. First, there are "many" of them (1:10), indicating that the opposition has substantial numbers (see also 2 Timothy 3:1-2; 4:3). Although their "minds and consciences are corrupted" (1:15), Paul still holds out some hope that, after rebuking them, they will become "sound in the faith" (1:13). They seem to be linked with Judaism (1:10, 14), although there is no indication here that they are pressing the Pauline issue of works of the law (see Romans 3:19-31; Galatians 3:10-29). Instead, these people seem to be influenced by Jewish myths and genealogies. Again, Paul's refusal to engage his opponents in debate prevents the interpreter from identifying their theology with greater precision.

They are also charged with "ruining whole households" (1:11), but there is no specific indication of how these families are being "ruined." It may be by means of quarrels and divisions initiated by the opponents (3:9), by moral corruption (3:11), or by destroying their faith (1:9; 2:1). If the rebels reject marriage (see 1 Timothy 4:3), there is a clear connection with "ruining" families since a refusal to marry undermines the family's very foundation. Also, the conviction that "nothing is pure" (1:15) may be the basis for the opponents' ascetic withdrawal from the material world (1 Timothy 4:4).

The opposite conviction, "to the pure all things are pure" (1:15), is found in numerous New Testament texts (Mark 7:14-23; Luke 11:41; Acts 11:9; Romans 14:14, 20; 1 Corinthians 10:23-30) and is based on a positive view of creation. The "pure" are those with pure or clean hearts (1 Timothy 1:5; 2 Timothy 2:22) and consciences (1 Timothy 3:9; 2 Timothy 1:3), not those who follow an ascetic lifestyle. By contrast, Paul condemns his opponents soundly as having corrupted minds and consciences (1:15). Indeed, he cites the words of one of their own prophets against them: "Cretans are always liars, evil brutes, lazy gluttons" (1:12). The prophet is not named, but later church writers identify him as Epimenides of Knossos, a sixth century B.C. seer and writer.

According to this chapter, the primary issue facing the Cretan church is that some of God's people are teaching "things they ought not to teach" (1:11). Such behavior is as an act of flagrant insubordination. The content of this teaching is not clearly indicated, yet it includes some theological speculations designed to ground their ascetic way of life. In any case, by challenging the church's basic authority structure and by forbidding marriage, the opponents are ruining the family structure that serves as the basic model for the local church.

Paul's harsh condemnation of his opponents on the island of Crete is unmatched in the Pastoral Letters. He employs a familiar racial slur that essentially dehumanizes his opponents as "liars," "evil brutes," and "lazy gluttons" (1:12). Then he instructs Titus to "muzzle" or "gag" them (Gk. *epistomizein*; NIV "silence"). Furthermore, all Cretans are included in this brutal condemnation. One can only imagine the impact such an attitude had upon Titus's missionary activities in Crete.

This passage sends two pairs of messages, one theological and the other ethical. First, the gospel message of God's goodness and loving-kindness (3:4) seems admirably suited to an island notorious for its wickedness. Indeed, Paul's own pre-Christian life was not unlike that of the Cretans as described here. He was also enslaved to various passions and pleasures, filled with malice and envy, and generally despicable (3:3). In spite of Paul's former life, God's goodness resulted in his salvation. Thus, there is hope even for the rebellious Cretans. Indeed, Paul holds out hope for their salvation (1:13) and insists that God's grace brings salvation to all (2:11; see also 1 Timothy 2:4-6). The extremely negative portrait of the Cretans illustrates the perils of disobedience and rebellion. Yet, this letter assures us that even "Cretans" are not outside the reach of God's goodness and salvation, even though Paul displays no great enthusiasm for the endeavor (3:10-11).

Second, this passage provides a model, albeit questionable, for church leaders. Titus and overseers are charged with the task of refuting or rebuking (Gk. *elegchein*) their opponents sharply (1:9, 13). Indeed, 1:10-16 sets the pace for this activity. But Paul's tone is exceedingly harsh as it is elsewhere when he delivers strident rhetoric (2 Corinthians 11:13-15; Philippians 3:2). By contrast, in 2 Timothy 2:25 Paul provides a more adequate approach for dealing with the opposition: one that advocates gentleness instead of invective. Surely this second model mirrors more accurately the actions of God and Christ (see 3:4; 1 Timothy 1:16).

Application, Teaching/Preaching Points

This portion of Scripture is so defined by its historical context that it can be difficult to imagine its relevance for the 21ˢᵗ century. Yet it does speak to our day, especially at the level of confusing faith with fanaticism, and the need for church leaders who have the gifts and graces necessary to cultivate faith communities.

Confusing Faith with Fanaticism. In many respects, we live in a day of fanaticism. There is very little to distinguish passionate—even violent—behavior from intense commitment to religious or ideological beliefs. Indeed, the two seem to go together. Today, many "true believers" are those most committed to forms of violence against "nonbelievers." This is not only true among Shiite terrorists, but also among Christian cults that demand great personal rigor and dedication from their adherents. Perhaps persons raised in an enlightened and tolerant context experience moral uncertainty and confusion. Such people grow hungry for moral clarity and spiritual purpose. If these are not available in their own world, they tend to seek them in another. As Johnson says, "It is the atmosphere of moral chaos and lassitude which provides the best ground for conversion to a cult or the eager embrace of a moral legalism" (1987: 121). Perhaps the real appeal of cults is that they offer the possibility of a human life with structure, coherence, clarity and, above all, choice and commitment. Thus, the great popularity of inhumane and intolerant creeds may well derive from a context of religious and moral instability. People are looking for a way to live and we can learn from Titus that what people most want is to be able to commit themselves to some value or cause that needs them. If so, we need to know what we believe and how we should act so that we have something to say to people who are searching for meaningful commitment today.

Five Vices Responsible Church Leaders Avoid. The brief list of vices to avoid (Titus 1:7) has often puzzled commentators because the standard seems too low; more like the basic standard appropriate for unbelievers than saints. However, such a reaction reflects a lack of realism. It is pointless to pitch standards so impossibly high that people in leadership get discouraged. A modern description of the people's behavior on the Island of Crete suggests that things have not changed much in 2000 years! The five vices to avoid are still appropriate for leaders in the 21st century. They are: 1) Avoid being overbearing; that is, stubborn or pigheaded. This describes people who stick to their opinion even when a ton of good reasons oppose it. 2) Avoid being quick tempered; that is, easily angered and then remaining angered forever and a day. 3) Avoid drunkenness; that is, church leaders should not overindulge in wine or any other drug that debilitates the senses. 4) Avoid being violent; that is, avoid striking out at people with either "fists" or "words." 5) Avoid pursuing dishonest gain; that is, refuse to make money in a disgraceful fashion like the Cretans who stick to money like bees to honey.

Wanted: Church Leaders With Convictions. Paul begins 1 Timothy with the false teachers; then he shifts to speaking about the kind of people who will replace them. He begins Titus with the matter of appointing church leaders; then he shifts to the issue of false teaching. What is clear in Titus is that any leader serving in the local church must clearly grasp the basics of the Christian faith. This entails more than remembering certain doctrines, signing a doctrinal statement, parroting them in an interview or regurgitating them for an examination. It is not enough to attend a course or obtain a degree from an accredited school. Leaders need to be devoted to the gospel with strong convictions and capable of recognizing deviations from biblical teaching. If they lack convictions, their leadership will lack purpose and direction and the faith community will suffer the consequences. This is a stronger statement than earlier requirements of elders and deacons (1 Timothy 3:2, 9). According to Titus, church leaders play a dual role in a faith community; namely, they encourage others with sound or healthy teaching and they refute those who oppose the gospel message.

The Power of God's Transforming Grace. Paul undoubtedly studied the Greek philosophers of his day, even as we study English literature. Sometimes we even recall it, to everyone's surprise. Here in Titus, Paul quotes Epimenides of Knossos, a Cretan philosopher from around 600 BC whom Aristotle called a prophet (see another Epimenides quote in Acts 17:28, "In him we live and move and have our being"): "Cretans are always liars, evil brutes, lazy gluttons." Then Paul says, "This testimony is true" (Titus 1:12-13). Paul's agreement with his philosopher "friend" reveals considerable down-to-earth realism on his part. It must have been a tough assignment for Titus to teach some of his Cretan converts to forsake their engrained cultural values, and become Christians who embody the values of God's kingdom. If we are amused by the shortcomings of the Cretans, perhaps we should turn the spotlight on ourselves. We are also influenced and shaped by the culture in which we live. All human nature is flawed and every culture has its own version of that marred nature. We can be so immersed in our own culture that we fail to see its shortcomings objectively, let alone repent of them. Perhaps people from other cultures might be better able to criticize us, although they are usually too polite to oblige. What is encouraging about Paul's approach here is that he doesn't write the Cretans off. Why? Because he believes in the power of God's transforming grace. And so should we.

Personal Reflection Questions
• Titus is to appoint elders who are blameless. DISCUSS: How are your church leaders chosen? For their gifts?

Their learning? Their character? Which is more important? Why? Is the quality of life expected of church leaders in the public eye too high or too low? In what ways do we expect more from them than we do from ourselves? How can we help them?

- According to Paul, some members must be encouraged and others refuted. DISCUSS: How can a church differentiate between members with shortcomings who require encouragement, and fundamentally corrupt members who require rebuke?

- "Cretans are always liars, even brutes, and lazy gluttons." DISCUSS: Paul would be accused of racism if he made these remarks today (1:12). Under what circumstances should Christian preachers use this kind of language?

CHAPTER TWELVE

The Pedagogy of God's Grace

The Text: Titus 2:1-15

You must teach what is in accord with sound doctrine. [2] *Teach the older men to be temperate, worthy of respect, self-controlled, and sound in faith, in love and in endurance.* [3] *Likewise, teach the older women to be reverent in the way they live, not to be slanderers or addicted to much wine, but to teach what is good.* [4] *Then they can train the younger women to love their husbands and children,* [5] *to be self-controlled and pure, to be busy at home, to be kind, and to be subject to their husbands, so that no one will malign the word of God.* [6] *Similarly, encourage the young men to be self-controlled.* [7] *In everything set them an example by doing what is good. In your teaching show integrity, seriousness* [8] *and soundness of speech that cannot be condemned, so that those who oppose you may be ashamed because they have nothing bad to say about us.* [9] *Teach slaves to be subject to their masters in everything, to try to please them, not to talk back to them,* [10] *and not to steal from them, but to show that they can be fully trusted, so that in every way they will make the teaching about God our Savior attractive.* [11] *For the grace of God that brings salvation has appeared to all men.* [12] *It teaches us to say "No" to ungodliness and worldly passions, and to live self-controlled, upright and godly lives in this present age,* [13] *while we wait for the blessed hope—the glorious appearing of our great God and Savior, Jesus Christ,* [14] *who gave himself for us to redeem us from all wickedness and to purify for himself a people that are his very own, eager to do what is good.* [15] *These, then, are the things you should teach. Encourage and rebuke with all authority. Do not let anyone despise you.*

The Flow and Form of the Text

After explaining the need for sound teachers (1:5-16), Paul provides Titus with examples of the sound teaching he and his colleagues must pursue. This teaching is

directed to various groups within the church (see
1 Timothy 5). While the teaching's content seems highly
moralistic, it is rooted in Paul's understanding of God's
grace. Therefore, after providing Titus with instructions
for older and younger men and women as well as slaves
(2:1-10), Paul relates the behavior he requires to God's
grace (2:11-14). The concluding verse (2:15), with its reference to "these things," provides a transition to the next
section (3:1-2).

An important pattern emerges in this chapter of Titus.
Paul provides his delegate with sound teaching (2:1-10)
and then explains the theological basis for the conduct he
urges (2:11-14). Indeed, in the next chapter he provides
another example of sound teaching (3:1-2) and again
explains why believers must act in a morally acceptable
manner (3:3-7). In each case, transitional statements occur
in 2:15 and 3:8. Thus, the instructions of 2:1-3:11, together
with their theological warrants, constitute the heart of
this hortatory letter, with chapter 1 playing an introductory role.

Flow of Titus 2:1-3:11

Sound Teaching	2:1-10
God's Grace	3:11-14
Transitional Statement	2:15
Sound Teaching	3:1-2
God's Grace	3:3-7
Transitional Statement	3:8
Sound Teaching	3:9-11

At one level, the list of virtues and vices comprising
2:1-10 is similar to the material of 1:5-9 (see also
1 Timothy 3:1-13). Except here, the virtues to cultivate
and the vices to avoid are presented as general ethical
instructions for specific groups rather than qualifications

for church leaders. The basic categories are age groups within the church (see also 1 Timothy 5:1-2). However, elements of the household management tradition can also be discerned here. The household code often treats relationships in paired groupings (husbands and wives, masters and slaves, parents and children), emphasizing the pattern of authority and subordination that defines the patriarchal family. The influence of this traditional structure is observed in the instructions to younger women (who are to be submissive to their husbands) and to slaves (who are to be submissive to their masters). With their patriarchal framework, these exhortations mirror the ethical ideals promoted by Greco-Roman and Jewish societies. The uniquely Christian elements are identified by means of the purpose clauses (Gk. *hina;* "so that") as seen in verses 5, 8 and 10. They include the traditional material cited in 2:11-14, which serves as the theological warrant for the teaching of 2:1-10.

The Text Explained

Examples of Sound Teaching (2:1-10). The NIV translation of 2:1 omits an important Greek word that contrasts Titus with the rebellious people of the preceding paragraph (Gk. *sy de;* literally, "But as for you"). Indeed, Paul sandwiches his description of the rebellious people (1:10-16) between two counterexamples of faithful people: the elders who are faithful teachers (1:5-9), and Titus who faithfully declares (Gk. *lalei;* NIV: "teach") what accords with sound doctrine (2:1-10). This concern for sound doctrine (Gk. *hygiainouse didaskalia;* literally, "healthy teaching") permeates the Pastoral Letters (1:9; 1 Timothy 1:10; 6:3; 2 Timothy 1:13; 4:3). However, it is important to note that the passage under consideration does not define doctrine, but rather the moral conduct that is consistent with it. Paul assumes that good behavior flows from sound teaching, whereas any deviation from this teaching can only produce morally flawed conduct. Thus, Paul engages the opposition at the level of praxis, not theory.

The instruction to older men begins with a triad of virtues ("temperate, worthy of respect, self-controlled") that emphasizes moderation, an ideal extolled by Paul and his culture (2:2). Elsewhere in the Pastoral Letters, the same virtues are presented as requirements for both men and women in church leadership (see 1 Timothy 3:2, 8, 11). Here they define the behavior of all older men, likely understood to be men over 60 years of age. The next triad of virtues ("faith, love, and endurance") are more readily identified as Christian. Here, however, "endurance" replaces "hope" as the third virtue (2:2; see also 1 Timothy 6:11; 2 Timothy 3:10; cf. 1 Corinthians 13:13; Galatians 5:5-6; Colossians 1:4-5; 1 Thessalonians 1:3; 5:8). This is not the traditional Pauline endurance (Gk. *hypomone*) expressed as patience in the face of affliction, for no persecution is even mentioned in this letter (cf. Romans 5:3; 2 Corinthians 1:6). The context in Titus suggests instead either a patient waiting for the hope of eternal life to be fulfilled (see 1:2; 2:13; 3:7), or an endurance that applies to doing what is good (see 2:14; 3:1, 8, 14), or an adherence to the truth (see 1:1; 1:14). The emphasis is surely on the issue of sound doctrine or healthy faith, a sharp contrast with the opponents (see 1:13).

Earlier exhortations to older women are echoed in this passage, but with different language. Here they are exhorted not simply to the modest and decent behavior expected of all Greco-Roman women (see 1 Timothy 2:9), but to the "reverent" (Gk. *hieroprepeis*) behavior appropriate for holy persons. This word does not suggest that "older women" have a priestly role within the church; it connotes no more and no less than the "holy" behavior expected of all Christians (1 Timothy 2:15; 2 Timothy

2:21). Paul aims to draw as sharp a contrast as possible between a Christian woman's conduct and the defiled (1:15), loathsome (1:16) behavior of the rebellious teachers. Older women are also warned about excessive talk. In particular, they are not to be "slanderers" (Gk. *diabolous*), a characteristic of the moral decay peculiar to the last days (see 2 Timothy 3:3). It is also the chief trait of Satan, called "the Slanderer" (Gk. *ho diabolos*; NIV: "devil") in passages such as 1 Timothy 3:6-7 and 2 Timothy 2:26. Drunkenness is a frequently mentioned vice in these letters (see 1:7; 1 Timothy 3:3, 8, 11). However, only here does Paul warn against addiction (Gk. *dedoulomenas*; literally, "enslaved") to wine (2:3), a likely contrast with enslavement to God (1:1; see also 3:3).

An entirely new virtue is mentioned next as Paul urges the older women "to teach what is good" (Gk. *kalodidaskalous*; sole occurrence in the New Testament). Clearly, this teaching is distinct in several ways from what Paul has prohibited in 1 Timothy 2:12. It is to be done in the home context, not in the corporate worship setting. Its content is domestic matters, not doctrinal issues. Finally, the students are younger women, not the gathered community.

Some interpreters understand the older women of Titus 2 to be in the same category as the female deacons of 1 Timothy 3, with the teaching responsibilities described here signifying one of their assignments within the community. To be sure, the expected virtues of women deacons and older women do overlap, but there is no indication in Titus that the older women hold a leadership position within the church even though the behavior they teach benefits the community (3:5b). Indeed, the teaching of domestic skills mentioned here is the typical provenance of older women in Greco-Roman society.

The behavior encouraged of younger women is the goal of the older women's domestic teaching. In fact, the pattern of parallel instructions to various age groups is broken here. Unlike the instructions for the other age groups, those for the younger women are quite specific to their life situation. Indeed, the sheer length of these instructions implies a special interest in this group. Perhaps the damage to homes by the opponents (1:11) was especially acute among the families of these younger women, prompting Paul to focus his remarks to them on matters designed to strengthen the family structure.

The specific instructions to younger women open and close with comments pertaining to a proper relationship between wives and their husbands (3:4-5), encouraging a standard of domestic behavior that is the ideal in Greco-Roman and Jewish cultures. Interestingly, there is no corresponding set of instructions to the husbands. Loving one's husband (and children) as well as submitting to him is a widely praised virtue. The early Christian adoption and adaptation of the household code (see Ephesians 5:22-6:9; Colossians 3:18-4:1; 1 Peter 2:18-3:7) is likely designed to counter the perception that the Christian message undermines the family's traditional patriarchal structure (see Matthew 23:8-12; Galatians 3:28; 1 Corinthians 7:1-17). Of course, the false teachers' ascetic message does indeed undermine the family unit, as Paul indicates (1:11; see also 1 Timothy 4:3). In contrast, Paul urges behavior that reinforces the family unit in order to counteract his opponents' teaching and enhance the legacy of his own message.

The NIV appropriately translates the next item in the section on young women ("to be busy at home;" 2:5; 1 Timothy 5:14). The Greek term (*oikourgous*) describes one who works at home, doing work like grinding flour, baking, laundering, cooking, nursing children, making beds, spinning wool, keeping the house, as well as being hospitable and caring for guests. In the culture of Paul's day, women are praised for fulfilling such domestic responsibilities. Grammatically speaking, the Greek word *agathas* either qualifies the young women's domestic work or, more likely, stands alone as a separate item as the NIV translates it ("to be kind"). Thus, Paul encourages gentleness, a spousal quality deemed important. Like the older and younger men, the young women are also encouraged to be self-controlled (Gk. *sophronas*), a favorite trait in the Pastoral Letters (see 1 Timothy 2:9). When applied to young women, it carries the sense of sexual restraint, a point reinforced with the word "pure" (Gk. *hagnas*) on this virtue list. In this literary context, the term does not refer to sexual abstinence but to a wife's sexual fidelity to her spouse.

The list of virtues prescribed for young women concludes with the first of three clauses that state the purpose of the instructions to the various age groups: "so that no one will malign the word of God" (2:5, 8, 10). Paul is primarily concerned that Christian women who do not behave according to the standards of Greco-Roman society will damage the church's task of proclaiming the gospel (see also 2:10; 1 Timothy 5:14; 6:1). This possibility is enhanced by the widespread fear in Roman society that new religious movements like Christianity will upset family relationships and undermine society's political and domestic structures. To eliminate potential suspicion of the Christian message, Paul encourages Titus to teach the young women to exhibit contextually appropriate domestic behavior (see 2:9-10) and charges his opponents with undermining family norms (see 1:11). Paul's instructions have the added benefit of strengthening the church's social fabric at a time when "many" (1:10) are ruining it by promoting the ascetic life.

The instructions for young men are relatively brief by comparison with those for young women (2:6). Using the only imperative in 2:2-10, this group is exhorted to exercise "self-control," a very significant character trait in

these letters. Although the instructions to the various age
groups are now concluded, the words to Titus supple-
ment the exhortation to young men. Indeed, Titus is
urged to be a model for young men, and probably for the
entire faith community (see 1 Timothy 4:12).

The behavior Paul urges upon Titus contrasts sharply
with his opponents who are "unfit for doing anything
good" (1:16). Titus is to model Christian behavior: "In
everything set them an example by doing what is good.
In your teaching show integrity, seriousness, and soundness of speech that cannot be condemned" (2:7-8a). It is
difficult to determine whether Titus is to show integrity
and seriousness in the method (see 1:11; 2 Timothy 3:6-7)
or content of his teaching (cf. 1:9). Fee is undoubtedly correct: "Here teaching…has to do with the activity of teaching, not its content…" (1988: 189). Hence, integrity and
seriousness are to characterize his teaching style. The
next phrase points to the content of his teaching. If it is
healthy teaching ("soundness of speech"), it will be
above condemnation for it will foster proper Christian
conduct (cf. 1:9; 2:2). A second purpose clause follows the
list of virtues: "so that those who oppose you may be
ashamed because they have nothing bad to say about us"
(2:8b). Here, unlike the other two purpose clauses which
focus on society's reaction to the behavior of Christian
women and slaves (2:5, 10), the instructions relate to the
impact Titus's behavior will have on other church leaders. His opponents are the specific adversaries named
earlier in the letter (see 1:9). If Titus's teaching and behavior are above reproach, his opponents will have no
ammunition to attack him when he criticizes their behavior (1:10-16).

The final group (slaves) derives from a new category,
one not based on age but on a family role. The influence
of the household management tradition is most evident
here. A standard feature is a slave's submissiveness and

obedience to his or her master (see Ephesians 6:5-9; Colossians 3:22-4:1; 1 Timothy 6:1-2; 1 Peter 2:18-25). Again, as in 1 Timothy 6:1-2, a set of parallel instructions to masters is omitted. Paul's focus here is the subordinate status of slaves in relationship to their masters. The concern for submissiveness, emphasized at various points in this letter (2:5, 9; 3:1), is likely intended as an antidote to the rebellious behavior endangering the faith community (1:10). If "stealing" is a stereotypical Greco-Roman view of a slave's behavior, "talking back" (Gk. *antilegontas*) is a trait of the opponents (1:9). Similarly, the injunction to "try to please them," although a pretty straightforward expectation of slaves, reflects the exact opposite behavior of the opponents.

Although the words to slaves are clearly shaped by the portrait of the rebellious people, the instructions about slaves close with a definition of their purpose: "so that in every way they will make the teaching about God our Savior attractive" (2:10). By their submissive, pleasing and honest service, slaves will commend the Christian faith to outsiders. For the Christian faith will be perceived to produce people whose behavior is utterly appropriate to their rank and station in society. Indeed, outsiders will not only not condemn the gospel but be attracted to it by the believer's behavior.

Living Between the Times (2:11-15). In verse 11, the word "for" (Gk. *gar*) introduces the theological basis for the preceding set of instructions given in 2:1-10. It is quite likely that 2:11-14 (a single sentence in the original Greek), with its lofty tone and distinctive theological terms found nowhere else in the Pastoral Letters, derives from the church's liturgical context. In its present literary context, however, it makes three theologically important points about the behavior urged in the preceding verses: first, this behavior serves God's plan for bringing salvation to all; second, it is rooted in God's grace and signifies the presence of God's transforming grace within the community; third, it is based upon Jesus Christ's redemptive death. Although the ideas found here are well attested in the other Pauline writings, the specific terms used are peculiar to Titus.

First, Paul connects the behavior urged in verses 2-10 with God's desire to save all people (see also 1 Timothy 2:4; 4:10). The behavior described in the preceding passage is commended because it makes the Christian message attractive to outsiders; it promotes God's plan to save them. In this way, Paul reinforces the points made in verses 5 and 10: that Christian behavior, when it conforms to society's highest standards, enhances the church's witness to the world.

Second, the behavior urged in verses 2-10 concretely evidences the presence of God's transforming grace. This idea is expressed by means of the term "instructs" or "trains" (Gk. *paideuein*; NIV: "teaches"), a process involving discipline and instruction (see also 1 Timothy 1:20; 1 Corinthians 11:32; 2 Corinthians 6:9) that is viewed here as moral improvement. Although Paul's theology supplies the eschatological framework for this progress, the language used derives from Greco-Roman philosophy. That is, as in Paul's other letters (Romans 6:1-5; 1 Corinthians 7:29-31), God's grace is understood as a power that brings about a real moral transformation in the present. As a result, grace empowers believers to look forward with hope to Christ's second coming, described here as his second epiphany or "appearing" (see also 1 Timothy 6:14; 2 Timothy 4:8), and to eternal life (1:2; 3:7).

Three cardinal virtues describe the transformed life: self-control, upright (lives) and godly lives (2:12). The first, self-control (Gk. *sophronos*; literally, "responsibly, with moderation"), reiterates a virtue mentioned three times in the previous exhortations where it applies to older men, younger women and younger men (see

2:2, 5, 6). The second virtue, "upright" (Gk. *dikaios*; literally, "uprightly or righteously"), elsewhere named the goal of Christian training (see 2 Timothy 3:16), depicts a person whose life conforms to established norms (see 1 Timothy 1:9). The third, godliness (Gk. *eusebos*), the opposite of the rejected ungodliness (2:12; Gk. *asebeia*), infers a devotion to God together with the kind of behavior appropriate to such devotion (see 1 Timothy 2:2).

Paul also portrays the Christian life as a time of waiting for Jesus Christ's second coming, here described as "the blessed hope" and his "glorious appearing" (2:13). Glory, the visible sign of God's presence, is ascribed to the risen and returning Christ (see Mark 8:38; 13:26). Earlier, God was called Savior (see 2:10); now Christ is given the same title (see also 1:3-4). Indeed, the returning Christ is called "God," one of the very few passages in the New Testament to explicitly do so (see also John 20:28; Hebrews 1:8). While the Greek phrase permits a translation that distinguishes between "God" and "our Savior," the single article and single personal pronoun of the Greek text unites the nouns (God and Savior) and favors an interpretation that attributes the whole phrase to Christ (cf. Ephesians 5:5). Also, the sentence continues in the next verse to describe Jesus' work alone. Although Paul does not stop here to develop this phrase's christological implications, elsewhere in the Pastoral Letters he calls Christ's first coming an epiphany of God's grace (2:11; 2 Timothy 1:9-10) as well as an epiphany of "the kindness and love of God our Savior" (3:4). Thus, the phrase "great God and Savior" of Titus 2:13 refers to Jesus Christ, providing us with New Testament evidence of Christ's deity (see Harris 1980: 271).

The final clause of 2:11-14 uses traditional Christian language to interpret Jesus' death as a sacrifice: "who gave himself for us" (2:14; see also Isaiah 53:12; Mark 10:45; Galatians 1:4; 2:20; Ephesians 5:2; 1 Timothy 2:6). It emphasizes the goal or consequences of Christ's self-giving act: "to redeem us from all wickedness and to purify for himself a people that are his very own, eager to do what is good" (2:14). This passage likely derives from a Jewish-Christian liturgy, for its language reflects the Jewish Scriptures. While Paul frequently speaks of Christ's death as an act of redemption (Romans 3:24; 1 Corinthians 1:30; 6:20), the first phrase ("redeem us from all wickedness") almost directly quotes Psalm 130:8. The second phrase ("to purify for himself a people of his own") is influenced by texts such as Ezekiel 37:23; Exodus 19:5; and Deuteronomy 7:6. Finally, even as the goal of Israel's election is defined in terms of obedience (see Deuteronomy 6:20-25; 10:12-16; 26:18), so the goal of Jesus' self-giving is to produce a people who are "eager to do what is good." The contrast with the opposing teachers is clear, for their teaching produces people "unfit for doing anything good" (1:16). Thus, Paul's exhortations (2:1-10) conform to the moral purpose of Christ's sacrificial death.

Paul ends this chapter by emphasizing the importance of his exhortations: "These, then, are the things you should teach" (2:15a). "These things" (Gk. *tauta*) refers primarily to the contents of chapter 2, but also to the similar message of 3:1-11. Titus is to "encourage and rebuke" (2:15b), verbs that echo both Paul's earlier instructions to church leaders as well as this letter's overarching and complimentary goals (1:9, 13; 2:6). Further, Titus is to encourage and rebuke "with all authority." The word "authority" (Gk. *epitage*) means to command or order "with all impressiveness." In this way, Paul reinforces his insistence upon respect for order that is found in his instructions to the younger women (2:5), slaves (2:9) and the whole church (3:1). Finally, Paul warns Titus against letting people "despise" him, an exhortation similar to his warning to Timothy (see 1 Timothy 4:12), but without reference to Titus' age. This warning connects with this letter's general concern for rebellion against authority (1:6, 10), a thought that Paul carries over into the next chapter (3:1-8).

Application, Teaching/Preaching Points

A careful and sympathetic reading of the text is the best way to understand how it might be heard in the church today. The second chapter of Titus continues several applicable messages for today's church.

Why Live a Godly Life? This letter repeatedly exhorts God's people to "do what is good" (2:3, 7, 14; 3:8, 14; 1:16). Why should Christians live godly lives? The New Testament contains no Leviticus with its set of rules. Instead, the New Testament supplies theological motive for Christian living. The first reason for godly living is that God himself has appeared in human history, bringing us light to show us how to live and granting us his grace to do so (2:11). Walking in this light means saying "No" to ungodliness and worldly passions. The second reason for godly living is Jesus' promise to return (2:13). Christ's second coming will be a dramatic consummation of world history. He will come to receive his own people; but he will also come to judge everyone, including the family of God (2 Corinthians 5:10; 1 Peter 4:17). Here then is another motive for godly living: What will Christ find us doing at his second coming (see Matthew 24:45-51; 2 Peter 3:11-12)? The third reason for godly living is Christ's redemption for us (2:14). He came to set us free (redeem us) from all wickedness. The anticipated result of Christian faith in Jesus Christ is changed lives. His death motivates us to obey him. If we continue to live in sin, we deny his purpose in dying. The final reason for godly living relates to Christ's goal of "purifying a people for himself" (2:14). If we stress Jesus as personal Savior, we may forget that godliness is to be shared by the whole Christian community. Our individualism often obscures the fact that the Bible expects us to be more than a motley crew of patched up individual sinners; we are to be a whole redeemed community with a corporate life reflecting God's goodness and grace. Anyone who has ever wondered what human life is all about should be able to check out God's redeemed community and find out!

Jesus is God. Does 2:13 explicitly teach that Jesus Christ is God? Does Paul speak of the appearing both of God and Jesus Christ, two distinct persons of the Trinity? Or, does he state that Jesus Christ is God? The single definite article "*the* great God and Savior" seems to control both nouns. And in the New Testament, "appearing" is never used of God apart from Jesus. Thus, it seems that Titus 2:13 calls Jesus Christ "our great God and Savior." Harris claims this is "a verdict shared, with varying degrees of assurance, by almost all grammarians and lexicographers, many commentators, and most writers on New Testament Christology, although there are some dissenting voices" (1980: 271). Of course, the New Testament doctrine of Christ's deity does not stand or fall on the number of times Jesus is called God. Harris writes: "Faith in the deity of Jesus does not rest on the existence or validity of a series of 'proof-texts' in which Jesus may receive the title God (Gk. *theos*) but on the general testimony of the New Testament corroborated at the bar of personal experience" (1980: 271).

Changing Cultural Contexts Changes Things. Have changing cultural contexts made "subjection to husbands" (Titus 2:5) irrelevant in our world? Greek women remain in their own part of the house where they never meet any man apart from their husband. Their primary role is to be at home, raising the children. They rarely go out unaccompanied. So Paul encourages Cretan women to live Christianly in their cultural context. It would be nonsensical to urge them to go out, get a career, pay off the mortgage or, if the marriage fails, to set up shop as single parents! But what principles can we apply in today's world? Surely the general message of Paul's words remains applicable: that love, self-control, purity, kindness and relating appropriately to husbands and children are also virtues worthy of wives and mothers today. In North American culture, phrases like "be subject to their husbands" and "submission" can carry overtones of cringing surrender to "the man of the house." And certainly, Christian communities today cannot adopt these household directives carte blanche without causing a great ado. Just because Paul says younger women should be good housewives does not mean that women today should be limited to domestic functions. As social structures change (as they must to remain functional in shifting historical circumstances), so do social roles and the ways of fulfilling them. Also, we should not assume that the present North American nuclear family kinship system is the only one in the world. Perhaps ancestral kinship systems in Ghana or Uganda make Paul's advice pertinent and even progressive, but I have no first hand knowledge of that.

Personal Reflection Questions

- Paul gives some pretty specific instructions to older men and women as well as younger men and women. DISCUSS: If you are an "older person," how do you respond to Paul's directives in 2:2 and 2:3? If you are "younger," how do you relate to older people? What do you do to help the other group? If you are a "younger woman," how do you live out 2:4-5? What positive help is there in these verses for you?

- The text claims that we can "train" others to love appropriately. DISCUSS: Can people be "trained" to love their relations—spouse, children? If so, how can it be done?

- Titus is exhorted to set an example for others in the church. DISCUSS: Do people look to us as examples of Christian living (2:7)? If so, make a list of the people in your life (work, home, church, neighborhood) who are your examples of Christian devotion. What Christian virtues do you see in them as you watch them live their lives?

- The early church viewed the witness of slaves as a key factor in their outreach. DISCUSS: To what extent do we neglect the key role of Christians in the workplace? If we have Christians who are models in the entertainment industry, whom do we have in the business and work world?

- Grace teaches us to live godly lives. DISCUSS: How does the message of 2:11-14 give shape to a Christian lifestyle? Make a list of beliefs and actions that should be shared by your entire faith community (see 2:14) and another list that can only be applied to you as an individual? Which of the two lists is longer?

CHAPTER THIRTEEN

God's Transforming Grace

The Text: Titus 3:1-15

> *Remind the people to be subject to rulers and authorities, to be obedient, to be ready to do whatever is good,* [2] *to slander no one, to be peaceable and considerate, and to show true humility toward all men.* [3] *At one time we too were foolish, disobedient, deceived and enslaved by all kinds of passions and pleasures. We lived in malice and envy, being hated and hating one another.* [4] *But when the kindness and love of God our Savior appeared,* [5] *he saved us, not because of righteous things we had done, but because of his mercy. He saved us through the washing of rebirth and renewal by the Holy Spirit,* [6] *whom he poured out on us generously through Jesus Christ our Savior,* [7] *so that, having been justified by his grace, we might become heirs having the hope of eternal life.* [8] *This is a trustworthy saying. And I want you to stress these things, so that those who have trusted in God may be careful to devote themselves to doing what is good. These things are excellent and profitable for everyone.* [9] *But avoid foolish controversies and genealogies and arguments and quarrels about the law, because these are unprofitable and useless.* [10] *Warn a divisive person once, and then warn him a second time. After that, have nothing to do with him.* [11] *You may be sure that such a man is warped and sinful; he is self-condemned.* [12] *As soon as I send Artemas or Tychicus to you, do your best to come to me at Nicopolis, because I have decided to winter there.* [13] *Do everything you can to help Zenas the lawyer and Apollos on their way and see that they have everything they need.* [14] *Our people must learn to devote themselves to doing what is good, in order that they may provide for daily necessities and not live unproductive lives.* [15] *Everyone with me sends you greetings. Greet those who love us in the faith. Grace be with you all.*

The Flow and Form of the Text

After giving instructions that pertain to different

church members, Paul exhorts Titus to teach everyone to be subject and obedient to rulers and authorities (3:1-2). He then provides a lengthy theological warrant for this exhortation that is reminiscent of a familiar Pauline pattern: "once we were ... but now we are." It is designed to remind Titus that once we were foolish and disobedient (3:3), but now we are heirs to eternal life (3:4-8a) through God's grace and mercy. The moral life is predicated upon change in the very person of the believer. Here is the clearest statement of justification by grace in the Pastoral Letters, displacing the idea that Paul has simply substituted grace for good works in these letters. It is God's grace that saves and justifies the believer. It is the gift of redemption that enables believers to live different lives than they did in the past; this is the reason they must subject themselves and be obedient to rulers and authorities.

In the letter's closing section (3:8b-15), Paul returns to the theme of "good works." Verse 8b is a transitional sentence that refers to the previous exhortations ("these things") and repeats the earlier emphasis on "doing what is good" (1:16; 2:7, 14; 3:1). It anticipates the concluding exhortation of 3:14. If false teachers pursue genealogies and discussions over the law, Paul wants those who trust in God to devote themselves to "doing what is good" since it benefits everyone (3:8). Those who follow Paul's teaching devote themselves to good works because God's grace has trained them to do so. By contrast, the false teachers are simply unfit for any good work (1:16).

The Text Explained

The Exhortations Proper (3:1-2). Paul admonishes Titus to remind the entire community to submit (Gk. *hypotassesthai*) to "rulers and authorities" (Gk. *archais [kai] exousias*), presumably the Roman Empire's civil authorities (see Romans 13:1). This exhortation corresponds nicely with the submissive behavior expected of various household members in the previous chapter (2: 5, 9). The Greco-Roman world of Paul's day understands that the household and the state are inextricably connected. Order in one arena fosters order in the other, and disorder in one creates chaos in both.

The second phrase calls the entire community to obedience, focusing on civil behavior. The Greek infinitive specifically means obedience to those in authority (Grk. *peitharchein*). In the third phrase, however, Paul shifts the focus from the political arena to the Christian life in general, calling believers "to be ready to do what is good" (3:1). By contrast, his opponents are "unfit for doing anything good" (1:16). The concept of authority seems to link the believers' various arenas of daily life. Submission and obedience to political authorities (3:1), to church authorities (2:15), and to family authorities (2:5, 9) are all interrelated. Indeed, obedience in all these arenas is regarded as crucial to a healthy system's maintenance.

Paul calls the community to avoid vices and to cultivate virtues already familiar to us from other vice and virtue lists in the Pastoral Letters (1 Timothy 3:3; 1:20; 6:4; 2 Timothy 3:3; Titus 3:9; 2 Timothy 2:23; 3:2-4). For example, slander (Gk. *blasphemein*) or evil speech is a characteristic of the opponents (1 Timothy 1:20; 6:4; 2 Timothy 3:3). Bishops are exhorted to be peaceable and considerate in 1 Timothy 3:3. However, the focus here is not on relationships with external authorities in the political arena, but on relationships within the Christian community. Indeed, the external situation seems to be free of tension. The exhortation of 3:1 simply defines the parameters of Christian behavior while the internal tensions seem to shape Paul's argument here.

Theological Warrant for the Exhortations (3:3-8a). In the previous chapter, Paul provides a theological warrant (2:11-14) for the exhortations of 2:1-10. Now he again supplies a theological justification for his instructions of 3:1-

2. The connection between the exhortation and its theological basis is quite simple: God's mercy toward sinners models how Christians should deal with outsiders.

The passage opens with a list of vices that picture the pre-Christian life (see also Romans 1:29-31; 1 Peter 4:2-3). The list is illustrative, not definitive. The reminder of former disobedience (Grk. *apeitheis*) follows on the heels of an exhortation to obedience (3:1). The final two items on the list are almost synonymous: "hated" (Gk. *stygetoi*) and "hating one another," portray a complete absence of concern and affection for others and hence an absence of community. They contrast sharply with the aim of Paul's exhortations (2:4-5; 3:1-2) and with his description of God as filled with "kindness and love" (3:4).

This passage's critical feature is its description of God's saving action. Again, Paul refers to the first coming of Jesus as an epiphany (Gk. *epephane*; NIV: "appeared"). Here it is an epiphany of God's "kindness and love" (3:4), not of God's grace. Of course, "kindness and love" are synonyms for "grace," but the two new terms are selected to serve this theological passage's intended purpose.

Paul uses "grace" almost exclusively to define God's saving act. But the terms "kindness and love" (Gk. *chrestotes kai philanthropia*) were widely used by contemporary Hellenistic writers to describe a ruler's most prized virtues. Indeed, in Hellenistic Jewish writings, "kindness and love" are presented as models for human actions, which is the intended application here. Believers are to be kind and loving in all their interactions with one another and especially toward outsiders. This is how they experienced God's action in their own lives when they themselves were "outsiders." Paul's use of terms associated with both human and divine acts to define God's nature enhances this moral application.

Another theological point important to Paul's argument is the very Pauline message that God "saved us, not because of righteous things we have done, but because of his mercy" (3:5a; see Romans 3:24, 28; 4:2-5; 11:6; Galatians 2:16, 21; Ephesians 2:8-9). In a letter that mentions good works so frequently (2:7, 14; 3:1, 8, 14), a reminder that God's grace is granted quite apart from "righteous things we have done" is very important. Thus, Paul assumes that good deeds result from God's grace, but they do not evoke his grace and mercy.

In this passage, Paul speaks of "God our Savior" (3:4) and God's saving act (see also Ephesians 2:5-7). Elsewhere, Paul speaks of God having justified us, with salvation reserved for the future (see Romans 3:24; 5:9-10). This eschatological tension is preserved here for, though "saved," the believer possesses only "the hope of eternal life" (3:7; see also 1:2) rather than its complete reality.

A string of words rather loosely linked together associates the act of salvation with water (Gk. *loutron*; literally, "washing"), rebirth, renewal and the Holy Spirit. In early Christian writings these same terms are commonly linked with the act of salvation (see John 3:3-8; Romans 6:4; Ephesians 5:26; 1 Peter 1:3-5). Paul does not develop these associations here even though they are connected with the believer's moral life. This is one of the very few places in the Pastoral Letters where Paul speaks of the Holy Spirit (see also 1 Timothy 4:1; 2 Timothy 1:14). He only alludes to the Spirit's role in the work of moral renewal (see Romans 8:1-17; Galatians 5:16-26) and its connection with the hope of eternal life (see Romans 5:5; 8:15-17; 2 Corinthians 1:22; 5:1-5). The Spirit's role is simply one of several ways Paul understands the work of transformation in the lives of believers. Grace is certainly part of the process (2:11), as is sound apostolic teaching (1 Timothy 4:6) and Scripture (2 Timothy 3:16). Indeed, godliness, which is the goal of transformation, also plays a role as an agent of it (see 1 Timothy 4:7-8; 2 Timothy 3:5). Paul concludes his theological message with a familiar endorsement: "This is a trustworthy saying" (3:8a).

Final Exhortations Concerning the Opponents (3:8b-11). Before Paul concludes his words about the opponents, he repeats his earlier exhortations to Titus to promulgate the instructions he has received (see 2:1, 15). Here, however, he uses a far more emphatic verb (Gk. *diabebaiousthai*; literally, "insist on," or "make a point; NIV: "stress"). A purpose clause, summarizing the goal of the exhortations of 2:1-3:8a, urges the faithful to devote themselves to things that are profitable (Gk. *ophelima*) and excellent (Gk. *kala*). Thus, the relationship between the exhortations and the church's witness is not repeated here as in 2:5 and 10.

If the faithful are to devote themselves to what is "excellent and profitable" (3:8b), Titus is to avoid what is "unprofitable and useless" (3:9b). Paul defines the former as "doing what is good"; the latter as "foolish controversies and genealogies and arguments and quarrels about the law" (3:9a), things which characterize the disputes and debates of the opponents. This leads to a set of instructions on how to deal with these opponents, should they choose to persist in their actions. Although these verses contribute nothing new to the portrait of the opponents, together with 1:10-16, they frame the exhortations to orderly obedience with warnings about the opponents' disruptive activities.

With this final reference to the opponents, Paul returns to the harsh tone of 1:10-16. The moderate behavior mandated in 3:2, insofar as it is relevant for dealing with opponents within the Christian community, seems to be set aside by the two admonitions Titus is instructed to give (3:10). These admonitions correspond to the sharp rebukes mentioned in 1:13, but Paul's focus shifts from the expectation of successful correction to the expectation of failure: "After that, have nothing to do with him" (3:10).

Elsewhere, Paul is concerned with divisive behavior within the church (see Romans 16:17-20; 1 Corinthians 1:10-13; Philippians 2:1-4) and he reflects theologically on the problem (1 Corinthians 1:18-31; Philippians 2:6-11). But here he offers only concrete suggestions, including silencing the opponents, correcting them, treating them gently, and then avoiding those who persist in their divisive behavior. Paul shows no desire for substantive debate. If the rebukes are not successful, Titus is to terminate contact with the opponents. Paul does underscore the social consequences of the opponents' behavior (causing divisions) and responds with punishment (exclusion). Indeed, the letter's final personal instructions picture what inclusion looks like, as if to underscore the social implications of exclusion.

This is one of the many places in the Pastoral Letters where the opponents are depicted as engaging in vacuous verbal debates instead of profitable actions (1:10; 1 Timothy 1:4; 6:4, 20; 2 Timothy 2:23). The references to genealogies and the law (3:9) repeat earlier comments linking the opponents to Judaism (1:14; 1 Timothy 1:4, 7), but they add nothing concrete to the nature of the connection. The important point for Paul is the contrast between the opponents' worthless discussions and the solid actions he himself advocates. Titus is literally urged to go out of his way to avoid (Gk. *periistasthai*) such discussions, but he and the rest of the faithful are to put before themselves the goal (Gk. *proistasthai*) of good works spelled out in this letter.

As in 1 and 2 Timothy, Paul holds out some hope that the opponents may be dissuaded from their speculations (1 Timothy 1:20; 2 Timothy 2:25), for he encourages Titus to give two warnings before taking stronger measures (see also Matthew 18:15-17). However, Paul seems pessimistic that they will reform and focuses on what to do when an opponent is not persuaded to change his behav-

ior. The solution is simple: "Have nothing to do with
him" (3:10). Avoidance is a somewhat milder response
than that described in 1 Timothy 1:20 where certain persons are "turned over to Satan." However, even turning
someone over to Satan is intended to have a pedagogical
effect (see also Titus 1:13) whereas here the offender's status seems irreversible. The present tense of the verb "sinful" (Gk. *hamartanei*) implies that such a person is
"warped" (literally, "turned inside out, entirely altered)
and persists in sinning. Although it is Paul who insists on
the separation, he calls his opponent the one who is
"divisive" (Gk. *hairetikon anthropon*; literally, "a heretic, a
schismatic"), not only because his teachings destabilize
the community (1:11), but also because they bring the
separation upon themselves (NIV: "he is self-con-
demned"). From Paul's perspective, this avoidance strategy is designed to eliminate internal divisions and restore
order; he would not recognize his own behavior as divisive.

The adjective used in 3:10 to describe the opponents
(Gk. *hairetikos*) derives from a verb that means, "to
choose." As defined here, however, the choice is one that
affects the community's integrity, and the word has the
additional nuance of factious or divisive behavior. Since
the opponents are earlier identified as those who reject
the truth (see 1:14), the Greek word almost carries the
meaning of its English cognate, "heretic." However, the
emphasis in this passage is on the divisive results of their
behavior, not their doctrinal error (see also 2 Peter 2:1).

Travel Arrangements and Greetings (3:12-15). This
letter ends as most of Paul's letters do: with travel plans,
greetings, a final exhortation and a benediction (see
Romans 15:22-16:23; 1 Corinthians 16:5-24). Several individuals are mentioned, two of whom are known from
other New Testament writings. Tychicus is named elsewhere in the New Testament as one of Paul's traveling

companions and coworkers (Acts 20:4; Ephesians 6:21; Colossians 4:7; 2 Timothy 4:12). He or Artemas, an otherwise unknown person, is to replace Titus on Crete. The earlier descriptions of Titus's assignment on Crete do not mention his imminent replacement and seem to presume a lengthy stay (see 1:5, 13; 2:15). The requests for Titus to do his best to join Paul (similar to the request made of Timothy in 2 Timothy 4:9) and to send Zenas and Apollos "on their way," provide the immediate rationale for the letter, which is otherwise filled with exhortations of no immediate urgency.

There are several cities in the ancient world named Nicopolis ("Victory City"). Paul likely refers to the Nicopolis on the western coast of Greece. It is close to Paul's known travel circuit, although there is no other evidence that he ever visits that city. It is customary to avoid sea travel in the winter, when seasonal storms make sailing particularly dangerous (see Acts 27:12; 28:11; 2 Timothy 4:21).

Zenas is also unknown apart from this reference, but Apollos is a prominent figure in the early Christian mission in Corinth (Acts 18:24-19:1; 1 Corinthians 3:5-15; 16:12). The reference to Zenas and Apollos likely identifies them as the bearers of the letter. It also functions as a letter of introduction for them. The request to Titus and the Cretan church to "send them on their way" uses a Greek word (*propempein*) that has become almost a technical term in early Christianity for providing financial assistance for the trip. In Acts and the letters, various church workers are "sent on their way:" that is, they are given hospitality (food and lodging) and money to support them for the next leg of their journey (Acts 15:3; 21:5; Romans 15:24; 1 Corinthians 16:6, 11; 2 Corinthians 1:16; 3 John 6).

The exhortation to good works in 3:14 repeats the previous words of 3:8, but now to support the concrete

request of Christian hospitality. God's people are to provide for the "daily necessities" (Gk. *tas anagkaias
chreias*)—the necessities of life—for traveling Christian
workers. To do so is to be "productive" or fruitful, a reference to the tangible results of an active faith that
expresses itself in generous deeds of service to others.

Application, Teaching/Preaching Points

Titus provides us with a profound articulation of the
gospel that is unmistakably Pauline. Several aspects of
Paul's remarks here in this third chapter call for further
elaboration and homiletic development.

On Integrating Word and Deed. According to Paul,
"all men" (read, "all people") are to be treated with a gentle and considerate courtesy (3:2). With this phrase,
which repeats the universal emphasis of 2:11, Paul
includes all non-Christians. Although Paul does not
make this point explicit here, this charitable attitude can
promote the gospel as much as the socially prescribed
respect for order encouraged in 2:2-10 (see especially,
2 Timothy 2:24-26), for courteous actions by Christians
directly mirror the gospel message of God's kindness and
love for all people. To be sure, Paul's perspective of this
theological grounding of Christian behavior is depicted
elsewhere, but it is surpassed here. In Romans, for example, Paul encourages Christians of the capital city to
"welcome one another ... just as Christ welcomed you"
(15:7). Thus, in imitation of Christ, believers are to provide a gracious welcome to other Christians with whom
they disagree (see Romans 14:10). Even so, Paul does not
extend the application to outsiders. Here, however,
Christian courtesy is to be extended to all men, inclusive
of outsiders to the faith. Of course, the text's wording
extends this peaceable and considerate attitude to all
other Christians, even rebellious opponents, for the
phrase "all men" (3:2) is all-inclusive. Yet this message

stands in tension with the way Paul actually treats the rebellious teachers. His description of them (1:10-16) and the instructions to muzzle and rebuke them (2:11, 13) can hardly be described as courteous. All of this suggests an astonishing lack of integration of word and deed. Perhaps Paul had only non-Christians in mind when he wrote these words in 3:2. Perhaps he simply encourages behavior that promotes the gospel in Greco-Roman society. If so, Paul implies that where truth and the community's integrity are at stake, harsher methods have his tacit approval. Yet 2 Timothy 2:24-26 explicitly states that opponents are to be corrected with gentleness. These letters appear to offer a mixed ethical message.

Portrait of a Healthy Church. Two very important messages emerge from the personal requests and greetings section of this letter (3:12-15). The first is the ethical message found throughout these letters: Christian faith must result in concrete acts of charity or "good works," here exemplified by sharing resources to meet the basic needs of traveling Christians. The second message is more subtle. The opponents have just been charged with divisive activities, quarreling and dissension. As a consequence, they have been ejected from Christian fellowship. By contrast, the letter's final verses paint a portrait of a healthy Christian fellowship which includes companionship, affection and material support for a wide network of coworkers. This vigorous and supportive group bears visible fruit, while the opponents' squabbling is "unprofitable and useless" (3:9). Paul uses the traditional features of the letter's closure to send an object lesson on social behavior that corresponds with God's goodness and loving-kindness.

Living in the World as Christians. How should Christians live in the world? The Pauline Letters maintain the distinctively Pauline eschatological tension: Christians live between the times; the full consummation of God's kingdom is "not yet." But nowhere does Paul advocate a sectarian attitude toward the world. Christians should not go "out of the world" (1 Corinthians 5:9), and that attitude pervades Titus as well. Paul wants the members of God's community to shape up their internal affairs and their life in the home, but he does not want them to withdraw from personal contact with "outsiders," nor from the structures of society. He calls the internal opponents of the faith community corrupt. He speaks of the believer's former life as one of hostility, but now he wants God's people to be peaceable and considerate toward all people. They are not to speak ill of people outside the community. Here is a message for Christians who want to create a competing "Christian" culture so they can live "holy lives" and, from birth to death, never have to speak to or interact with non-Christians. Instead, they advocate Christian educational systems, medicine, science, art, music, literature, jewelry, etc. This approach to Christian identity is very close to the code of purity advocated by Paul's opponents so that some things and people and places can be labeled "clean" and others "unclean." By contrast, Paul wants these young Christians to see that God's love purifies them; while living in the world, they can see all things as clean and do good deeds. They are to stay in the ordinary structures of the world, fulfilling their obligations to the home and empire. He encourages them to participate in the political order, to do more than submit, but also to obey and to be ready to do what is good. By implication, he calls for Christians to work creatively within the political process. They are not to drop out of the world in sullen witness to its systemic corruption. Such abdication only allows corruption to increase. Nor are they to work single-mindedly for a state, which is the perfect realization of the kingdom. They are simply to work within the real, messy, complex structures of the political process as those who can "do good deeds" because they have been shaped by God's gifts of kindness and love.

The Transforming Power of God's Love. It is strange for us to hear such confident assertions about the transforming power of God's grace as we find here in Titus 3, especially when we look at our own staid lives in the Christian community. Yet Paul underscores the reality of this transformation. The Spirit of God does transform our consciousness; he does give us capacities we did not have before. So why are we so chary of celebrating this reality? After all, we recognize that experiencing trust, acceptance, love and kindness can effect a deep change in our personality structure, so that a formerly hostile person learns to accept him or herself, as well as others, in trust and love. So why do we hesitate to acknowledge that this is "the gift of God" operative among us? For many of us, a single revelation of love is so powerful that it enables us to speak of our lives in terms of before and after, of a change from fear and compulsion to freedom and joy. If God was at work to save when Jesus "gave himself for us," why do we think God is not at work now whenever any one of us "gives himself" for another? If such a gift can change our hearts, then we can be convinced even now of God's work in our own story and in the stories of others in the world. Paul clearly teaches that a person initiated into the Christian community can and does experience God's grace to the extent that the community lives in gentleness, mutual acceptance and self-service. And if the community lives this way, then it "demonstrates" the power of the gift of God to all people. The church is called to make the gift of God's kindness and love visible to all people.

Personal Reflection Questions

- Obedience to the state is normative in the Pastoral Letters. DISCUSS: Given the larger context of this whole letter to Titus, to what extent should Christians always obey the state authorities? What exceptions might there be? Why?

- Paul calls believers to live transformed lives. DISCUSS: How can we recapture Paul's urgency to see transformed lives in our churches? How can this transformation happen? If we are saved by God's grace, why are good works so important to us as individuals and as communities of faith?

- Warn a divisive person once or twice and then have nothing to do with him, says Paul. DISCUSS: Are splits and divisions a feature of our church life today? How can these issues be tackled in the light of Paul's letter to Titus?

SELECT BIBLIOGRAPHY

Commentaries

Barrett, C. K. *The Pastoral Epistles*. The New Clarendon Bible, ed. H. F. D. Sparks. Oxford: The Clarendon Press, 1963.

Bernard, J. H. *The Pastoral Epistles*. Cambridge Greek Testament for Schools and Colleges. Cambridge: University Press, 1899.

Bassler, Jouette M. *1 Timothy, 2 Timothy, Titus*. Abingdon New Testament Commentaries. Nashville, TN: Abingdon, 1996.

Calvin, John. *1, 2 Timothy and Titus*. The Crossway Classic Commentaries, ed. Alister McGrath and J. I. Packer. Wheaton, IL: Crossway Books, 1998.

Collins, Raymond F. *I & II Timothy and Titus: A Commentary*. The New Testament Library. Louisville, Kentucky: Westminster John Knox Press, 2002.

Donelson, Lewis R. *Colossians, Ephesians, 1 and 2 Timothy, and Titus*. Westminster Bible Companion. Louisville, Kentucky: Westminster John Knox Press, 1996.

Earle, Ralph. "1 and 2 Timothy" *The Expositor's Bible Commentary*. Frank E. Gaebelein (General Editor). Volume II. Grand Rapids, Michigan: Zondervan, 1978, 341-418.

Ellicott, Charles, J. *A Critical and Grammatical Commentary on the Pastoral Epistles with a Revised Translation*. Andover: Warren F. Draper, 1860.

Fee, Gordon D. *1 and 2 Timothy, Titus*. New International Biblical Commentary. Peabody, MA: Hendrickson Publishers, 1988.

_____. *1 and 2 Timothy, Titus*. Good News Commentaries, ed. W. Ward Gasque. San Francisco: Harper & Row Publishers, 1984.

Griffith, Michael. *Timothy and Titus*. Baker Bible Guides. Grand Rapids, Michigan: Baker Books, 1996.

Guthrie, Donald. *The Pastoral Epistles*. The Tyndale New

Testament Commentaries, ed. R. V. G. Tasker. Grand Rapids: William B. Eerdmans Publishing Company, 1957.

Hiebert, D. Edmond. "Titus" *The Expositor's Bible Commentary*. Frank E. Gaebelein (General Editor). Volume II. Grand Rapids, Michigan: Zondervan, 1978, 421-449.

Houlden, J. L. *The Pastoral Epistles: I and II Timothy, Titus.* TPI New Testament Commentaries, ed. Howard Clark Kee and Dennis Nineham. London: SCM Press, 1989.

Hultgren, Arland J. *I-II Timothy, Titus.* Augsburg Commentary on the New Testament. Minneapolis: Augsburg, 1984.

Huther, Joh. Ed. *Critical and Exegetical Handbook to the Epistles of St. Paul to Timothy and Titus.* Translated by David Hunter. Edinburgh: T. & T. Clark, 1881.

Johnson, Luke Timothy. *1 Timothy, 2 Timothy, Titus.* Knox Preaching Guides, ed. John H. Hayes. Atlanta: John Knox Press, 1987.

_____. *Letters to Paul's Delegates: 1 Timothy, 2 Timothy, Titus. The New Testament in Context.* Valley Forge, Pennsylvania: Trinity Press International, 1996.

Kelly, J. N. D. *A Commentary on the Pastoral Epistles.* Black's New Testament Commentaries, ed. Henry Chadwick. London: Adam and Charles Black, 1963.

Knight, George W. *The Pastoral Epistles: A Commentary on the Greek Text.* New International Greek Testament Commentary, ed. I. Howard Marshall and W. Ward Gasque. Grand Rapids: William B. Eerdmans Publishing Company, 1992.

Lea, Thomas D. and Hayne P. Griffin, Jr. *1,2 Timothy, Titus.* The New American Commentary, ed. David S. Dockery, no. 34. Nashville: Broadman Press, 1992.

Lock, Walter. *A Critical and Exegetical Commentary on the Pastoral Epistles.* The International Critical

Commentary. Edinburgh: T. & T. Clark, 1924.

Marshall, I. Howard. *The Pastoral Epistles.* The International Critical Commentary, ed. J. A. Emerton, C. E. B. Cranfield and G. N. Stanton. Edinburgh: T. & T. Clark, 1999.

Mounce, William D. *Pastoral Epistles.* Word Biblical Commentary, ed. Bruce M. Metzger, David A. Hubbard and Glenn W. Barker, no. 46. Nashville: T. Nelson, 2000.

Oden, Thomas C. *First and Second Timothy and Titus.* Interpretation. Louisville, Kentucky: John Knox Press, 1989.

Quinn, Jerome D. and William C. Wacker. *The First and Second Letters to Timothy.* Grand Rapids: William B. Eerdmans Publishing Company, 2000.

Scott, E. F. *The Pastoral Epistles.* ed. James Moffatt. New York: Harper and Brothers Publishers, 1946.

Stott, John R. W. *Guard the Gospel: The Message of 2 Timothy. The Bible Speaks Today.* Downers Grove, Illinois: InterVarsity Press, 1973.

Towner, Philip H. *1-2 Timothy & Titus.* The IVP New Testament Commentary Series, ed. Grant R. Osborne. Downers Grove, IL: InterVarsity Press, 1994.

White, Newport J. D. *The First and Second Epistles to Timothy and the Epistle to Titus. The Expositor's Greek Testament,* ed. W. Robertson Nicoll, Vol. 4. London: Hodder and Stoughton, 1897-1910. Reprint, Grand Rapids: William B. Eerdmans Publishing Company, 1974.

Ward, Ronald A. *Commentary on 1 and 2 Timothy & Titus.* Waco, Texas: Word Books, 1974.

Books

Balch, D. *Let Wives Be Submissive: The Domestic Code in 1 Peter.* SBL Monograph Series 26, Chico, California:

Scholars Press\ 1981.

Banks, Robert. *Paul's Idea of Community.* Revised Edition. Peabody, Massachusetts: Hendriksen Publishers, 1994.

Bailey, James L. and Lyle D. Vander Broek. *Literary Forms in the New Testament: A Handbook.* Louisville, Kentucky: Westminster/John Knox Press, 1992.

Bolsinger, Tod E. *It Takes A Church To Raise A Christian: How the Community of God Transforms Lives.* Grand Rapids, Michigan: Brazos Press, 2004.

Davies, Margaret. *The Pastoral Epistles. New Testament Guides.* Sheffield, England: Sheffield Academic Press, 1996.

Dawn, Marva and Eugene Peterson. *The Unnecessary Pastor: Rediscovering the Call.* Grand Rapids, Michigan: Eerdmans, 2000.

France, R. T. *Women in the Church's Ministry: A Test Case for Biblical Interpretation.* Grand Rapids, Michigan: Eerdmans, 1995.

Gritz, S. H. Paul, *Women Teachers, and the Mother Goddess of Ephesus.* Lanham: University Press of America, 1991.

Harding, Mark. *What Are They Saying About The Pastoral Epistles?* New York, New Jersey: Paulist Press, 2001.

Hayter, Mary. *The New Eve in Christ.* London: SPCK, 1987.

Hanson, Anthony Tyrrell. *Studies in the Pastoral Epistles.* London: SPCK, 1968.

Hurley, James. B. *Man and Woman in Biblical Perspective.* Grand Rapids: Zondervan Publishing House, 1981.

Kostenberger, Andreas J., Thomas R. Schreiner, and H. Scott Baldwin. *Women in the Church: A Fresh Analysis of 1 Timothy 2:9-15.* Grand Rapids, Michigan: Baker Books, 1995.

Kroeger, Richard Clark & Catherine Clark Kroeger. *I Suffer Not A Woman: Rethinking 1 Timothy 2:11-15 in Light of Ancient Evidence.* Grand Rapids, Michigan:

Baker Book House, 1992.

Malherbe, A. J. *Moral Exhortations: A Greco-Roman Handbook*. Philadelphia: Westminster Press, 1986.

Matera, Frank J. *New Testament Ethics: The Legacies of Jesus and Paul*. Louisville, Kentucky: Westminster John Knox Press, 1996.

Polhill, John B. *Paul and His Letters*. Nashville: Broadman and Holman Publishers, 1999.

Reicke, Bo. *Re-Examining Paul's Letters: The History of the Pauline Correspondence*. Edited by David P. Moessner and Ingalisa Reicke. Harrisburg, PA: Trinity International Press, 2001.

Ramsay, William M. *Historical Commentary on the Pastoral Epistles*. Edited by Mark Wilson. Grand Rapids, Michigan: Kregel Publications, 1996.

Stackhouse, John G. *Finally Feminist: A Pragmatic Christian Understanding of Gender*. Grand Rapids, Michigan: Baker Academic, 2005.

Towner, Philip. *The Goal of Our Instruction: The Structure of Theology and Ethics in the Pastoral Epistles*. Sheffield, England: JSOT Press, 1989.

Young, Frances. *The Theology of the Pastoral Letters*. New Testament Theology, ed. James D. G. Dunn. Cambridge: Cambridge University Press, 1994

Journal Articles/Chapters

Bowman, Ann. "Women in Ministry: An Exegetical Study of 1 Timothy 2:11-15." *Bibliotheca Sacra* 149 (1992): 193-213.

Coupland, Simon. "Salvation Through Childbearing? The Riddle of 1 Timothy 2:15." *The Expository Times* 112 (September 2001): 302-3.

Falconer, Robert. "1 Timothy 2, 14.15. Interpretive Notes." *Journal of Biblical Literature* 60 (1941): 375-9.

Fee, Gordon D. "Issues in Evangelical Hermeneutics, Part

III: The Great Watershed-Intentionality & Particularity/Eternality: 1 Timothy 2:8-15 as a Test Case. *Crux.* December 1990/Volume XXVI, No. 4, 31-37.

Harris, Murray J. "Titus 2:13 and the Deity of Christ" *Pauline Studies.* Edited by D. A. Hagner and M. J. Harris. Grand Rapids, Michigan: Eerdmans, 1980, 262-277.

Jebb, S. "A Suggested Interpretation of 1 Ti. 2:15." *The Expository Times* 81 (July 1970): 221-2.

Kimberley, David R. "1 Tim 2:15: A Possible Understanding of a Difficult Text." *Journal of the Evangelical Theological Society* 35 (April 1992): 481-6.

Köstenberger, Andrew J. "Ascertaining Women's God-Ordained Roles: An Interpretation of 1 Timothy 2:15." *Bulletin for Biblical Research* 7 (1997): 107-44.

Ladd, George Eldon. "Why Did God Inspire the Bible?" *Scripture, Tradition, and Interpretation.* Edited by W. W. Gasque and W. S. LaSor. Grand Rapids, Michigan: Eerdmans, 1978, 49-59.

Porter, Stanley E. "What Does It Mean to be 'Saved by Childbirth' (1 Timothy 2:15)?" *Journal for the Study of the New Testament* 49 (1993): 87-102.

Thomas, David. "Saved by Childbearing!" *Notes on Translation* 10 (February 1996): 52.

Toews, John E. "I Permit No Woman to Teach" *Your Daughters Shall Prophecy: Women in Ministry in the Church.* Edited by J. E. Toews, Valerie Rempel, and Katie Funk Wiebe. Winnipeg, Manitoba: Kindred Press, 1992, 137-156.

Waltke, Bruce K. "1 Timothy 2:8-15: Unique or Normative?" *Crux.* March 1992/Volume XXVIII, No. 1, 22-27.

Ancient Writers and Texts

Aristotle. *History of Animals, Books VII-X.* Translated and Edited by D. M. Balme. The Loeb Classical Library, ed. G. P. Goold. Cambridge, Massachusetts: Harvard University Press, 1991.

Augustine. *De Trinitate.* A Select Library of the Nicene and Post-Nicene Fathers of the Christian Church, First Series, ed. Philip Schaff, Volume 3. Grand Rapids: William B. Eerdmans Publishing Company, 1978.

Chrysostom, St. John. *Homilies on Timothy.* A Select Library of the Nicene and Post-Nicene Fathers of the Christian Church, First Series, ed. Philip Schaff, Vol. 13. Grand Rapids: William B. Eerdmans Publishing Company, 1979.

Gregory of Nyssa. *De Virginitate.* A Select Library of the Nicene and Post-Nicene Fathers of the Christian Church, Second Series, ed. Philip Schaff and Henry Wace, Vol. 5. Grand Rapids: William B. Eerdmans Publishing Company, 1972.

St. Jerome. *Letter 107.* A Select Library of the Nicene and Post-Nicene Fathers of the Christian Church, Second Series, ed. Philip Schaff and Henry Wace, Vol. 6. Grand Rapids: William B. Eerdmans Publishing Company, 1954.

Visotzkey, Burton L., trans. *The Midrash on Proverbs.* Yale Judaica Series, ed. Sid Z. Leiman. New Haven: Yale University Press, 1992.

Grammars, Lexicons, Wordbooks and Reference Books

Bauer, Walter. *A Greek-English Lexicon of the New Testament and Other Early Christian Literature.* 3rd Ed. Revised and Edited by Frederick William Danker. Chicago: University of Chicago Press, 2000.

Blass, F., and A. Debrunner. *A Greek Grammar of the New Testament and Other Early Christian Literature.* Translated and Revised by Robert Funk. Chicago: The University of Chicago Press, 1961.

Foerster, Werner, and Georg Fohrer. "sw/vzw, swthriva, swthvr, swthvrio." In *Theological Dictionary of the New Testament.* Edited by Gerhard Friedrich, Translated and Edited by Geoffrey W. Bromiley, Volume 7, 965-1023. Grand Rapids: William B. Eerdmans Publishing Company, 1971.

Freed, Edwin D. *The New Testament: A Critical Introduction.* Belmont, CA: Wadsworth Publishing Company, 1986.

Guthrie, Donald. *New Testament Introduction.* 4th Ed. Downers Grove, IL: InterVarsity Press, 1990.

Harris, M. J. "Prepositions and Theology in the Greek New Testament." In *The New International Dictionary of New Testament Theology.* Edited by Colin Brown. Volume 3. Grand Rapids: Zondervan Publishing House, 1978.

Harrison, Everett F. *Introduction to the New Testament.* Grand Rapids: William B. Eerdmans Publishing Company, 1964.

Kümmel, Werner Georg. *Introduction to the New Testament.* Translated by Howard Clark Kee. Nashville: Abingdon Press, 1973.

Liddell, Henry George, and Robert Scott, compilers. *A Greek-English Lexicon.* Oxford: Clarendon Press, 1968.

Metzer, Bruce M. *A Textual Commentary on the Greek New Testament.* New York: United Bible Societies, 1971.

Moule, C. F. D. *An Idiom Book of New Testament Greek,* 2nd Ed. Cambridge: Cambridge University Press, 1939.

Moulton, James Hope, and George Milligan. *The Vocabulary of the Greek Testament Illustrated from the Papyri and other Non-literary Sources.* Grand Rapids: William B. Eerdmans Publishing Company, 1930.

Oepke, Albrecht. "diav." In *Theological Dictionary of the New Testament,* Edited by Gerhard Kittel, Translated and Edited by Geoffrey W. Bromiley, Vol. 2, 65-70. Grand Rapids: William B. Eerdmans Publishing Company, 1964.

Rienecker, Fritz and Cleon Rogers. *Linguistic Key to the Greek New Testament.* Grand Rapids: Zondervan, 1980.

Robertson, A. T. *A Grammar of the Greek New Testament in the Light of Historical Research.* 4th Ed. Nashville: Broadman Press, 1934.

Schneider, J. and C. Brown. "Salvation, Savior." In *The New International Dictionary of New Testament Theology,* Edited by Colin Brown. Volume 3. Grand Rapids: Zondervan Publishing House, 1978.

Smyth, Herbert Weir. *Greek Grammar* [1910]. Revised by Gordon M. Messing. Cambridge, Massachusetts: Harvard University Press, 1956.

Thiessen, Henry Clarence. *Introduction to the New Testament.* Grand Rapids: William B. Eerdmans Publishing Company, 1955.

Turner, Nigel. *Syntax.* Volume 3, *A Grammar of New Testament Greek,* ed. James Hope Moulton. Edinburgh: T. & T. Clark, 1963.

Wallace, Daniel B. *Greek Grammar Beyond the Basics: An Exegetical Syntax of the New Testament.* Grand Rapids: Zondervan Publishing House, 1996.

Zerwick, Maximilian. *Biblical Greek Illustrated by Examples.* Translated by Joseph Smith, 4th Ed. Rome: Editrice Pontificio Istituto Biblico, 1963.